Samuel Johnson
1696 - 1772

Samuel Johnson
of
Stratford
in New England

1696-1772

by
Don R. Gerlach
Professor Emeritus
The University of Akron
with
George E. DeMille
Late Canon of Albany

Manufactured in the United States of America

Publisher's Cataloging-in-Publication Data

Gerlach, Don R., 1932-
    Samuel Johnson of New England, 1696-1772 / Don R. Gerlach.
      p.:   ill.:   cm.:
    Includes bibliographical references and index.
    ISBN 0-9777148-8-8
    1. Johnson, Samuel, 1696-1772. 2. Anglicans – Connecticut – Biography. 3. Clergy – New
England – Biography. 4. Church of England – United States – History – 18th century. 5. Columbia
University – Presidents – Biography.

BX5995.J59 2009
283.092—dc22

Typeset by Allyn R. Jenkins Typography, Inc.
Athens, GA
Printed by Piedmont Impressions
Athens, GA

The typeface is Berkeley and the text is printed on Lynx Opaque Text

Frontispiece: The Reverend Samuel Johnson by Thomas McIlworth
Used by permission of Columbia University

Table of Contents

Preface

Mention Samuel Johnson to even an educated audience, and they conjure up an image of the English lexicographer. But Dr. Johnson of "Stratford in New England," as he so often dated his letters, deserves a comparable recognition. "Revere his name, and be what he has been" was what Myles Cooper wrote of the Connecticut parson when he composed the inscription for the old priest's burial marker. Yet the name is probably not much revered because it has not been much known. And if Johnson's posterity is unfamiliar with his life and work, his failures and accomplishments, they can neither revere his life nor know how to be what he has been.

This book has two purposes. One is to make known to the intelligent reading public an appealing and likeable man – indeed a sizable figure, who strangely enough has had no modern biographer. Johnson is known, but apparently only to specialists. But in spite of this, and of deserving a better reputation, Johnson has not stimulated much research. Historians have been too enamoured of indisputably greater leaders, like Jonathan Edwards and Benjamin Franklin, and as a consequence men like Johnson have been left in the shadows. E. Edwards Beardsley's biography of him is about one hundred years old;[1] it is not readily available, or very inviting to twentieth century readers. Herbert and Carol Schneider published a fine edition of Johnson's writings in 1929, but this material has hitherto not been exploited.[2] Although several graduate students have recently undertaken studies of Johnson for doctoral dissertations, and although there have been a few monographs directly or indirectly concerned with Johnson as an intellectual figure,[3] we need to see the varied facets of the man presented as parts of a whole: Churchman, missionary and theologian, author, philosopher and educator.

The easiest way to identify Johnson for most people has been to designate him as the first president of King's College. In that capacity he did accomplish something, but he cannot be called a particularly great college president.

Other historians who have dealt with him have considered Johnson primarily as a philosopher, a proponent of Bishop Berkeley's Idealism, or a representative of the colonial mind in transition. Isaac Woodbridge Riley devoted to him a long chapter in his history of American philosophy.[4] How the philosophers view him is eloquently summed up in the introduction to the second volume of the Schneiders' magnificent collection of Johnson's writings:

> Samuel Johnson was one of those pathetic, but dramatic, figures who are caught between two worlds. The puritan world was crumbling. Johnson early escaped from its ruins and sought refuge in the urbane learning, the orderly government and rich civilization of the Anglican church and the British nation. But this complacent world was itself about to crumble, and he failed completely to understand the new forces which were impinging on it. Freethinking, liberty, whiggism, the new lights, independent reflectors – all these were terms of abhorrence to him.[5]

This is an incisive estimate, and it well expresses the view of Johnson held by many scholars other than intellectual historians. Both James Truslow Adams, who sketched his life for the *Dictionary of American Biography*, and Claude Newlin come to a similar conclusion.[6] Carl Bridenbaugh thought of Johnson primarily as the leader of "Anglican aggression" (which liberty-loving Dissenters vigorously fought in order to thwart an ecclesiastical tyranny more imaginary than it was real).[7] They all were convinced that he was a noble failure.

There is a certain plausibility in this attitude toward Johnson. To

Adams, Newlin and the Schneiders he was primarily a philosopher and political thinker whose views ran counter to prevailing American currents. His *Elementa Philosophica* apparently had little influence in Johnson's own day. As a political thinker, he was an ardent imperialist, loyal to King and country. Within three years of his death the War of Independence erupted, and the first British Empire was shattered. And Johnson died without accomplishing what was perhaps his major goal – an Anglican episcopate in America.

But Samuel Johnson cannot be so simply written off. Although he was not as great, powerful or distinguished as some eighteenth century leaders, he was one of three very remarkable men who clearly emerged from the intellectual mediocrity of North American colonists – men who distinguished themselves above all others: Benjamin Franklin, Jonathan Edwards, and Johnson. All three were involved in the founding of colleges; Johnson and Franklin developed a friendship through correspondence, and Johnson and Edwards shared certain intellectual and philosophic interests, despite the fact that they were poles apart in theology. For these reasons then we must attempt to assess how Johnson deserves to be ranked with Franklin and Edwards.

The other purpose of this book is to portray Johnson as he was. I have endeavored to present such a portrait as will show him in the perspective of his native Connecticut, of Anglican expansion in the northern colonies, of the Great Awakening, the development of colonial higher education, and of the American Revolution. Most scholars have looked at him from the wrong angle. We can be sure that if one had asked Johnson what ideas he most wanted to propagate, what system he was most zealous to extend, he would not have answered "Berkeleyan Idealism," or "the British Empire;" or "a new college curriculum," but "the welfare of the best of churches." And here lies the focus of his life and work, and the point of emphasis in this book. Johnson was first of all a priest of the Church of England, and, it is in this capacity that he must be judged. Indeed, all other facets of his career are but sides of a great and good Churchman and missionary whose influence was as deep as it was diverse.

No book of any merit requires an apology to introduce it. But I would probably be remiss if I did not offer a caveat to the reader who has a right to expect good craftsmanship in what he reads. This work is what some critics may call an exploratory biography, for I have not consulted the voluminous Johnson manuscripts at Columbia University or his papers held by the New York Historical Society. Instead, I have relied upon the Schneiders' four-volume edition of Johnson's papers which no one has hitherto exploited to write a life of the Connecticut parson. I have, of course, used other major primary sources which, though less voluminous, are important to the story. Some of these have been published; others have not.

This work was undertaken with the enormous aid and encouragement of the Reverend George E. DeMille, late Canon of Albany; our collaboration resulted in several articles which were published in *The Historical Magazine of the Protestant Episcopal Church*, *The Connecticut Historical Society Bulletin*, and *Connecticut History*. Canon DeMille left me the task of publishing our joint efforts.

I have been anxious to introduce the American Dr. Johnson to a wider public – to stress the varied facets of his career without overemphasizing or discounting any of them beyond what seems to be appropriate to suggest his most important work. By this means I trust that these efforts, if judged deficient, may prompt others to a more detailed study of his important figure's life. I have attempted to be scholarly without being pedantic; I have sought to account for Johnson's life in a way that might interest others as it has interested me. I have tried to be thorough and balanced in coverage and judgment, without attempting to be exhaustive – and without exhausting the reader. Like George Savile, Marquess of Halifax, a seventeenth century moralist and political writer, I agree that "There is no stronger evidence of a crazy understanding than the making too large a catalogue of things necessary." And without being blind to my hero's defects, I make no apology for believing that *nemo nisi per amicitiam cogniscitur* – one must be a man's friend to understand him.

D. R. G.

Chapter I

THE BACKGROUND:
A LAND OF STEADY HABITS

1. The Colony

We cannot begin to understand the life and work of Samuel Johnson without a clear picture in our minds of the environment from which he emerged and in which he spent the greater part of his life. At the time of his birth in 1696 much of Connecticut was still a vast wilderness dotted with little communities in which life was dominated by the Puritan ethos. The history of the colony had dual beginnings with settlements established along the Connecticut River (some in the upper valley and one at Saybrook at the river's mouth) in 1635 and at New Haven in 1638. The first began when a party of Massachusetts colonists under John Oldham settled at Wethersfield during the winter of 1634-35. In the spring a group of Dorchester people located Windsor, and in the ensuing October the first of the Reverend Thomas Hooker's followers moved to Hartford. In May 1636 Hooker, pastor of the Newtown church in the colony of Massachusetts Bay, led a large part of his flock down through the wilderness to join the founders of the town of Hartford.[1] Hooker's followers were attracted to the west, whence reports of fertile lands had roused their imaginations and ambitions. Their immigration was in part an expression of protest against life in Massachusetts and especially its restricted suffrage.

In the Bay Colony, only church members could vote, and it must be remembered that while every inhabitant was compelled by law to attend the worship of the established church and to support its ministry, church membership, and with it the privilege of voting, was confined to the elect. When Hooker set out on his trek to Connecticut, the majority of the inhabitants of Massachusetts Bay were not members of the church there, and therefore not voters. Now Hooker was not, as he has sometimes been represented, a believer in democracy. Democracy was as much a term of objurgation to an orthodox Puritan divine of the Seventeenth Century as Communism is in some quarters of American society today. But Hooker objected to the extent of the discretionary power exerted by Massachusett's magistrates. To see just what he had in mind for the governance of his people in their new wilderness home, we must turn to the Fundamental Orders, the framework of the government under which the colony of Connecticut operated.

The Fundamental Orders did not appear immediately, however. At first the Connecticut settlers were governed by a commission of eight men empowered by the Massachusetts General Court to summon the inhabitants of the new communities for the holding of a court – the term then used for a legislative and electoral body. When the first of these courts assembled in 1637, the six magistrates and nine deputies from the three towns proceeded to act as an *ad hoc* government, levying taxes, naming a treasurer, and ordering quotas of men from each town to serve in war against the Pequod Indians. Moreover, they decided to create a lasting government consistent with Hooker's principles which he elucidated in a sermon preached to the members of the court in May 1638: the election of public officials with powers defined by a body of freemen as large as "consistent with the will of God;" the unity of church and state; and a moral test for admission to "freemanship" or the suffrage.

The 1638 General Court devised the Fundamental Orders for the maintenance of liberty and the "purity of the Gospel," as well as for the governance of the three Connecticut River valley towns. Adopted at Hartford in January 1639 by a convention of "free planters" from Hartford, Wethersfield and Windsor, they made voting, and all participation in government, not a right but a privilege, granted to

2

certain individuals. This participation was established on two levels – the local and the provincial. A general court met twice a year; in April all the freemen assembled to elect a governor and his assistants or magistrates; in September the governor, assistants and deputies from the towns gathered to act as a legislature. At the town level, the inhabitants who subscribed to an oath of fidelity were to choose deputies to the general court, but deputies were required to be freemen and not mere inhabitants. Each of the towns chose selectmen or magistrates to govern local affairs between annual town meetings. Charles M. Andrews summed up the distinction between inhabitants and freemen in a capsule statement:

> the "admitted inhabitants" were the householders in the towns, including also the adult males, married or unmarried…, who as landowners and Trinitarians, were the substantial and godly men in their respective communities; the "freemen" were only such of the "admitted inhabitants" as were deemed by the general court fit to take part in the affairs of the commonwealth itself.[2]

Three things are to be especially noted about this form of government. The voting privilege was not specifically restricted to members of the church, but in practice only church members were recognized as freemen. On the town level, the suffrage was fairly inclusive, and in the town meeting there was general participation in the management of affairs. On the colony level, however, the freemen were expected to select the better sort to hold office, and then to let them carry on the government. Although the governor's term was only one year (and he was not permitted to succeed himself), the same men were elected to office by the freemen with great regularity. From 1639 to 1643 John Haynes, Edward Hopkins and George Wyllys served as governor; from 1643 to 1655 two men only held this office; John Haynes was elected in odd-numbered years, and Edward Hopkins in even-numbered. Here, then, was no democracy in the modern sense, but a political aristocracy which recognized only the sovereignty of God, with not so much as a nod to the King of England.

The colony of New Haven had its beginning in 1638 with the Reverend John Davenport as its leading organizer. Having despaired of more thorough reformation of the Church of England, Davenport ended his services to her, wandered in Scotland several years, and developed valuable contacts with London merchants Samuel and Theophilus Eaton. With a band of some fifty adherents he came to Boston in 1637, but soon decided that this was not the place to promote the religion of his conception. Moreover, Massachusetts was undergoing the convulsions of dissidents like Roger Williams and Anne Hutchinson, and the results were disturbing. Davenport's associate, Theophilus Eaton, and others explored the coast of Connecticut for a more suitable settlement. In March, 1638, Davenport and his coterie moved to Quinnipiack, and so began the colony of New Haven.

Davenport was a man of dominating personality, utterly rigid in his convictions, a perfectionist without an ounce of compromise in his make-up. He proceeded to shape the colony of New Haven in his own image. It was to be a theocracy of the purest sort possible, in which "the rules set forth in scripture" were to be the basis of all law, both ecclesiastical and civil. In 1639 the New Haven leaders drafted their fundamental articles with more theocratic rigor than had their northern neighbors. The Word of God was to be their rule of conduct, and if English traditions (such as trial by jury) were found to conflict with it, the Bible was to be preferred. Church and state were to be one and the same thing, with only church members voting or holding office. "The towns and Colony political organizations were but the machine by which this church-state was supported. None but the regenerate could vote in town meetings, or for the Governor and magistrates and deputies to the Colony Court. Church members ruled the New Haven state, and nonconformity to the churches was treason to the state itself."[3] Eaton served as governor from 1639 to 1657, and only two others held that office until 1662, when New Haven was annexed to Connecticut.

When Puritans worked at state-building, the pillars of the church covenanted a civil organization in which they served as magistrates. This they enlarged in October 1643 when Milford, Guilford, and Stamford joined New Haven under a constitution in which it was agreed

> That, as in matters that concern the gathering and ordering
> of a church, so also in all public offices, which concern
> civil order, as choice of magistrates and officers, making
> and repealing laws ... they would, all of them, be ordered
> by the rules which the scripture held forth to them.[4]

Meantime, another group of adventurers led by John Winthrop, Jr., son of the Governor of Massachusetts, had established a trading post at Saybrook at the mouth of the Connecticut River. Armed with a patent originally given to the Earl of Warwick by the Council for New England, a land-granting corporation, these men planted a community which early began to cooperate with the upper Connecticut River towns. In 1644 Connecticut bought a share in the Saybrook patentees' interests, thus opening the mouth of the river to their trade and paving the way for amalgamation of the Connecticut communities. Young Winthrop became governor of Connecticut in 1657, and when he was reelected in 1659, he began a tenure that lasted until 1676. The restrictive clause of the Fundamental Orders was altered to permit a well-respected leader to remain in office, even before Connecticut got its royal charter in 1662.

For two and a half decades Connecticut and New Haven grew as two independent colonies. Their populations increased, towns were organized and churches established; there was trouble with the Dutch in New Amsterdam, who claimed Connecticut territory as part of New Netherland. There were also difficulties with the Indians from time to time. And in order to deal with such common problems, Connecticut, New Haven, Plymouth and Massachusetts Bay formed a confederation which attempted solutions to them. The dreams of Davenport and Hooker seemed to have become realities. Then came the first major event to affect the history of both the Connecticut colonies alike.

The restoration of Charles II to his father's throne in 1660 brought some startling changes for the American colonies, and especially in Connecticut. New Haven was particularly concerned for want of any official title to the lands it encompassed. Connecticut had only the sanction of the Bay Colony, whose General Court had permitted the first settlers to move west under the pledge that they would remain under the political and religious jurisdiction of Massachusetts, and that they take with them some form of church organization. But the inhabitants of both colonies had reason to be concerned what the new King's reactions would be to their dubious origins, and to Puritans' abuses of non-Puritans. Moreover, there were conflicting boundary claims with Roger Williams's colony of Rhode Island and Providence Plantations.

Connecticut took the initiative to insure its survival. In 1661 Governor John Winthrop, Jr., set out for England to assure Charles II that Connecticut recognized him as rightful heir to the throne, whose previous occupant the English puritans had beheaded. Winthrop also carried a petition requesting a charter. And when the charter was issued in April 1662, New Haven and Connecticut were united as one province.

Some of New Haven's people were not as willing to join Connecticut as Connecticut's leaders were to have them, although various towns broke away from the former to join the newly-chartered colony. Governor William Lette of New Haven and Benjamin Penn, who chaired a committee to argue against incorporation, disliked Connecticut's franchise (which was limited to freemen), and relaxed requirements for church membership, and they believed joining her was inconsistent with their oaths to maintain their own commonwealth. Moreover, they feared the union would tend to separate church and state.[5]

Controversy and correspondence between the two old colonies were exchanged until January 1665, when New Haven finally and formally submitted. The controversy may have gone on indefinitely but for the King's land grant to the Duke of York and his sending four commissioners to seize New Netherland in 1664. The grant gave the Duke lands west of the Connecticut River, and the commissioners had power to investigate New England affairs – a power that endangered the religious underpinnings of its governments. New Haven and Connecticut found a mutual interest in cooperating to prevent the loss of their jurisdictional claims. Under the charter of 1662 they might share strength, determination and survival.[6] This unsettled interlude set the religious and political stage on which Samuel Johnson finally made his debut. New Haven settlers had good reason to fear a diminution of their theocratic ways. Traditional religious beliefs were to be eroded by more liberal practices, and the result by the end of the century was restlessness, turmoil and confusion which finally held to the Saybrook Platform, the "apostacy" at Yale, and ultimately the upheavals of the Great Awakening. This jealous rivalry between Connecticut and New Haven was to have a considerable effect on the life and fortunes of Samuel Johnson.

The 1662 charter designated Winthrop as governor (and also named a deputy and twelve assistants or magistrates), but the general court of two freemen from each town retained the privilege of electing Connecticut's governor annually thereafter. This was important in several respects. In neighboring colonies like New York, and Massachusetts after 1691, the governor was appointed by the crown, was almost invariably an Englishman and therefore a member of the Church of England, and surrounded by a hierarchy of English – and Anglican – officials. Thus in such colonies Anglicanism frequently became a sort of status symbol. To belong to the Church of England was the mark of an aristocrat, if also occasionally a stigma in the eyes of ambitious and discontented provincials. This was not so in Connecticut. The new charter confirmed Connecticut's magistrates in their control of religious matters, which remained Puritan, not Anglican, although it also required that Connecticut's laws be "not contrary to the lawes of this Realme of England...."[7] And in Connecticut the Congregational-Presbyterial order at the time when Johnson was born still maintained a largely unquestioned supremacy.

2. The Standing Order

The dominant feature of the environment in which Samuel Johnson was born and reared was Puritanism. Any attempt to define a complete and all-inclusive religious system in so brief a space as this must of necessity be a partial failure, but such an attempt we must make. Puritan theology originated largely from the brain of one great intellectual, John Calvin, and it bears throughout the impress of Calvin's personality. Having demolished the infallibility of Pope and Church, Calvin substituted another infallible authority – the Bible as interpreted by John Calvin and other right-thinking elders of reformed Christian bodies. The essence of any theology is, of course, its doctrine of God, and Calvin's doctrine was very clear-cut, supremely logical, and to most moderns not a little repulsive. Calvin's God was the absolute sovereign of the universe He had created, so towering in His majesty, so awful in His might, that man shrank into insignificance before Him. Man, fallen man, was utterly depraved; he had altogether lost his freedom of will. Before John Jones was born, God had determined what manner of man Jones would be, had predetermined his character, his career, and therefore his eventual destination in the world to come. It followed from this premise that the church of the Puritans was not the ark of salvation for all mankind, but the gathered company of the elect – the chosen few whom God had predestined to eternal happiness. And the elect could be identified by certain manifest signs; they were the "visible saints" who could testify by word and deed that they were God's elect.

This austere theology found its outward and visible form in a correspondingly austere worship. Puritan worship was purely an act of the mind, and therefore doomed from its conception to fail, for surely the nature of man is not one of so exclusively an intellectual cast. No such sensual trifles as organs, or statues, stained glass, incense or vestments were allowed to come between the Puritan and his God. In the bare meetinghouse the minister prayed long "conceived" prayers and preached hour-long sermons, while the laity sat in silent concentration. This theology and worship were built on a thorough-going Biblicism. The Bible as the Word of God contained within its covers all necessary truth, which any intelligent man might plainly recognize for himself, with proper hints from his minister. The Bible was the supreme guide to belief, to worship, even to the forms of civil society. And the strict and legalistic code of conduct laid down in the Old Testament – the Puritan tended to fight shy of the New Testament – was to be observed with the utmost rigidity.

But Puritans did not look only to Calvin. Hooker and Davenport themselves helped crystallize the creeds and platforms of New England Congregationalism, as did men like Richard, Increase, and Cotton Mather, and John Cotton.[8] Theirs were the writings defining a church and church membership, forms of worship and ordination, and the role of church councils. At first every local congregation was a thing unto itself, choosing and ordaining its own ministers by the laying on of hands by the laity. The first generation of Puritan clergy, who had been priests of the Church of England, renounced their priesthood in the new world; their successors were chosen by the local congregations formed by solemn covenants or agreements made with one another and with God after the example of the ancient Hebrews as recorded in the Old Testament.

Congregationalists participated in three covenants – grace, civil and church. The first was an invisible system of spiritual ties shared by those who had experienced salvation by faith as God's elect. The second was "merely the physical enforcement and public advancement of whatever the churches desired." And the church covenant was the visible means by which the elect pledged obedience to God, the church and the state. The three were so intertwined as to be one, for "the Church Covenant gave form to the Covenant of Grace, and the Civil Covenant gave power to the Church Covenant."[9]

The local autonomy of congregations suggests that there could be diversity in the Puritan Way, but practices were frequently so similar as to produce general uniformity. New England Congregationalists agreed to the doctrine of the "visible saints" – that is, that the church consisted of "persons who had felt the stirrings of grace in their souls," – the conviction that they were God's elect – "and could demonstrate that to the satisfaction of other saints."[10] Thus "united into one body, by a holy covenant," the saints pledged themselves to "the publick worship of God, & mutuall edification one of another, in the Fellowship of the Lord Jesus."[11] Their "pastors, teachers, elders, deacons, and widows … obtained their office by the holie & free election of the Lordes holie and free people."[12] But those who were thus chosen must demonstrate their qualifications of learning and moral living. They were expected to be men of sobriety, virtue and education, and their influence as leaders reached into most every corner of colonial life.

Such was the general atmosphere of New England Puritanism. By 1660 it was firmly established by law in Connecticut, and no other religious group was tolerated. A statute passed in 1644 required all citizens to contribute to the support of the Congregational Church and its ministers. Connecticut delegates cooperated with others from Massachusetts, Plymouth and New Haven in drawing up an agreement at Cambridge in 1648. The Cambridge Platform recognized the independence of each congregation, and provided that offenders against ecclesiastical order might suffer deprivation of church rights, but not civil rights. But it also provided for the collection of church taxes, by the magistrates if necessary, and that civil authorities should not compel church membership but enforce godliness and ecclesiastical orders against heresy and dissent. Quakers were thus discouraged from tarrying in Puritan communities. In 1658 a second Connecticut law reinforced the first by requiring that any group desiring to form a church must receive the permission of neighboring churches and the General Court. Although church suffrage was extended to all baptized persons, the local minister determined who might be baptized, and he was often very selective in exercising this power.[13] Not until 1708 did the colony recognize the right to dissent from the established order; at that time the General Court passed a toleration act which granted liberty of conscience in recognition of the English Toleration Act of 1689; the latter allowed freedom to Trinitarian dissenters from the Church of England, but not to Roman Catholics or Unitarians. Dissenters from Connecticut Puritanism might form their own churches if they registered with their county court. But no provision was made to exempt them from taxes to pay the clergy of the standing order until 1727.[14]

Yet Puritanism was losing the force that it once had in New England, and in Connecticut. Symptomatic of this decline was the reassessment of requirements for church membership exemplified by the Halfway Covenant. Church members were expected to give proof of their conversion in order to enjoy the full privileges of membership, and ministers grew concerned that children were left unbaptized and that baptized adults were not completing their covenant by giving evidence of conversion. These were falling outside the bounds of the religious-political state. A synod of clergymen, largely of Massachusetts and Connecticut, hammered out a compromise between 1657 and 1662, known as the Halfway Covenant. It declared that baptized children could become full church members after reaching maturity and professing the covenant. These who failed to complete the covenant but who had been baptized might have their children baptized, but they could not receive communion until they made a public profession of faith and gave proof of their conversion. Such would be "half-way members" because they were allowed only partial enjoyment of church privileges, although they would still be subject to the watch and discipline of the church. They were to have no vote in church matters, nor could they hold any ecclesiastical office.[15]

Although the Connecticut General Assembly urged all the churches to follow it, the Halfway Covenant encouraged dissension instead of stopping it. Some congregations refused to accept it, and others split between factions which would and would not do so. Dissidents withdrew from the churches in Hartford, Windsor, Wethersfield and Stratford; in Greenwich a minority left the church because their minister refused to baptize children of non-communicants.[16] Critics feared the Halfway Covenant made church membership and discipline too lenient. Amidst the rising difficulties the Connecticut Assembly passed the law of 1658 which forbade the formation of any church without the consent of both the Assembly and the neighboring churches. Succeeding generations of Puritans were losing some of the zeal of their fathers; there was less devotion to the Standing Order, more factionalism, more questioning of authority and government, and consequently a decline in religion. A number of originally strong churches found themselves "without ministers for protracted periods".[17]

To deal with such problems the Connecticut clergy finally devised the Saybrook Platform with the sanction of the General Court in 1708. The Saybrook system enhanced the ministers' authority by forcing congregations in each county into a consociation of clergy with the power to vote and lay delegates with the power to debate only. The consociation was an appeals court for settling disputes of discipline, and any church daring to disregard the decision of this body "lost the legal right to raise taxes to support its pastor."[18] Although the 1708 platform said nothing about ordination, it clearly indicated that ordinations had become more and more the exclusive privilege of the clergy. It made formal the practices that had grown customary years before. Ordinations at the hands of the laity were gradually discontinued, and gradually the clergy omitted asking for the laity's consent to major decisions. The Cambridge Platform of

1648, stressing congregational autonomy, was thus discarded. Connecticut Puritanism became basically Presbyterian – not Congregational – more republican than democratic. Yet not all the Connecticut ministers and churches would agree to follow the Saybrook Platform in every detail, and some totally rejected it. Moreover, the religious scene was complicated by the fact that every church had Halfway members, and by 1699 standards of admission had become so relaxed that the Connecticut Assembly gave "the householders" of each town, church members or not, a voice in the selection of the town minister.[19] Into his religious system Samuel Johnson was born and bred. It did not long prove satisfying to his questioning mind.

By the end of the seventeenth century, the period when our story really begins, Connecticut had assumed a shape that was to last without too much change up until the Revolution. The colony in 1700 consisted of some twenty-odd townships, located on Long Island Sound and in the valleys of the Connecticut, the Housatonic, and the Thames Rivers. The population had grown from about 800 in 1636 to an estimated 30,000.[20] The basic industry was of course farming, and farming was never too easy a way of earning a living on Connecticut soil. Also in the colony there was the inevitable sprinkling of artisans and small tradesmen. In the early days of the New Haven colony, an attempt had been made to develop the communities lying along the Sound into seaports, but the attempt failed, and Connecticut had therefore no such class of wealthy merchants and shipowners as had sprung up in neighboring Massachusetts. Nor was there anything like the class distinction as in Virginia and South Carolina between planter, indentured servant and slave, or in New York between landlord and tenant. It was not that Utopian dream, the classless society, but it approached it more nearly than any other American colony. The distinctions that existed were not so much between the rich and poor, employer and employed, as between old settlers and newcomers, between the godly and not-so-godly. And yet there was a social elite consisting of well-to-do farmers, merchants and clergy, who dominated political and religious activities. The lower class masses, small farmer, yeomen and a few slaves, were known for their coarse manners, and intellectual and social backwardness.[21]

Connecticut of course had its unique social, religious and political characteristics, as did every other colony. And intellectually, it was no worse than most of the others. If its achievements in education were limited in scope and productivity, it was largely because opportunities were also limited. Books, schools and teachers were few in number, and the masses had little more than rudimentary knowledge of reading, writing and arithmetic. For Puritans the catechism and the Bible received the most attention. Knowledge was valued "not simply as a polite accomplishment, nor as a means of advancing material welfare, but because salvation was impossible without it."[22] The best educated men were tutored by their ministers and then sent to Harvard or to college abroad. Their learning centered in mathematics, Greek, Latin and Hebrew, surveying, logic and metaphysics. Scientific pursuits were rare, and the theories of Bacon, Newton and Locke were considered heretical and much to be avoided. Calvinist theology and an unsophisticated study of natural law, known as physicks, completed the higher education of the day. Thus, the best educated had but a limited breadth of knowledge, largely theological, and increasingly obsolete. Although Connecticut was Puritan and provincial, it was not static; the religious order was shaken by decay and schism. And the value placed on learning carried with it the promise of even greater change.

3. The Collegiate School

One of the great virtues of the Puritan was his passionate belief in learning. The necessity of education, especially the education of the clergy, was indeed inherent in the Puritan system. The clergy were meant to hold in that system a prominent, almost a dominant position. But the Puritan clergy, unlike some other religious hierarchies, could not base their claim to superiority on the possession of an apostolic succession, or their monopoly of a mysterious and imposing ceremonial. Their high place in society depended on sheer learning and aptitude of spiritual leadership, demonstrated by their sermons. The first generation of Puritan clergy in the new world had been almost to a man graduates of Oxford or Cambridge. They possessed therefore the best learning of their day. Their successors were not their equals in this respect. True, Harvard College had been founded, mainly to provide a godly and learned ministry, but Harvard could not begin to match the English universities in scholarship. The second generation of New England clergy were therefore far less learned than their predecessors and the best of them realized the truth. And so both Hooker and Davenport, clerical leaders of the two colonies in Connecticut, different as were their views in many respects, had foreseen the coming need, and had dreamed of a good educational system for their colonies. But in 1700, these projects were still mainly in the world of dreams.

By that year, something else was giving the demand for a Connecticut college a new urgency. At Harvard there were two young tutors, John Leverett and William Brattle, who, in the face of the bitter opposition of Increase and Cotton Mather, were modernizing and liberalizing the antiquated course of study. The Mathers, and those who agreed with them, rightly saw in this modernization a threat to Puritan orthodoxy. The events proved that the Mathers were right. They, and their Connecticut brethren, therefore felt that a new college was needed in New England, a college that would bring up its sons in the Puritan way, uncontaminated by the heretical tendencies of Locke and Newton.

The first actual step toward the founding of what was to develop into Yale University was taken in the year 1701. Early in October a group of ministers met in Branford, and resolved on the immediate formation of a college, or rather, what they preferred to call a "Collegiate School." All were agreed on this. But when the question was raised as to where that school was to be located, the old feud between northern and southern parts of the colony, between Hartford and New Haven, a feud which had troubled the life of the colony ever since their forcible union, flared out once more. Neither faction among the clergy who were to be the trustees could bear to see the new institution located in alien territory. For a time, then, the question was left in abeyance, but for years thereafter it lifted its ugly head to plague the planners of the infant institution. In October 1701, the colonial assembly, prodded into action by the clergy, passed an act to incorporate the school, empowering a self-perpetuating board of trustees to erect the collegiate school. This act was of doubtful legality, for it was by no means clear that the assembly, whose existence depended upon the royal charter, had such a power of incorporation. Ten trustees were named in the act (eventually there were to be eleven) – all ministers of the established church. Significantly, the incorporation made no mention of the location of the school.[23]

In the middle of the following month the trustees, who possessed neither corporate funds nor property, met in Saybrook and took measures to make the projected school a reality. They elected one of their number, the Reverend Abraham Pierson, to be rector, and set the tuition at thirty shillings a year for undergraduates and ten shillings for graduate students. They also determined that at least temporarily the school should be located at Saybrook. This was plainly an evasionary measure; no one was jealous of little Saybrook. In March 1702, Pierson opened the school with one student in attendance. But not in Saybrook. As pastor of Killingworth, his only income came from his congregation,and it refused to release him to live at Saybrook; hence, he continued to live and teach in his Killingworth parsonage. As Pierson was a man of parts and reputation, more students came, and by the middle of 1705 some twenty boys were boarding wherever they could find accommodation in Killingworth and its surrounding farms, and getting their education in Pierson's parsonage. The prospects for the school were steadily brightening when, in March 1707, Pierson died.

Since Pierson's support had come almost wholly from his congregation, and since the trustees had no money in hand to pay for the full-time support of a successor, they were forced into a curious makeshift. The Reverend Samuel Andrew, pastor of the church at Milford, was made titular rector of the school – an office he continued to hold for some years. He taught the seniors at his home in Milford. The rest of the students were now domiciled at Saybrook, under the care of Phineas Fiske, who had been named tutor. This was obviously an unsatisfactory solution to the problem of locating the school, and the result was that attendance dwindled for several years. Then in 1714 there came a gleam of light. Nine students entered the freshman class at Saybrook.

4. Anglican Underground

So far, the picture we have been attempting to paint, the picture of colonial Connecticut at the close of the Seventeenth Century, has largely been one of Puritan colors. Indeed, except for its comparative poverty, Connecticut was at that time, even more than the mother colony of Massachusetts, the ideal Puritan theocratic state. But there was one fly in the ointment.

In the year 1639 seventeen families had come to Connecticut together, not like most of the early Connecticut settlers, via Massachusetts, but directly from England. Their leader was the Reverend Adam Blackman or Blakeman – the name is written both ways in the documents. Blackman is something of a mystery man. He was, like all of the Puritan clerical leaders of the first generation of immigrants, a priest of the Church of England. While the evidence is not too clear, there is some indication that he was less of a Puritan than a conformist. Blackman and his followers formed a community named Stratford, located some ten miles west of New Haven, at the point where the Housatonic River empties into Long Island Sound. Here Blackman may have conducted services according to *The Book of Common Prayer* until his death in 1665. He was naturally succeeded as pastor of Stratford by clergymen ordained in the Congregational fashion. But in spite of this, the evidence suggests that a number of the inhabitants of Stratford – Hawleys and Beardsleys among them – were convinced Anglicans, who though they may have conformed to Connecticut Puritan order, still treasured copies of *The Book of Common Prayer* brought from England, and used them in the bosom of their families. This tradition they handed on to their children.[24]

The first overt act of rebellion of this group against the Standing Order, the first open manifestation of these underground Anglicans, occurred as early as October 1664, when seven men of the township of Stratford, by a document that still exists, petitioned the General Assembly of the colony, as "Members of the Church of England," for the privileges of "Our Mother Church" and especially for the two essential sacraments of Baptism and Holy Communion. They insisted that they were "not under the due care of an orthodox ministry" that would duly administer the sacraments, and they requested that in future no law should force them to contribute to the support of any church or ministers "that will neglect or refuse to baptize our children, and to take care of us as of such members of the Church as are under … their charge and care." As might have been expected, the Assembly offered little satisfaction. Noting that some petitioners were "grieved that they are not interteined in church fellowship," the Court suggested that the clergy and churches "consider whither it be not their duty to enterteine" those persons of "honest and godly conversation" and ask them to join "in church fellowship, by an explicit covenant … ." Here was no more than a suggestion that the Anglicans of Stratford place themselves under the "care and watch" of the Standing Order by accepting the Puritan covenant. Evidently this did not settle the matter, for in May 1669, petitioners "of the Church of Christ at Stratford with many of the Inhabitants" informed the General Court that "uncomfortable Differences have too too long bin and yet remain amongst us …." Again they asked the Court to "doe something for our Settlement," – a clear indication that not only were there divisions among the Congregationalists over the Halfway Covenant, but also that the Anglicans remained dissatisfied.[25]

Then for a long period we hear no more of the activities of the Stratford Anglicans. But by the beginning of the eighteenth century it is evident that these tenacious souls longed for the ways of the Church of England, if outwardly they succumbed to Connecticut non-conformity. In 1702 David Humphreys, secretary of the newly founded missionary agency of the Church of England, the Venerable Society for the Propagation of the Gospel in Foreign Parts, stated that he had received a petition from certain Churchmen living in Stratford, asking that the Society (commonly called the S. P. G.) send them a priest of the Church of England to function as their missionary."[26] From this point on, the activity of the Stratford resistance grew steadily greater. In 1703 - 1704 it was rumored that the Reverend John Reed, minister of the Congregational Church in Stratford, had made the remarkable statement that he would gladly journey to England to receive there ordination by a bishop.[27] Whatever the truth of the matter, Reed was finally forced out of his parish. Then the Congregationalists of Stratford, vividly aware of the Anglican threat, resolved to get themselves the strongest minister available. In 1709 they determined on the Reverend Timothy Cutler, a Harvard graduate and reputedly one of the best and most orthodox preachers in Massachusetts. Time proved that they could hardly have made a worse choice from their point of view.

Meantime, the Stratford Anglicans continued to agitate. In September 1705 they again drew up a petition. This one was addressed to the Reverend William Vesey, first rector of Trinity Church, New York, and asked his help in procuring for them the services of a clergyman of their faith. This had some result. In November the Reverend George Muirson, a missionary of the S. P. G. at Rye, New York, with a sort of roving commission, made a foray into Connecticut to explore the missionary prospects. In September 1706 he visited Stratford, evidently for the first time. It was the first time many of the Stratford Anglicans had ever seen a priest of the Church of England. The devoted band received him joyfully, and before he left he had baptized twenty-four adults and children. (One of the standing grievances of Connecticut Anglicans arose from the refusal of Congregational ministers to baptize children of Anglican parents.) From this time on until his death in 1708 Muirson visited Stratford several times each year; thus the Church of England people in Stratford were at last in regular contact with their beloved mother church. Encouraged by this, they planned to go a step farther. It appears that by the end of March 1707 they had organized themselves as a parish. In April they again sent a petition, this time to the Bishop of London, asking for an exemplary missionary to be settled with them and equipped to "silence the cavils" of their enemies. The nineteen men who signed the document "in behalf of the rest" of the Stratford Anglicans cited their inability to maintain "a minister of our Church, by reason of some laws which compel us to pay our money to the support of Dissenters, and empower them, as sometimes they do, to take our goods by distress."[28]

The Stratford Churchmen had not only persevered, organized and petitioned for support; they had found allies. The Reverend William Vesey and the provincial governor of New York had taken an interest in them. And sixty miles west of Stratford, just over the border of the colony was the village of Rye, New York. By 1700 Rye had become an active center of Anglicanism. Here Muirson lived, and here was located an even more important person for Anglican expansion. Colonel Caleb Heathcote was lord of the manor of Scarsdale, including much of Westchester County, one of the wealthiest and most influential Anglican laymen in the colonies, and a convinced Churchman. Several times Heathcote accompanied Muirson on his visits to Stratford, and extended over him a protecting arm. Moreover, he interceded with the S. P. G. for the colonial laity who needed and desired the ministry of the Church. In January 1708 Heathcote wrote to the secretary of the S. P. G. from Stratford, reporting that the Episcopalians there were about to erect a church building, and that it would probably be open for services by the following September.[29] He was over-optimistic. The death of Muirson in October 1708 put an end to this hopeful project and to S. P. G. plans to send him to Connecticut, and the church in Stratford had to wait for the coming of Samuel Johnson.

Meantime, in September 1708 the Churchmen of Stratford, and all their fellow Churchmen scattered about Connecticut, achieved a sizable victory. Their continual proddings and petitionings had finally done their work, and in that month a reluctant General Assembly passed a toleration act. It was, like its English predecessor of 1689, a grudging toleration only. It provided that non-members of the established church might worship unmolested where and how they pleased, if they "qualified" themselves under the English Toleration Act of 1689. Otherwise, they must still attend the services of the established church. Moreover, the new law "Provided ... that nothing herein shall be construed to the prejudice of the rights and privileges of the churches 'as were established by law' or to the excusing any person from paying any such minister or town dues, as are now, or shall hereafter be due from them."[30] In effect, for the Connecticut of 1708, this was a toleration the benefits of which extended to Stratford only, for only there was there a sufficient number of zealous Anglicans even to attempt to meet the conditions of the act. But at least a precedent had been set; the long reign of complete intolerance and exclusiveness was coming slowly to an end. And most of the credit for this accomplishment must be given to the annoying Anglican "resistance" of Stratford.

But this limited toleration was not enough. Having achieved so much, the Churchmen of Stratford again took the offensive against the Standing Order. Now they began a prolonged attack on another of the bastions of the establishment – the law which compelled all taxpayers to contribute to the support of the Congregational minister of the locality. This issue was raised time after time; protests were made in the town meetings. Some Anglicans flatly refused to pay the tax, and were in consequence imprisoned.[31] But they persisted, and eventually were to achieve their aim; the law was modified in 1727.

There was one peculiar feature of the Congregational establishment which was to prove eventually a great advantage to Anglican advance in New England. The establishment was intolerant; that was no novelty in the world of the Seventeenth Century. So was the Church of England, so was the Roman Catholic Church, so were other religious bodies. But in all these other establishments, one purpose of intolerance was to force everyone, in the area where the church was established, to *belong* to the church. The community was to be a religious monolith. Not so the Puritan establishments of Massachusetts or Connecticut: they were at once established and *exclusive*. Everyone in the community must attend the church; everyone must support the church financially. But membership, with all that this meant of participation in government, was a jealously guarded privilege. A letter, written by Colonel Heathcote in January 1709/10 to the secretary of the S. P. G. shows graphically just how exclusive the established church was in Connecticut: "In some of their Towns amongst 100 sober people, not ten will be admitted to the Sacrament, and vast numbers are denied Baptism. I am told that in a Town called Newhaven within 14 miles of Stratford there are near 1000 unbaptized...."[32] The numbers here might well be exaggerated; but they represent a sub-stratum of hard fact.

After the death of George Muirson, the Stratford Churchmen were for several years without even the occasional services of a priest. But by the end of 1712 the S. P. G. at length had sent to Stratford a resident missionary. Unfortunately the Reverend Francis Phillips, an Englishman whom the Society selected for this key post, proved to be completely unfitted for the work, and left after a brief and troubled pastorate.[33] But the way was being prepared for the coming of the man who was to make of Stratford what it eventually became, the heart of a rapidly growing Anglican Church in Connecticut. East of New Haven was the village of Guilford. Here lived "a good religious man" named Samuel Smithson, "lately settled at Guilford," and a convinced member of the Church of England. In the year 1716 he gave to young Samuel Johnson, just graduated from the collegiate school, a copy of *The Book of Common Prayer*.[34]

5. The S. P. G.

In the following pages the reader will find times without number the initials S. P. G. They stand for The Society for the Propagation of the Gospel in Foreign Parts. For two hundred years after the Reformation, missions to non-Christians were almost entirely confined to the Roman Catholic Church. It is one of the glories of the Church of England in the supposedly lax and inactive – as far as Christianity is concerned – Eighteenth Century, that at the very beginning of that century the Church of England began active missionary work.

In 1700 the Bishop of London sent as his commissary to Maryland the Reverend Thomas Bray. Bray remained in the colonies only a few months, but he took back with him to England a vision – the notion that here in the colonies was a vast field for missionary work, an opportunity that the Church of England must seize. Therefore in 1701 he founded the Society for the Propagation of the Gospel in Foreign Parts. Its first meeting was held in Lambeth Palace on January 27, 1701, with Archbishop Tenison presiding, and a goodly number of bishops and other noted divines in attendance. The Society was duly chartered by the king. Its object, as set forth in this instrument, was to be the provision of godly ministers for the administration of God's word and Sacraments among the king's loving subjects beyond the seas. It also planned active missionary work among Indians and Negroes.[35]

The founders of the S. P. G. at once began a campaign for funds – a campaign which continued from year to year, and was so well managed that by the outbreak of the American Revolution it had amassed well over £300,000 – a tremendous sum for those days.

This money was carefully spent in providing stipends for both priests and school teachers. Leaving aside Virginia, where the

Church by reason of its endowed status needed no financial help, the Society subsidized missionaries throughout the other colonies, granting normally a stipend of fifty pounds a year for a priest – enough, with what the local congregation could raise, to support him in reasonable comfort.

Furthermore, the Society did one other thing most necessary for the health of the Church in the colonies. It exercised discipline. Each priest and each school teacher was required to make periodical reports to the secretary of the Society, and these reports were carefully scanned. The Society demanded results, and if the recipient of a stipend failed to produce results, he was incontinently dismissed. The result was that the Society's priests were the most active and diligent of the colonial clergy. Furthermore, the reports, which were carefully kept and filed, are one of our best sources for the history of the colonial church. Over and over again, in tracing the life of Samuel Johnson, we shall be quoting from his letters to the successive secretaries. In fact, it was the existence of the Society, and its efficient operation, which made possible his life's work for the Church.

Chapter II

THE FORMATIVE YEARS

1. Boyhood

Samuel Johnson was born in the little Connecticut village of Guilford on October 14, 1696.[1] Guilford lies on Long Island Sound about sixteen miles east of New Haven, and is the center of a township consisting of a stretch of fertile coastal plain, with an upland of wooded hills. It boasted a small and rather shallow harbor; it was eventually made a port of entry. The original settlers of Guilford, like so many of the Puritan colonists, had come from England as a corporate group under the leadership of a minister, the Reverend Henry Whitefield. They had maintained their existence as a separate colony until forced to merge with the nearby colony of New Haven. New Haven, as we have seen, was under the leadership of the Reverend John Davenport, the quintessence of Puritanism. At the time of Samuel's birth the village was built around the characteristic New England green. Many of the houses were built of local stone. Stone likewise was the meetinghouse, a box-like structure with a thatched roof and a porch. This had been erected in 1643, and therefore by 1696 began to have a semblance of antiquity. Not as old was the school, built in 1677. Around these two buildings revolved the life of the pioneer community. The population of the township at the time of Samuel's birth was about 540.

The members of the Johnson family were not among the original settlers of Guilford. Robert Johnson, the great-grandfather of Samuel, came to America from Kingston-upon-Hull in Yorkshire, and was one of the founders of New Haven in 1637. In 1653 Robert's son William moved to Guilford and set up in business as a fuller – or dresser of cloth – an important occupation in a community which aimed to be as far as possible self-contained in its economy. William soon became a man of standing in the community, for at one time he held the important position of town clerk. He was also a deacon in the established church; this was a testimony of his orthodoxy, his regular practice of religion, and his uprightness of life. He was followed in the family business by his son Samuel.[2] According to our Samuel, his father was not a particularly good businessman, but obviously he was sufficiently successful to provide adequately for his large family. The cloth-dressing business remained the possession of the Johnson family until well into the Nineteenth Century.

The elder Samuel, who like his father was a deacon in the church, in 1694 married Mary Sage of an influential Middletown family. It was a period when a large birth rate was paralleled by an equally large death rate. Mary Johnson bore eleven children, six of whom survived to maturity. Samuel was her second child, and the eldest survivor in a family of five brothers and five sisters. It seems to have been an exceptionally happy family circle, and made Samuel what he was throughout his life, a man with strong family ties. Samuel, tall, strong, and healthy, did the things normal for a village boy of his generation. He rode horseback, and on one occasion his horse ran away with him. He swam and fished. Three times he escaped drowning. In winter he skated, and inevitably fell through the ice. All this was usual. But Samuel was an unusual boy. His brief *Autobiography* tells us what made him different.

> This Samuel was early taught to read by the care of his grandfather, who was very fond of him and, being apt to learn, he taught him many things by heart, beginning with the Lord's Prayer and Creed, and as he delighted to read the Scriptures, he got many passages of them by heart, which his grandfather, carrying him about with him to visit the ancient people, his contemporaries, made him

recite *memoriter*, in which he much delighted. One of the first things he remembered of himself was an impatient curiosity to know everything that could be known; so that he was very inquisitive. His grandfather had a book in which there were several Hebrew words, the meaning of which he was very desirous to know, but to his great mortification nobody was able to tell him And these inclinations in him made his grandfather, who lived till he was six years old, very desirous he should be bred to learning in the College which was about that time founding.[3]

It is a graphic picture, in spite of the involved pronouns, which this passage gives us – the precocious little boy trotted out to display his mixture of piety and learning before a circle of admiring grown-ups. It was the sort of process which might well have made of him an insufferable little prig. It is an indication of Johnson's essential balance and sanity that nothing of the sort came about. But the real importance of the passage, and the key to much of Johnson's life, lies in the one phrase – the "impatient curiosity to know everything that could be known." The boy was already possessed by a passionate thirst for knowledge. This thirst was to be one of the driving forces of Samuel Johnson's life, a quality that makes him worth our attention today.

Grandfather William died in 1702, when Samuel was six years old. Samuel's parents seem to have been less interested than the grandfather in their child's drive for scholarship. According to the *Autobiography*, the father attempted to train the boy up in the family business of clothdressing. Fortunately, Samuel showed no interest or aptitude for the business. He "could think of nothing but books, so his father let him follow his inclinations."[4]

Fortunately, this happened in New England, where almost every village, however small, had its local school, usually taught by the minister. And the minister of Guilford was no ordinary man. The Reverend Jared Eliot, a graduate of the Collegiate School in 1706 and grandson of John Eliot who helped Hooker found Connecticut, already at the age of twenty-one gave promise of an unusual career. He was reputed to have been Rector Pierson's favorite pupil. He eventually extended his interest from theology to science, became, like a number of his co-clergy, a practising physician, and was considered the best of the sort in Connecticut. His scientific interests and achievements eventually secured for him the honor of election to the Royal Society of London. While at Guilford Eliot married the daughter of Samuel Smithson, the Churchman who gave young Johnson his first *Book of Common Prayer*.[5] Contact with such a mind must have been a stimulating experience for eleven-year old Samuel. Unfortunately, in 1707 Eliot left for another pastorate, and the school in Guilford was temporarily closed. The family, having decided that Samuel must have schooling, sent him to the Reverend Joseph Smith of North Middletown, where he found the teacher "such a wretched poor scholar ... that he in a manner lost half a year." He then returned to Guilford, where

> the next master he had was one Mr. [Daniel] Chapman who for near two years taught him much better but the next year he had the good fortune of being taught by one Mr. James who though a very odd sort of man yet having been bred in England he was a very good classic scholar, both in Latin and Greek by whose help he made much better proficiency than usual, for the condition of learning ... was very low in these times indeed much lower than in the earlier time while those yet lived who had had their education in England...[6]

The biographer of Johnson's contemporary and later antagonist, Thomas Clap, sums up ably the content of secondary education for the Connecticut student who in those days was preparing for college. Since all schooling in New England was then dominated by the entrance requirements for Harvard and the Collegiate School, Johnson must have been subject to the same regime as Clap. A thorough grounding in Latin was the basic requirement. The pupil must know Latin grammar as found in Cheever and Lily, and he must be able to read with facility Cicero, Vergil, Terence, and Ovid. He must be able to write passable Latin prose. In addition, it was well if he knew enough Greek to read the New Testament.[7] Since Samuel Johnson had had the two advantages of a superior mind and superior teaching, by the autumn of 1710 he was ready to enter the Collegiate School at Saybrook. He was then fourteen, a fairly normal age at that time for college entrance.

2. College Days

When Johnson entered the Collegiate School, it was at one of its lowest points. There were only ten students registered, and they were divided into two groups – the freshmen, sophomores, and juniors at Saybrook, the seniors at Milford under the tuition of Rector Samuel Andrew. The tutors at Saybrook were two in number, Phineas Fiske and Joseph Noyes. Fiske left during Johnson's time at Saybrook, and was replaced by William Russell. These were all men in their early twenties; their chief qualification, and of all the tutors of this early period of the school, seems to have been to be related to a trustee. Of Russell we know very little, but Fiske, in his later days, had the reputation of being the dullest preacher in Connecticut. He could hardly have been an inspiring teacher.

What was life like in this incipient Yale in the year 1710? Saybrook itself, located on a tiny peninsula jutting into the Connecticut River, was even smaller than Guilford. It consisted of barely a dozen farmhouses, facing the usual green. At the tip of the peninsula was the old stone fort, erected in 1648 when there was still danger from attack by Indians. At the other end of the community was Lion Gardner's windmill, dating from 1636.[8] The tutors lived and held classes in the large frame house formerly owned by Nathaniel Lynde, and now the property of the trustees of the school. The students – all boys in their late teens – boarded wherever they could find accommodation.

The college day began at sun-up, with morning prayers – not to be confused with Morning Prayer. At this time the scriptures were duly read and expounded by one of the tutors. Classes began at six-thirty, with time off a little later for breakfast. For freshmen, the morning was then devoted to a solid drill in Greek and Latin grammar and prose composition. The students were expected by the end of the year to write passable Latin, and even to carry on a conversation in that tongue. The drill was followed by reading in Tully and Vergil; some work was done in elementary Hebrew. The mastery of these three languages would equip the boys with the necessary tools for a life of ministry or public service in an orthodox Calvinistic commonwealth. Dinner, at noon, was a hearty meal of meat and vegetables, washed down by plenty of beer or cider. This was followed by an hour or so of recreation. Then the boys were back at the grind, which ended after supper with evening prayers and a second sermon. By nine o'clock, everyone was in bed.[9]

It was a hard life, and the course of study made it no easier. Apart from the three learned languages, which at least had the merit of bringing the student into contact with the classics and the scriptures, the curriculum was unbelievably barren. The trustees had solemnly ruled that theology was to be taught, not from Calvin's *Institutes*, but from watered-down Calvin. The theological textbooks were a Latin Catechism, William Ames's *Marrow of Sacred Divinity* and the same worthy's *Cases of Conscience*. The logic of Peter Ramus was taught from the Latin manual of Bergersdicius. To these studies were added, for practical purposes, simple arithmetic, surveying, and what passed for science. The science text was a set of notes compiled by former Rector Pierson. It is an amazing fact that in the year of Our Lord 1710, when Copernicus had been in his grave two hundred years, the boys in the Collegiate School were still being taught that the sun goes round the earth. Coming to the school with the two advantages of a first-class mind and good preparation, young Johnson soon discovered that he knew far more already than the average student, and sometimes more than the tutors. A contemporary of his at the school testified that "the greatest proficient in the Hebrew and in the other languages also was Dr. Johnson."[10]

However, there were some compensations. There were weekly disputations, which taught the student something of the art of arranging and applying his knowledge. And where modern college education tends more and more to an extreme specialization, the Collegiate School had inherited from the universities of the Middle Ages the basic idea that knowledge was essentially one, and that all one had learned in college might be combined into a synthesis. Each student was expected, as a sort of diploma piece, to write up such a synthesis. And so we find Johnson writing in Latin, some time before he graduated, A Synopsis of Natural Philosophy in the form of ninety-two questions and answers. A typical item was:

> Q. 84. What is there to be observed about the element of fire?

A. About the element of fire there is to be observed (1) that it is in the uppermost place of changing nature. It is near the third heaven, not beneath but above the vault of the moon from which it extends to the third heaven, comprising the second ... or starry heaven. (2) When condensed it burns or shines….[11]

Even at sixteen or seventeen, young Johnson found this not quite satisfactory. He discarded his synopsis, and embarked on a still more ambitious program, which he called *An Encyclopedia of Philosophy*. This consisted of no less than 1271 numbered assertions, in which he aimed to sum up all knowledge as he then possessed it. Having finished this, he sat back to contemplate himself and his opus with something of wonder and admiration. Looking back at this work from the perspective of maturity, he appended to it this charming note:

N.B. When I was at College I was taught nothing but to be a conceited coxcomb like those that taught me. Indeed we had no books and our ignorance made us think almost out of our own brains as a certain Gent. (Mr. Noyes) of those times used to say was his way.[12]

It was said of Thomas Clap, Johnson's contemporary, that "he never grew – he was cast." Now one reason why Samuel Johnson is worth our consideration today is that the opposite was true of him. His whole intellectual life was a prolonged voyage of discovery. The two notes we have quoted above are the indication of the first of these discoveries, discoveries that would turn Samuel Johnson into something rather different from Tutors Noyes and Russell. From the day when his proud grandfather had displayed the six-year old boy until now, he had been at the head of the class. He suddenly discovered that he was at the foot. Somehow in his last year at Saybrook he chanced to get hold of a copy of Bacon's *Advancement of Learning*, perhaps the only copy in Connecticut. Here was totally different intellectual fare from the chaff he had been handed out. It is a clear indication of Johnson's real intellectual superiority that he could at once perceive the greatness of Bacon. It is also an indication of Johnson's innate modesty that, having perceived that superiority, he could abase himself before it. In his *Autobiography* Johnson graphically described what Bacon meant to him:

> the reading and considering Lord Bacon soon brought down his towering imaginations; he soon saw his own littleness in comparison with Lord Bacon's greatness whom he considered over and over again so that he found himself like one at once emerging out of the glimmer of twilight into the full sunshine of open day.[13]

Perceptivity, receptivity, humility – these three qualities Johnson here demonstrated. And these are the qualities of a true scholar. This discovery of Bacon, and all that it meant, was the beginning of the intellectual emancipation of Samuel Johnson, the beginning of that process by which he freed himself from his native provincialism, and became the outstanding intellectual of the colony. Until this point, he had been doing the ordinary thing in a better than ordinary way. Thereafter he proceeded to do the extraordinary thing.

Something else of value Johnson gained from his stay at Saybrook. Throughout his life he was a gregarious person, a person with a gift for friendship. Here on Saybrook Point he met a kindred spirit – Daniel Browne. Browne had entered the Collegiate School in the same class with Johnson. Like Johnson, he had a better than average mind; like Johnson, he was eager to go a-voyaging in the world of books and thought. And so there was begun between the two a friendship of heart and mind, a friendship that endured while the two traveled together on the intellectual exploration, and that ended only when Browne lay dead in far-off England.

There is a bit of mystery about Johnson's senior year at the Collegiate School. Normally he would have gone to Milford to finish his course under the direction of Rector Andrew. But on January 5, 1714, Johnson was back in Guilford, where the selectmen had hired him to teach the local school at a salary of forty shillings a month. Johnson, as is evident throughout his entire career, was a born teacher. That he was successful in this, his first venture at teaching, we know from the best evidence. In the spring the selectmen – and Connecticut selectmen were an economical lot – raised his pay to forty-five shillings a month. It is just possible that Johnson was so far ahead of his fellow students that he was allowed to spend this last year studying on his own. Whatever the reason, the fact remains that he did not go to Milford.

On September 8, 1714, Commencement was held in the meeting-house at Saybrook. The Rector "presided, flanked in the deacons' seats by such Trustees as could come, in their full-bottomed wigs, white bands, black coats and small-clothes, black stockings and shoes with silver buckles."[14] Commencement was an all-day affair, beginning with a long conceived prayer. The students were given a chance to show off by giving their disputations – in Latin of course. Finally, nine youths, Johnson and Browne among them, were given their degrees. Of the nine, three eventually became Anglicans. Mean-time, two other events which influenced Johnson's future were taking place – the school's acquisition of the Dummer Library and a student revolt.

3. The Dummer Library

While young Johnson was thus doing what in modern "pedaguese" would be called "enriching the curriculum" by his fascinated reading of Bacon, on the other side of the Atlantic something was happening which was to have an incalculable effect on his future. It became customary for some American colonies to maintain in England an agent – a sort of lobbyist who would look after the interests of the colony, see that the King thought favorably of it, and attempt to make sure that Parliament passed no laws which would affect the colony unfavorably. The agent of Massachusetts at this time was one Jeremiah Dummer, Harvard graduate and man about town, who knew everyone of importance in London, and was well received in London society.[15] The years when Johnson was at Saybrook were bad years for the finances of the Collegiate School; in 1712, for example, the General Assembly voted only £100 for it instead of the former grant of £120. It therefore occurred to the Reverend James Pierpont, who of all the trustees took the most active part in furthering the interests of the school, that Dummer might be able to raise money for it in England. To give Dummer a status in the matter, Pierpont induced the General Assembly of Connecticut, in October, 1712, to appoint Dummer the agent of the colony.[16] Dummer at once busied himself about the affair. His most promising prospect seemed to be Elihu Yale, American-born Governor of Fort St. George in India, who had returned to England with the fabulous wealth of a nabob. But Yale's purse strings were not easy to loose, and it was some time before he gave money to the Collegiate School – not much, but enough to induce the authorities to rename it Yale College.

The quest for money was not very successful; Dummer then turned his efforts in another direction. So far, the library of the school consisted only in the few books given at its very beginning. Realizing, apparently, that the school needed books as much as it needed money, Dummer began to hunt for them. Here, beginning in 1713, he was very successful. Sir Richard Steele gave a beautifully bound set of the *Spectator Papers*, Isaac Newton the second edition of his *Principia*, and such eminent scholars as Bentley, Whiston, and Halley contributed liberally from their personal libraries. Governor Yale gave forty volumes. In all, Dummer managed to amass close to a thousand volumes – a collection the like of which was seldom to be seen in the American colonies.[17] The collection was a well-rounded one. English literature was represented by Spenser and Milton and Jonson and Butler, science by Boyle, Euclid, Huygens and Newton, Latin literature by Horace and Ovid. There were the Church Fathers in ponderous Latin and Greek tomes. Inevitably, there were numerous volumes of controversial divinity. Keith, Barclay, and Penn were here to speak for the dissenters, and for the Anglicans writers like Hooker, Potter, Jeremy Taylor, Stillingfleet, and Wake. Titles included provocative subjects like *A Rationale Upon the Book of Common Prayer*, *Canons of the Church of England*, *A Vindication of the Rights of Ecclesiastical Authority*, and *A Discourse Concerning Election and Reprobation*. Here was a whole new world of thought waiting for the student. Here was also dynamite.

The first shipment of books arrived just in time for the Commencement of 1714. Its appearance posed an immediate and urgent question. Where were these books to be housed? There was obviously no place for a library of a thousand volumes in any of the country parsonages where school had at times been kept, nor even in the house owned by the trustees at Saybrook. The question, so often deferred, of a permanent location for the Collegiate School now had to be faced. Such a location, and an adequate building, would cost money, and money the trustees had never had. They therefore twice appealed to the General Assembly of the colony, and twice their appeal failed to elicit any useful response. But then came a sudden gleam of sunshine. In 1715 a boundary dispute which had been dragging on for years between Connecticut and the mother colony of Massachusetts was finally settled, and the younger colony found itself the owner of over a hundred thousand acres of disposable land. Encouraged by this windfall, the Assembly voted £500 from the sale of the lands for the erection of a permanent "college house."[18] The first intention was that this building should be located in neutral Saybrook, where there were now twenty-five students in residence.

On October 17, 1716, the trustees met to take action appropriate to this grant. They must now come to a decision about location. It was found that they were divided into three warring factions. A small group of temporizers preferred to keep the school at Saybrook. But this was no longer possible. The remainder of the trustees were divided into two strong factions, fighting for the opposing claims of Hartford and New Haven. The trustees finally referred the matter to the General Assembly, which decided in October 1717 that the college ought to be located at New Haven. The decision came when the New Haven faction, fortified by a promised subscription of the sizable sum of £2000 from residents of that community, given with the attached string that it would be available only if the school were moved to New Haven, managed to put through a majority vote for the move. As so often happens in human affairs, the long purse won. This decision arrived at, the trustees also resolved that work should be started at once on the erection of a building.[19] But the trustees in favor of the Hartford area did not accept their defeat as final, as we shall see.

4. The Students Revolt

During the same time that the trustees were thus divided over location, the affairs of the Collegiate School suffered another complication. The twenty-five late teen-agers who were assembled at Saybrook were no play-boys. College to them was a serious matter

– a ladder to climb out of the hard physical labor of a Connecticut farm. They wanted education, and they wanted it badly. And, as Johnson's testimony makes abundantly clear, they were getting at the Collegiate School a very inferior brand of it. Added to a bare and antiquated curriculum was the uninspiring teaching of the various tutors. Nor were they much better off in their senior year under Rector Andrew. Andrew was a scholarly recluse, who intensely disliked and consistently avoided contacts with people, and was happy only in his study with his nose in a book. Furthermore, the boys suffered from bad living facilities, and bad food. They therefore showed that they were of the same make as the students of Paris and Oxford in the Middle Ages, of those of Columbia and Harvard in 1968-69. They staged a student revolt. It seems to have taken the form, not of a sit-in, but of a walk-out. Some of the boys gradually drifted to Wethersfield for instruction arranged by the Reverend Messers Woodbridge and Buckingham of Hartford, two trustees who wanted the college moved from Saybrook to Wethersfield. Others put themselves under Johnson's tuition at Guilford. Thus the turmoil was related to the dispute over the location of the school. The schism was serious enough to extort from the trustees a very queer permission indeed. The students were to remain at Saybrook for three years. But in their senior year, they might go wherever they could find teaching to their liking. Those who elected to go to Wethersfield, just out of Hartford, found that the Reverend Elisha Williams, Harvard graduate of some five years' standing, was showing signs of the intellectual leadership that would eventually make him rector of Yale. Williams was assisted as tutor by Samuel Smith, who had graduated from the Collegiate School in 1713, and apparently had teaching ability. Several, we do not know how many, went to Johnson at Guilford.[20] So matters stood until the decision was made to locate the school at New Haven and while the building there was under construction.

5. Dissent from Dissent

The intellectual revolution wrought in Samuel Johnson by his discovery of Bacon was marked by a slower change in his religious ideas. Brought up in a pious and happy home, we have seen how as a boy of six he had begun that avid reading of the scriptures which he was to continue as long as he lived. He went to Saybrook an orthodox Calvinist. But during his Saybrook days there were signs of a growing dissatisfaction with what passed for orthodoxy in colonial Connecticut. With obvious disapproval Johnson wrote that the students "were not allowed to vary an ace in their thoughts from Dr. Ames's *Medulla Theologiae* and *Cases of Conscience* and Wollebius which were the only systems of divinity that were thumbed in those days and considered with equal if not greater veneration than the Bible itself...."[21] Already he was showing the true scholar's desire to go back to the sources.

Nor was he much pleased by the type of religious manifestation common among the students at the Collegiate School. Throughout his life, he constantly showed a deep dislike for "enthusiasm" – the public outpouring of religious emotion and ministers' extemporaneous prayers. It was customary for the boys at Saybrook to supplement the stated religious exercises of the school by holding prayer meetings. On these, Johnson commented (with his autobiographical use of the third person pronoun):

> But what first prejudiced him against this way was his observation, when at college of its great tendency to promote and nourish self-conceit and spiritual pride. The scholars had private meetings for prayer and reading and such as had something of a knack that way could not forbear appearing vain of it; one especially who excelled at it was even so vain as to talk of his gifts; on the other hand some modest youths of good sense...were apt to be despised and discouraged. He also often observed many impertinent and indecent and sometimes almost blasphemous expressions dropt, which were very shocking to him, which gave him early disgust and led him to think surely it must be much better that our prayers be pre-composed in the best manner possible.[22]

This was treading on dangerous ground, for the "conceived" prayer was rooted deeply in the Puritan notion of acceptable worship. Returning to Guilford after graduation in this frame of mind, Johnson was ready to look for an alternative. And just at this crucial time in his mental development, Mr. Smithson gave him a copy of *The Book of Common Prayer* – the most insidious piece of propaganda the Anglican Communion has ever put out. Johnson read it, and the spell of Cranmer's magnificent translations and compositions from the Latin seized upon him. Furthermore, biblical student that he was, he now became vividly aware how filled was the Prayer Book with subtle and beautiful biblical allusions, and how greatly it made use of the Scriptures in Psalms, lessons, epistles, gospels. This was the beginning of a love affair that would last throughout Johnson's life.

The books that Dummer had collected in England lay in Saybrook, boxed, unshelved. Nevertheless Johnson must have managed to gain access to them. Among them was Archbishop King's *Inventions of Man in the Worship of God*, a defence of the Prayer Book system. In 1715 Johnson read this, and found it convincing. The "*extempore* way in which he had been brought up" Johnson had already decided was very wrong, for the use of "well-composed forms" gave "no occasion to rack our invention in finding what to say...." Johnson thought it admirable that worshippers would "have nothing else to do in prayer but to offer up our hearts with our words which is indeed the proper and only business of prayer."[23]

With his family background, his education, and his own innate bent toward religion, it was only natural that Johnson should at this point begin to think seriously about entering the ministry of Connecticut's established church. Therefore in 1715 he applied for and received a license as a lay preacher in that church. His first sermon was delivered on May 22, 1715, in the Guilford meeting house. It makes very interesting reading. Like most sermons of beginning preachers, it is more than a bit pedantic. It contains quotations in Latin, in Greek, in Hebrew. (Boys of nineteen like to display their scholarship.) It is overlong for the modern taste. But it has certain remarkable characteristics. One sometimes wonders, reading the Puritan divines, whether they had ever heard of the New Testament. But this is a New Testament sermon. Written on the text from Isaiah, "Behold, a virgin shall conceive," it is an exposition of the person and work of Jesus Christ. A careful search can discover only a phrase here and there which betrays the fact that it was delivered in a Puritan meeting house. And Johnson rose in places to a real eloquence, as in this passage:

> Now Christ therefore the eternally begotten Son of God, became man, did subsist in one person, inseparably and so to subsist to all eternity ... Behold! O Christian, by the eye of thy faith, the most wonderful sight that was ever seen in the world, yea truly admirable! The creator and the creature, the maker and the thing made, God and man, the potter and the clay, infinite and finite, eternal and temporal, unchangeable and changeable, naming but one person! And whom having not seen with your bodily eyes, ye love, and whom though now ye see not yet believing ye rejoice with joy unspeakable and full of glory.[24]

Not from William Ames did these antitheses come. Johnson, when he wrote them, was plainly moving from the orthodoxy of his father and his grandfather to a much older orthodoxy. It is difficult to avoid the conclusion that when Johnson wrote these words he had found in the boxes of the library at Saybrook the Decree of the Council of Chalcedon.

During the two years he taught at Guilford, Johnson continued to preach at intervals, but when he was called back to the Collegiate School as tutor he had not proceeded to ordination.

Chapter III

BEGINNING A CAREER

1. Election as Tutor

The trustees of the Collegiate School met October 17-20, 1716 to grapple with several problems, not least of which was the issue of locating the school. By a vote of five to two the decision was made for New Haven, but the trustees applied to the General Assembly to "nominate the place," evidently hoping that it would sanction the resolution of a thorny issue. Other important matters were also decided. Eight of the trustees were present; the Reverend Moses Noyes, minister of New Haven, presided. It was now necessary to do something radical about the teaching staff. No longer was the relationship to a trustee to be the sole qualification for a tutor, and it was deemed necessary that the tutors scattered in several towns be brought to some common ground. The Reverend Mr. Andrew, in spite of his reluctance, was continued as rector "for the present," although he did not live in New Haven. But two new tutors were appointed to assist him, and indeed, to carry most of the teaching load. The minutes of the trustees' meeting are revealing. The question was put:

> Whether we approve Sir Johnson of Guilford for Tutor for the Collegiate School?

Yes. Mr. Ruggles, Mr. Davenport, Mr. Webb, Mr. Russel, Mr. Andrew, Mr. Noyes.

Mr. Buckingham saith he hath nothing to object against him on account of his qualifications.

Mr. Woodbridge saith, he doth not account it convenient to mention him, because of Newark call.

Sir Johnson was desired to appear before the Trustees, & the ofer [sic] of a Tutor of the School was made to him, & he desired to consider of it.[1]

On the following day Johnson appeared before the trustees and accepted the position. But the discerning reader will note that in some strange way, Johnson's teaching career was involved with the burning question of the ultimate location of the school. The two trustees, Buckingham and Woodbridge, who failed to concur in the appointment, were the die-hard opponents of the move to New Haven. The majority, having won their main point, however, were apparently in a conciliatory mood. They elected as Johnson's fellow tutor Samuel Smith, who had been assisting Elisha Williams in the rival school at Wethersfield. The trustees sent Johnson to persuade Smith to bring his scholars to join the school. But in spite of the special embassy to induce him to accept the tutorship, Smith refused. Again, at the trustees' meeting at the end of October, 1716, an olive branch was extended to the Hartford faction, when Elisha Williams was offered the post of senior tutor.[2] He declined. In the upshot Johnson, with only temporary and make-shift help, was compelled to carry on the work of the New Haven school almost single handed; he was assisted by Moses Noyes, the town minister. What the stipend was for Johnson's work the records do not make entirely clear. In April 1717 he was paid by vote of the trustees £17. And in the following September the minutes show that the treasurer was instructed to pay Johnson £23, "being the whole due him to his services the year past."[3]

In October 1716, Samuel Johnson, having arrived at the mature age of twenty, moved to New Haven to begin his brief career as tutor in the Collegiate School. Taller than average, he was strongly built with a complexion somewhat florid, and a facial expression that somehow combined a natural dignity with a great deal of approachable friend-liness. Wearing the wig and black gown that were the badges of his office, he presided over his first classes.[4]

It was no easy task that he faced. The schism in the student body, fomented by the industrious Hartford trustees, Woodbridge and Buckingham, was full-blown. Fourteen of the students were still at Wethersfield, Johnson had thirteen at New Haven, and four lingered in Saybrook. It was not until the January following Johnson's arrival in New Haven that work on the new building was even started. Meanwhile, the young tutor was compelled to hold classes in the house where he was then lodging. His own comment on the situation at this point was brief and to the point: "things looked dark and melancholy, and even spightful and malicious."

2. Revising the Curriculum

Pushing discouragement aside, Johnson went manfully to work at his serious problem while the schism over the school played itself out. Gradually matters began to improve. Johnson was a born teacher, who loved the art, and a natural leader of young men. Soon both his undoubted intellectual power and his sympathetic person-ality had their effect on the students. Disgusted with the curriculum from which he had suffered during the years at Saybrook, he now initiated a quiet revolution in the course of study. As we have seen, he had already dug deeply into the boxes containing the Dummer library. He brought more of these books with him to New Haven. Among them was Newton's *Principia*, the personal gift of its author. This Johnson, with his devouring curiosity, began to read, but he dis-covered that it was beyond his comprehension. The mathematics he had been taught at Saybrook was not up to the task. He therefore set himself to learn the necessary mathematics, and having mastered the tools, he could read the masterpiece with intelligent understanding. Of equal importance was his discovery, at about the same time, of John Locke. Now Newton and Locke were the two basic authors behind that many-sided movement of the human mind which we have come to call the Enlightenment. Forsaking Ames and Wollebius, Johnson threw himself into the current. But it was not to be the Enlightenment of Diderot and the French Encyclopedists.

Along with Newton and Locke Johnson discovered Catholic theology. All this newfound knowledge Johnson was doing his best to pass on to his students. During these exploratory years, he "began to introduce into the curriculum the empiricism of Locke, the inductive method of Bacon, and the cosmology of Kepler, Copernicus, and Newton ... During his three year tutorial stint, Johnson was eminently successful in establishing an up-to-date scientific tradition."[5] As a result the Collegiate School which had been in part founded to counteract the growing liberalism of Harvard, was itself developing even more rapidly the same trend toward a liberalized course of study.

In September 1717, the first commencement was held at New Haven. Four students were given their bachelor's degrees, and Johnson was made Master of Arts. At the same time a new tutor, the Reverend Joseph Moss, about whom we know very little, was added to the staff.[6]

The Commencement was graced by the presence of Governor Gurdon Saltonstall, a man who played a significant part in Samuel Johnson's formative years, as in those of Yale College. Saltonstall was born in 1666, ordained to the Congregational ministry, and settled as pastor at New London. While he was there, George Keith and John Talbot, Anglican missionaries, made their famous journey through the American colonies. In September 1702 they arrived at New London, and there occurred an extraordinary incident, which Keith recorded in his journal.

> Mr. Talbot preached there [September 13] in the forenoon, and I preached there in the afternoon, we being desired to do so by the minister, Mr. Gurdon Saltonstall, who civilly entertained us at his house, and expressed his good affection to the Church of England, as did also the minister at Hampton [John Cotton] and the minister at Salisbury [a Mr. Cushing], and divers other New England ministers did the like.[7]

Such is the evidence for Saltonstall's amiability and his talent for leading and mediating between men of differing persuasions. Saltonstall's leading parishioner at New London was Fitz-John Winthrop, governor of the colony from 1698 to 1701. During Winthrop's later years, he came to lean more and more on the advice of his pastor in political affairs. Late in 1701, Winthrop died. Whereupon the General Assembly of Connecticut exercised their power under the royal charter. Meeting on December 11, 1701, they asked Saltonstall to resign his parochial charge, and become Winthrop's successor as governor. He complied, was duly elected, and continued in office until his death in 1724.[8] Through the difficult days when the location of the Collegiate School was a burning question, he steadily favored its removal to New Haven, and proved a consistent friend to the college.

3. The New Building

During the college year 1717-1718 matters steadily improved. The New Haven section of the school was gradually finding funds to carry on its work. Dummer in England had been steadily working on Elihu Yale, and had finally secured from him a sizable gift, most of which was applied to the construction of the new college building. This was designed by Governor Saltonstall himself, and the builder was Henry Caner of Boston. Of no great architectural pretensions, it was nevertheless the most impressive structure in New Haven. It was a hundred and sixty feet long and twenty wide. Three stories in height, with a kitchen ell, it contained fifty studies for students and tutors, and a great room heated by two huge fireplaces, capable of containing the Dummer library. Writing to Dummer on October 31, 1718, the trustees grew fairly lyrical in their description:

> We are in hopes of having shortly perfected our Splendid Collegiate House, which was raised on the 8th instant. We behold its fair aspect in the Market-place of New Haven, mounted on an eminent place thereof, in length ten rods, in breadth 21 foot, and nearly thirty foot upright, a Spacious Hall & an equally Spacious Library.[9]

By the fall of 1718 Johnson was able to move himself and his students into the new building, named Yale Hall in compliment to the English donor – a name which of course was eventually applied to the college itself. And here, to his great joy, Johnson was joined by his closest friend and co-student, Daniel Browne, whom the trustees had appointed junior tutor. No longer was it necessary for him to carry on his silent intellectual revolution in solitude. Browne, with whom he had been in constant correspondence ever since their student days, was in complete sympathy with the Johnson reform of the curriculum.

4. Moving the Library

One of the main purposes of the erection of the new building at New Haven had been the necessity of providing space for the library collected by Jeremiah Dummer in England. Except for the books taken out by Johnson, these were still stored in the original boxes in Saybrook. They must now be brought to New Haven. But there was a certain turbulence about the comparative democracy of early Connecticut, and local pride and parochialism, as we have seen, were strong forces. The inhabitants of Saybrook, deprived by the removal of the Collegiate School of their one title to greatness, now took the remarkable stand that the books had been given to the school in Saybrook, and in Saybrook they must stay. Negotiation proved fruitless, and Governor Saltonstall was called in. He therefore ordered the county sheriff to seize the precious books, and bring them to New Haven. But the people of Saybrook refused to obey his behest, and a veritable riot ensued, in which some two hundred volumes were lost or destroyed.[10] But at long last the major part of the collection, easily the best college library in the American colonies, arrived safely at New Haven, and the books were duly shelved in the great library room which had been built to house them. A veritable feast of learning and literature were now readily available to the inquiring minds of men like Johnson and Browne.

5. The Students Again Revolt

The college authorities had long been patient with the schism in the student body. Now it was determined that it must end. In the fall of 1718, the building completed and the library lodged in it, the General Assembly, prodded into action by the governor, passed an act "ordering all the scholars to repair to the established college." The

"Act for the Encouragement of Yale College" was an attempt at "a final conclusion of ... differences and misunderstandings," and indeed it offered all parties some concession. The tutors at New Haven, Wethersfield, and Saybrook were to be paid "in proportion to the scholars under their tuition." The Wethersfield students nearing graduation were to be given their degrees at New Haven "without further examinations" and others admitted to the same standing at New Haven as they had had at Wethersfield. Hartford was to have £500 to build a statehouse, and Saybrook £50 for its town school.[11]

The students came to New Haven, but with rebellion in their hearts. Among them was a young man named Jonathan Edwards. And thus, for a brief moment, the two best theological brains in Connecticut, if not in all New England, came into contact. It might have been expected that the contact would prove a fruitful and amicable one. Edwards was eventually to make great use of Locke and Newton in his thinking, and in all probability Johnson was the man who introduced him to those thinkers. Edwards owed something to his teacher, but he disliked Johnson. And the Wethersfield students, resentful at having to come to New Haven, made themselves as obnoxious as possible, and refused to submit to discipline. Strangely enough, they seem to have made a dead set for Tutor Johnson. Why it is hard to explain. It is abundantly clear that throughout his life Johnson was an appealing, indeed a magnetic teacher. But whatever the cause, the rebels deliberately set out to "unhorse" him from his tutorship – and they succeeded. First they concocted "a list of all the deficiencies of the New Haven college, in which the doctrines and methods of Tutor Johnson had the most prominent place, and secretly despatched it to the minister of Hartford." The minister of Hartford was of course Timothy Woodbridge, who knew how to make effective use of such a document. Partly as a result of his machinations to stir up trouble for the New Haven school, whose location he had disapproved, on January 10, 1719, all the Wethersfield students except one walked out, and returned to Wethersfield.[12]

Faced with this new revolt, Governor Saltonstall took vigorous action. He called a joint meeting of the trustees of the college and the General Assembly of the colony. Their first decision was that the college must now have a real head, and a strong one who would reside at the school. Rector Andrew had long wanted to get rid of his thankless and disagreeable job. Their choice as his successor was the Reverend Timothy Cutler, who earlier had been called to the Congregational church in Stratford to put down the rebellious Anglicans.[13] He had not done this, but he had proved a successful pastor in that difficult community. Cutler was then thirty-six years old, moderately scholarly in his tastes, of a commanding presence and dignity, rather stiff in his manner, and above all a strong disciplinarian. He had already formed a friendship with Johnson, and had journeyed to New Haven to browse in the library. What was to be the result of those browsings we shall see. At the time, he appeared to the trustees the ideal man for the difficult task ahead. And in many ways he was. Becoming rector in March 1719, Cutler soon restored discipline, and the schismatic students returned. Jonathan Edwards, who could not see into the future, had comments to make. In a letter to his family he noted that "the Trustees ... have removed that which was the cause of our coming away viz; Mr. Johnson from the Place of a Tutor." And his report on Cutler was that the new rector was "extraordinarily courteous to us, has a very good spirit of government, and keeps the school in excellent order."[14] Cutler soon showed his talents as a disciplinarian. Again, in his first year, the students revolted, this time against the food in the commons. When they displayed their indignation by overturning Cutler's privy, they were expelled.

But the peace of the school required that Johnson be the sacrifice. It was all done in the most gracious manner. In March 1719, the governor and council consulted the trustees and

> Upon consideration of the state of the college, the trustees present did declare, that Mr. Johnson, against whose learning it had been reputed that the deserting scholars had objected, had been for some years employed as a tutor in the said college, and was well known to be a gentleman of sufficient learning ... and in that respect very well accomplished for the charge he is in.[15]

Thus Johnson's departure was the occasion for compliments and avowed regrets. The last entry concerned with him in the records of the trustees was dated September 9, 1719, when this minute was entered:

> Ordered that the Rev'd Mr. Samuel Andrew, Samuel Russell and Thomas Ruggles to adjust the account which is due Mr. Johnson for his service in the college and order him what shall be due out of the treasury, with our particular thanks for his good service, and that three pounds be ordered him for his extraordinary service. Voted and passed.[16]

It is a mark of the real largeness of spirit of Samuel Johnson that, although he bitterly resented the action of the students against him, he acquiesced in the action of the trustees, and remained throughout his life a loyal son of Yale, interested in her fortunes, and securing for the college more than one benefaction.

6. Ordination

The end of his career as a teacher at Yale brought sharply before Johnson the other alternative career he had been considering for several years. After graduation from college and returning to his native Guilford he had made a tentative advance toward the ministry of the Congregational Church, and then stopped. There were two reasons for this. The first was his obvious delight at being made a tutor in the Collegiate School. But there was a more important reason for his hesitation to proceed to ordination. His religious foundations, the stern Calvinism in which he had been brought up, which he had inherited from his deacon father and grandfather, were being undermined. He was going through a religious crisis. A book – *Bacon's Advancement of Learning* – had been the first instrument of Johnson's intellectual emancipation. A second book – *The Book of Common Prayer* Mr. Smithson had given him – had begun, in his student days, his reaction against Puritan worship – the beginning of his spiritual emancipation. On his dismissal from the faculty of Yale, Johnson went to live at West Haven – only an hour's walk from the college. Beginning in October 1719, the month after his leaving Yale, Johnson kept a list of the books he read, and the month when he finished each one. This list he continued at intervals until 1756, and it offers us an entrancing look into his growing mind. It is significant that the first book listed, in this October of 1719, was *The Liturgy of the*

Church of England. Of course he had read it before, but his placing it at the head of his readings was portentous. The list is varied. In general literature we find *Paradise Lost*, Cicero, the Spectator Papers. His omnivorous taste is indicated by Gordon's *Geographical Grammar* and Keil's *Anatomy*. But most of the titles show how his mind was drawn to controversial divinity. They included:

> Dr. John Potter on Church Government
> Mr. Lesley's Easy Method with Deists
> The Whole Duty of Man
> Fuller's Church History of England
> Mr. Pascal's Thoughts on Religion
> Dr. Taylor's Rules on Holy Living and Dying.

It is easy to see how his mind was running. Two particularly notable titles are St. John Chrysostom on the priesthood – he was discovering the Fathers – and Richard Hooker's *Laws of Ecclesiastical Polity*. Hooker was a kindred spirit; his quiet reasonableness was just the thing to appeal to the mind of Samuel Johnson.[17]

After an autumn of such reading, thinking, interior debate, during which he very possibly talked much with Cutler and Browne, he sat down on December 20 to write a most remarkable paper, which he entitled "My Present Thoughts of Episcopacy with what I conceive may justify me in accepting Presbyterial Ordination."[18] This paper was never, like so many effusions of religious converts, intended for publication. It was never designed to be seen by anyone save its author. We must therefore grant it the virtue of complete honesty. Its six printed pages are too long for complete quotation, but it demands careful summary here. In it Johnson stated as clearly and candidly as possible his theological position in 1719, with the aim of arguing out his reasons for and against his being ordained in the ministry of the Congregational Church. It is his debate with himself. It deserves to be told in his own words as much as possible.

The paper is divided into two parts, the first giving his arguments for Episcopal ordination, the second his reasons against it. He began logically by defining the nature of the Church: "there ought to be and originally was also an external and visible unity and in primitive times it was very much insisted on ... ." Therefore, "whoever needlessly separates and breaks off from a church so established, is certainly guilty of the great sin of Scripture ... ." But with pleasing charity he held that the reformers of the Sixteenth Century should not be blamed for their schism; they were compelled by events and conscience. Yet because the Church is a visible organization, a divine society, it "must be under the direction of officers to whom the management of the public affairs of it doth belong ... ."[19] Armed with what "good evidences" he could command, Johnson deduced that "Episcopacy was truly the primitive and apostolical form of church government, and that the apostolic office was designed to be a settled standing office in the church to the end of the world." He learned that in the primitive church the office of a bishop was to confer the Holy Ghost in the sacraments of confirmation and ordination, and that this power was reserved to bishops, presbyters taking only a subordinate part, and deacons none at all. Now Puritanism had always appealed to the primitive and apostolic Church for the justification of its polity and presbyterian practices. Johnson had accepted the appeal; he had gone back to the Fathers, and his decision was that Puritanism had lost its case. He concluded this section of his paper with the flat statement: "I would with a full approbation ... and with the greatest delight and satisfaction submit to the orders" of the Church of England.[20]

When he could write such statements as those in this paper, Samuel Johnson had become intellectually, not only a Churchman, but a High Churchman. But he was a High Churchman as the term was understood in the Eighteenth and early Nineteenth Centuries. He had little concern for ceremonial beyond what was decent and orderly; he knew nothing of Eucharistic vestments or incense pots. But he had a secure hold on the basic Catholic faith; he believed in the Church of England as a divine, not a man-made society; he was sure that only within the Apostolic Succession was there a valid ministry; he held the sacraments to be necessary vehicles of grace; and he was deeply attached to them as the expression of the catholicity of the Church of England. The Enlightenment had not made him, as it made so many, a compromising Latitudinarian.

Reading, reason, logic, had led Johnson so far, to a conclusion which would have been utterly shocking to his students, his neighbors, and his pious family. But logic has sometimes to give way to the force of circumstances. Except for the little, half-organized Anglican underground in Stratford, the Church of England was non-existent in the Connecticut of 1719. Episcopal ordination was not to be had in any of the English colonies. Therefore Johnson reached the practical conclusion that if he could not be ordained by the laying on of hands of a bishop, "God in his providence by placing me under such circumstances, does dissolve my obligation to the observance of this institution ... if at the same times I do it with a resolution to observe it, when the same Providence shall make it possible."[21]

Johnson next proceeded to marshall concrete reasons why he could in conscience be ordained to the Congregational ministry. The reasons he gave were eight in number, five of which were mere elaborations of the basic three. Leading the list was: "The passionate entreaties of a tender mother." Behind that bare phrase there lies a story of emotional Scenes deeply disturbing to a man with Johnson's strong family affections and reverence for his ancestral traditions. Second, he feared doing the Church of England more harm than good by announcing his conversion at that time. Profoundly aware of the strong anti-Episcopalian prejudice then existing in Connecticut, he knew full well the stir such a conversion would make. Moreover, such action could seriously damage the reputation of the struggling college to which he was so deeply attached. Less important were his fears of "many things to be compiled with which I do not sufficiently understand" about "taking Episcopal order" and his uneasiness about being "too much precipitated into these opinions"[22] But all were typical of the convert who wrestles with every aspect of his dilemma.

Thus reason and expediency had engaged in battle. For the moment expediency won. On March 20, 1720, Samuel Johnson, twenty-four years old, was ordained a minister in the Congregational Church.[23]

Having already a reputation that extended through the little colony, he was offered the choice of several pastorates. Though West Haven was one of the smallest, he chose it, basically because its nearness to Yale would enable him to continue his delvings in the college library. Now a man of great intellect may well be a bad pastor. Johnson proved a good one. He had a deeply personal religion, and was conscientious in the performance of his pastoral duties. He liked books; he also liked people, and people liked him. And soon his reputation as a pastor began to spread abroad, into neighboring communities. The Congregational minister of those days was judged, not only by his sermons, but also by his "conceived" prayers. Johnson prayed so eloquently, so fervently, that people came from far and wide to hear him. They little suspected what it really was they were admiring. Johnson, with the deep distrust and dislike of extemporary prayers that he had acquired as a student, had set himself to memorize great portions of *The Book of Common Prayer*. He was feeding his flock with Thomas Cranmer.

7. The Library Once More

Johnson chose the location of his first pastorate for a particular reason. In those days when walking was not a lost art, West Haven was within easy distance of New Haven, of Yale and the Yale library. For the next two years, every moment that he could spare from his pastoral work was spent in that library; thus he satisfied the intellectual curiosity, the passion "to know all that could be known" that was so deeply rooted in his being. The reading list which he began to keep in 1719 gives us the key to his intellectual adventures. It is an amazing list, and it shows much fine miscellaneous browsing. Law, science, mathematics, medicine, secular history – he dipped into each of these fields. But most of his reading fell into three main categories.

The pastor of West Haven began to discover the hitherto unknown world of English literature – a subject not taught in the New England college curriculum. It is, however, a grave mistake to think of Puritanism as anti-literary or anti-intellectual, for all the unsavory connotations the popular mind has given it. Many of the early English Puritans had been people with an excellent cultural tradition, as had their first-generation descendants in the New world. But during the ensuing years something had happened to that tradition, something had been lost. Out of the womb of Seventeenth Century English Puritanism sprang *Paradise Lost*. But Puritanism in New England gave birth to Wigglesworth's *Day of Doom*. This lost heritage of English literature Johnson was now recovering. In his reading lists of these West Haven years we find Milton, *The Spector*, Bacon's *Essays*, George Herbert, Butler's *Hudibras*, shocking to Puritan readers. He read and re-read such classical authors as Ovid, Horace, Cicero, and Virgil. In these two years "he learned something of the wealth of poetry and literature which England had produced during the seventeenth century, of which he had hitherto not the faintest notion."[24]

As one would expect, a large part of his reading was theological. It was by no means a one-sided quest. Pierce and Barclay and Penn and Calamy were there to speak out for various shades of non-conformity, and Shaftesbury for early free-thinking. But they were counteracted by a great mass of Anglican divines – Potter, Jeremy Taylor, Barrow, Tillotson, Pearson. We have already noted Hooker's *Ecclesiastical Polity*. More striking were the works of the non-jurors – Brett, Dodwell, Leslie, Nelson's *Feasts and Fasts*. Johnson had moved a long way in his intellectual voyage from good Dr. Ames's *Medulla Theologiae*.

And finally, to crown the whole, Johnson was devouring the ancient Fathers of the Church. He read Chrysostom, Clement of Rome, Ignatious of Antioch, Polycarp. Here as the primitive church speaking for itself, and speaking always the ancient Catholic tradition. In September 1722 he added Cyprian to his list with the comment:

> which with other ancient Authors and modern Authors read for these 3 last years have proved so convincing of the necessity of Episcopal Ordination, to me & my Friend, [Daniel Browne] that this Commencement Sept. 13, 1722, we found it necessary to open our Doubts to the ministers, from whom if we receive not satisfaction we shall be obliged to desist.[25]

8. The Group

Johnson, for all his intellectuality, was not the kind of intellectual who loved to go voyaging through strange seas of thought alone. He was essentially a gregarious person, who loved to discover ideas, but also loved to share his discoveries with others. We have already seen him discussing his early intellectual problems with his bosom friend, Daniel Browne. And now, during these fruitful years when he was journeying from West Haven to explore in the college library, he gradually became the center of a group of similar inquiring minds. Of course there was Browne, now settled in as a tutor at Yale. The most prominent of the group, though probably not its intellectual leader, was Timothy Cutler, whom Johnson had met before his coming to Yale, and who was proving himself the first effective head of that institution. Jared Eliot, Johnson's first teacher, and now in some sense his pupil, added his real mental gifts. Eliot's marriage to the daughter of Samuel Smithson may have contributed to his interest in the Anglican way. Three other Puritan clergymen drifted in; John Hart, pastor of East Guilford, James Wetmore of North Haven, Samuel Whittlesey of Wallingford. All but Cutler were Yale graduates.[26] We can easily picture them, during the winter of 1721-22, gathered around the roaring log fires in the great room which housed the library, or huddled around a candle-lit table. Thumbing through the ponderous Greek and Latin tomes, one would read aloud a passage such as "Let no man do anything connected with the Church without the bishop. Let that be deemed a proper Eucharist which is administered either by the bishop, or by one to whom he has entrusted it." Here was a meaty text to discuss, for this was no biased sectarian controversialist speaking. This was the voice of Ignatius, Bishop of Antioch, martyr for his faith, who had very likely learned that faith from the lips of Simon Peter. And how did this agree with either a Presbyterian or a Congregational form of church organization?

The debate, in Johnson's mind, as well as in the minds of other ecclesiastics, centered to a great extent on the vexing question of church polity. But these inquirers were learning something more, something more fundamental, than polity. Polity led to doctrine, and thus they met a new theology, a new God. Perry Miller, greatest of the intellectual historians of New England's colonial period, has well summarized the nature of their discovery. In the Puritan theology, "the elaborate proof of His [God's] rationality and of the intelligibility of nature built up by the scholastic doctors of the thirteenth century was swept aside by a dogmatic assertion that He was transcendent, terrible, incomprehensible, even while good and merciful." The group that centered about Johnson had come to realize that Anglicanism "turned back to scholastic conceptions and celebrated a God of reason and of beauty, the God of Hooker's *Laws* and of Herbert's poetry."[27]

Out of Johnson's coterie came converts to the Church of England, and one fact stands out about them. The Protestant Episcopal Church in the United States of America has been a prolific recipient of converts, as every parish priest well knows. They have come for many reasons – the structural beauty of the churches, the music and liturgy or the social eclat that sometimes hovers about the congregation of a Fifth Avenue Episcopal Church. But the Connecticut converts were moved by a basically intellectual experience. Except for Cutler, in all probability none of them had ever seen an Episcopal Church, had never witnessed a performance of its liturgy, and until the process was practically complete, had never seen a priest of that church. They had read and thought their way into her arms. And it is not surprising that their fervency of conviction or arduous labors on her behalf marked the fortunes of the American Episcopal Church forever after. By the spring of 1722, a great explosion was at hand.

Chapter IV

THE DARK DAY
AND ITS AFTERMATH

1. The Gathering Storm

By the spring of 1722 some report of what was happening in the Yale library had begun to spread abroad through the colony. Nothing which is shared by seven men can long remain a secret, and indeed, the seven seem to have made no attempt to keep their proceedings hidden. They were not conspirators, but honest seekers after the truth. And so, on the eve of what has been aptly called the most dramatic event in American church history, Connecticut was abuzz with rumors. On April 23 of the fateful year the Reverend George Pigot arrived in Stratford. He was the missionary of the S. P. G. who had been sent out to carry on the work there, which had lapsed since the death of Muirson. In June, Johnson visited him.[1] It was Johnson's first contact with a priest of the Church of England. In July, Pigot in turn journeyed to New Haven, and there met the entire seven, with whom he talked for an hour or so. It has been alleged that he was in part responsible for the coming conversions.[2] But this is unlikely; by this time the group had pretty well made up its collective mind. Pigot of course was thrilled by what he learned from this meeting, and at once sat down to report to the secretary of the S. P. G. :

> The leading people of this colony are generally prejudiced

against their mother church, but yet I have great expectations of a glorious revolution of the ecclesiastics of this country, because the most distinguished gentlemen among them are resolvedly bent to promote her welfare and embrace her baptism and discipline, and if the leaders fall in, there is no doubt to be made of the people.[3]

Pigot, as was only natural in his situation, rather overestimated what was to come. Even so, the result was dramatic enough.

Meanwhile, having heard rumors of the activities of the little band of inquirers, the trustees of the college requested that the group meet with the trustees to clear up the suspicions arising from their behavior.[4]

2. Commencement

On Wednesday, September 12, 1722, the Yale Commencement was held. Commencement was always an outstanding event in the colony's year, attended by all the dignitaries of Connecticut. This year, Pigot was also present by invitation. All went as usual until Rector Cutler rose to give the customary prayer. At its conclusion he uttered the significant words, "and let all the people say Amen." This might seem to be a very trivial thing, but in the circumstances, it was a veritable bombshell. As we have noted, it was one of the basic principles of worship in the Puritan meeting house that the function of the laity was to sit in silent contemplation, and not to make the service a Christmas game of versicles and responses. But worse was to come; on the following day occurred the real explosion.

Led by Rector Cutler, the seven men who had been reading together met the trustees in the college library and handed those dismayed officials this paper:

> To the Rev. Mr. Andrew and Mr. Woodbridge and others, our Reverend Fathers and Brethren, present in the Library of Yale College this 13th of September, 1722, –

> Reverend Gentlemen: Having represented to you the difficulties which we labor under, in relation to our continuance out of the visible communion of an Episcopal

Church, and a state of seeming opposition thereto, either as private Christians, or as officers, and so being insisted on by some of you (after our repeated declinings of it) that we should sum up our case in writing, we do, (though with great reluctance, fearing the consequences of it) submit to and comply with it: And signify to you that some of us doubt the validity, and the rest of us are more fully persuaded of the invalidity of the Presbyterian ordination, in opposition to the Episcopal; and should be heartily thankful to God and man, if we may receive from them satisfaction herein; and shall be willing to embrace your good counsels and instructions in relation to this important affair, as far as God shall direct and dispose us to do.

> Timothy Cutler
> John Hart
> Samuel Whittlesey
> Jared Eliot
> James Wetmore
> Samuel Johnson
> Daniel Browne[5]

This labored document is plainly not the work of a group of young firebrands, eager to cast off the shackles of inherited tradition and start a revolution against the establishment, but the result of a long and often painful process. They could do no other. It is also apparent from the document itself that within the group there was a division. Some were certain that Presbyterian ordination was invalid; some were merely unsure. The trustees were aware of this division. Sitting amongst the very books of the library which had induced the explosion, they required the dissenters "to declare truly how the case was from the youngest to the eldest...."[6]

Johnson made an entry in his diary four days after the document had been presented which allows us to see clearly into his state of mind:

> It is with great sorrow of heart that I am forced thus, by the uneasiness of my conscience to be an occasion of so much uneasiness to my dear friends, my poor people, and indeed to the whole colony. Oh God, I beseech thee, grant that I

may not by an adherence to thy necessary truths and laws as I profess in my conscience they seem to me, be a stumbling block or occasion of fall to any soul … Lead into the way of truth all those that have erred and are deceived....[7]

These are the utterances of a sincere and deeply religious man, who has not only the mind of an intellectual, but also the heart of a pastor.

Faced with the explosive document the seven had presented, the trustees ordered a special meeting to be held a month later, possibly with the hope that in the meanwhile the petitioners might think better of their position, or be moved from it by the pressure that was sure to be brought against them. The trustees also needed time to prepare themselves for the disputation to come. In the meantime, Johnson conferred with his friends and other ministers, who advised that the members of the dissenting group who were firmly convinced of the invalidity of Presbyterian ordination should abstain from ministerial functions.[8]

The defenders of the Standing Order had the more difficult task of marshalling the forces of distinguished Congregationalists to maintain the cause of Puritan orthodoxy. By early October the Reverend Joseph Webb of Fairfield, one of the Yale trustees, and the Reverend Joseph Moss of Derby had appealed for help to Cotton Mather, grand panjandrum of Congregationalism. Webb wrote:

> I apprehend the axe is hereby laid to the root of our civil and sacred enjoyments, and a doleful gap opened for trouble and confusion in our Churches. The Churchmen among us are wonderfully encouraged and lifted up by the appearance of these gentlemen on their side, and how many more will, by their example, be encouraged to go off from us to them, God only knows. It is a very dark day with us; and we need pity, prayers and counsel.[9]

Moss asked for books on Presbyterian ordination, and vowed it was time to "put on our armour and fight, or else let the good old cause, for which our fathers came into this land, sink and be deserted." Similar appeals were made by John Davenport of Stratford and Stephen Buckingham, minister at Norwalk.[10]

Mather obliged by addressing a letter to his Connecticut brethren, outlining a ten-point line of defense. Let the deserters be charged with teaching popery, with rash action, and with causing superstition and schism. They should not be allowed to continue in their pastorates, and their congregations should express dissatisfaction over being betrayed. Yet Mather suggested that the dissenters be heard; nothing should be done rashly, for "the peace of God ... in the utmost expression of reasonable Charity, should rule in such occasions...."[11]

3. The Disputation

Both as a constant friend of Yale College and as an ordained minister of the Standing Order, Governor Saltonstall was seriously concerned over the untoward events of Commencement week. Throughout this whole troubled affair he demonstrated that he was both a Christian and a gentleman, and acted with sobriety and charity. Wishing to keep firm control in his own hands, and hoping to reclaim the erring seven, on October 16, the day following the meeting of the General Assembly, he presided over the public disputation that the petitioners had requested. Johnson said that he "moderated very genteely."[12]

Because the disputation was concerned basically with the question of Holy Orders, it is well to review briefly the various theories that came into conflict. According to the strict Congregationalist theory, as held by the early Puritans of Massachusetts, each local congregation, being a completely autonomous body, elected their minister, and then ordained him. All of the early Puritan ministers in the Bay Colony had been ordained priests in the mother Church of England, but subsequently, at least in some cases, they were ordained by lay members of their congregation. By 1722, this theory and practice seems to have been almost wholly discarded in Connecticut in favor of the Presbyterian theory. According to this view, there was in New Testament times but one order of the ministry, the terms presbyter and bishop being synonymous; the presbyter therefore had the power of ordination. This was a claim, then, to a sort of apostolic succession. The Catholic theory, which Johnson and his associates were to defend, held on the contrary that in the New Testament bishop and presbyter were separate orders, and that the power of ordination was always reserved to the bishop. This theory has been held in common by the Anglican, Roman Catholic, and Eastern Orthodox Churches. It is worth noting that in the disputation some of the opponents of the seven, without the faintest leaning toward prelacy, expressed doubts about their own ordinations because there was a lay element in the strain.[13]

None of the many accounts of the disputation tell us who were the clergy who represented the Standing Order and defended Presbyterian ordination. Whoever they were, they worked at a great disadvantage. They knew the common arguments in favor of their view. But their seven opponents had spent two years in intensive study of the question; Johnson had spent more. They were filled with arguments and apt quotations. The seven wisely chose Johnson, the best brain of the group, as their spokesman, and he justified their confidence. Precisely and logically presented, with documentation from the Scriptures and the Fathers, his reasoning proved so formidable that the trustees and their allies seemed incapable of making an equally distinguished counterattack. The inevitable result followed. Worsted in argument, one of the older men among the defenders of the Standing Order lost his temper and descended to vituperation.[14] Whereupon Governor Saltonstall, seeing that nothing further was to be accomplished by debate, quietly adjourned the meeting. His wise attitude paid dividends. As the petition itself indicated, the seven were actually divided into two groups, the doubtful and the convinced. Now three of the petitioners, Eliot, Whittlesey, and Hart, announced that they had been reassured by the arguments on the Presbyterian side, and remained within the Standing Order, where they ministered acceptably the rest of their lives. There can be no doubt of their honesty and sincerity throughout. But for Cutler, Johnson, Wetmore, and Browne, the die was cast. Anglican ordination they must have.

On October 13, on the eve of the disputation, Johnson had confided to his diary his sorrow and his determination:

> If I am by what ordination I have had consecrated to God, yet I am not on this account guilty of sacrilege, for that I design yet to devote myself, my whole life to the service of

Christ, and his Church, and so promote the good of precious souls and this (if I might be allowed and so far as I
am allowed) in this place.

These considerations all laid together, it seems to be my
duty to venture myself in the arms of Almighty Providence, to cross the ocean for the sake of that excellent
church, the Church of England, and God preserve me, and
if I err, God forgive me.[15]

Thus it was Johnson's hope that his West Haven congregation, to
which he had become so attached, might follow him in his transfer
of allegiance. But this was too much to expect; most of them
remained within the Standing Order.

4. The Standing Order Reacts

Even in the retelling after the lapse of two centuries there is something a bit thrilling about the story of the Yale commencement of
1722 and its consequences. But to the small, tightly knit colony of
Connecticut, and indeed to all of Puritan New England, it was inex-
pressibly shocking. Here were both heresy and treason met together.
Letters dealing with the event flew about New England as thick as
falling leaves in Autumn. One of the ministers present at the disputation wrote that all there were "amazed and filled with darkness."
And when the news reached Cotton Mather, that worthy, never
mealy-mouthed nor noted for his tolerance, burst into transports of
rage. That this should happen at Yale College, which he had sponsored as the refuge of undefiled Puritanism against the mounting
liberalism of Harvard! Mather called the devil-possessed apostates
"cudweeds," "degenerate offspring," "deserters," who had set up as
their leading doctrine "that vile, senseless, wretched whimsey of an
uninterrupted succession." The "highflyers" were not merely persons somewhat mistaken in their theological views; they were the
agents of Satan himself, since "they will have none owned for ministers of Christ in the world, but such as anti-Christ has ordained for
him; such as the paw of the beast hath been laid upon."[16] Such foam-
ings at the Mather mouth stand in sharp contrast with the attitude of
Johnson as he bade sad farewell to his beloved flock at West Haven.

Johnson found "parting with people was very tender; they loved him and he them," he wrote. But they were too prejudiced to join his move, save for "four or five of them that could be reconciled to receive him again in orders," Nor could he persuade them otherwise when he revealed that his much admired preaching, instructions "and above all his prayers" had been from the Church of England.[17]

The Yale trustees of course had no choice but to take action. There must be no more dark days at the college, On October 27, they excused Rector Cutler from his office, and accepted the resignation of Tutor Browne. Then they did their best to secure the future orthodoxy of the teaching staff of the college by decreeing that all rectors and tutors should be required to accept *ex animo* the Saybrook Confession of 1708, and give full satisfaction that they were untainted by the twin heresies of Arminianism and prelacy.[18] This theological requirement was not entirely abolished until 1818.

5. Pilgrimage to England

Meantime, on October 23, 1722, Cutler, Johnson, and Browne had set out on their quest for apostolic orders. Wetmore, who had business and family affairs to arrange, would follow as soon as he could. This was no simple journey. The voyage to England in the Eighteenth Century was long, expensive, and not a little dangerous. Fortunately, we are able to follow the travelers day by day. When they set out, Johnson began a travel journal, which still exists in the library of Columbia University, its ink browned by the passage of two centuries, but still legible. On Sunday, October 28, the Feast of St. Simon and St. Jude, they were in Bristol, Rhode Island, where there was a strong parish of the Church of England. Filled with joy at what to them was a precious privilege, they joined in the public worship of the church they had chosen. Cutler, since he was a Harvard man, might well have attended King's Chapel. He had certainly seen it. But for Johnson and Browne, it was the first time they had ever seen an Anglican church, the first time they had participated in the actual services of *The Book of Common Prayer*. Johnson noted in his journal, "Here, being Sunday, I first went to church. How amiable are thy tabernacles, O Lord of Hosts."[19]

Taking with them a letter of introduction from the Reverend James

Oren of Bristol to the Secretary of the S. P. G., they moved on to Boston, where they spent several days. Their last in Boston was Sunday, November 4 – another red-letter day. Johnson wrote, "This day, by God's grace I first communicated with the Church of England. How devout, grand, and venerable was every part of the administration, every way becoming so awful a mystery."[20] Was this indeed their first communion? Perhaps Johnson at this time would have answered yes. The modern reader, with a different ecumenical approach, may differ. The question may be left to the dogmatic theologians.

The following day they embarked on the ship "Mary," commanded by Captain Thomas Lithered. It was a difficult journey, lasting five weeks and four days. Three times, on this "boisterous and uncomfortable voyage," they encountered serious storms. But they were not idle. They had brought with them a few books, and they read Kettlewell, Robert Nelson, Jeremy Taylor, and for comic relief *Hudibras*. On Sundays, Wednesdays, and Fridays, they read the daily office. Finally, on December 14 their troubles were at an end. "This day," Johnson wrote, "blessed be God, we first came in sight of land. The first we made was the Isle of Wight, having been ten days without an observation. We were marvelously conducted by the good hand of Providence through the fog thus far up the channel; *cui laus*."[21] Johnson, like every good New Englander of the day, was a devout believer in special Providences.

6. The Promised Land

On December 15, the pilgrims landed at Ramsgate, took horse there, and that night they were in Canterbury. The next day, Sunday, they enjoyed Prayer Book worship for the third time – in Canterbury Cathedral. It is not hard to picture the three travelers trudging up narrow Mercery Lane, and passing through Christchurch gateway. And there, across the green of the close, was the vast bulk of the Cathedral Church of Christ, with Bell Harry Tower looming against the English sky. They entered the cathedral by the south porch, and looked beyond the clustered columns of the mighty nave, past Prior de Estria's pulpitum, or carved stone screen, to the soaring vault of the quire. It is an experience which today can shake the casual tourist. But Johnson and his friends had seen nothing to compare with it in their lives. Puritan New England was eventually to develop an architecture of its own, an architecture of considerable charm. But this early in the Eighteenth Century, the Puritan meeting house was nothing more than a square or rectangular bit of a village carpentry. Canterbury was the glory, the majesty, the beauty of God, reflected in stone. These were in a very real sense Canterbury pilgrims. They had come home.

In the afternoon they went to Evensong, and again to Morning Prayer on Monday, missing no opportunity to join in Anglican worship. After service they went to the deanery and presented themselves to the Dean, Dr. George Stanhope. To their surprise they found that they were neither unwelcome nor unknown. "Come in, gentlemen," said the Dean, "you are very welcome, I know you well...." At the very moment when they knocked on the dean's door he and some of the canons were reading a newspaper account of the pilgrims' "declaration for the Church." They received the converts with open arms, and "made very much of them...." One more day was spent in Canterbury, attending services, being shown round the cathedral, and dining with the cathedral clergy." Passing through Rochester, they came by coach to London on December 20. Finding lodgings in Fetter Lane, they made the acquaintance of the New England Coffee House – as its name implies, a gathering place for travelers from the new world.

In London Johnson was able to indulge to the full one of his predilections. Always a social being, he found Eighteenth Century London a veritable paradise of society. The New England Coffee House seems to have been, as was natural, his favorite resort. But he recorded, with evident delight, how he ate at this tavern and drank a bottle at that. Unlike New England, there was in London no taboo on taverns; they were gathering places for transacting all kinds of business and for enjoyment while doing so. And he was making new acquaintances everywhere. It is amazing how the English, reputed to be so aloof, took Johnson and his companions to their bosoms. But then it was unusual that dissenting colonists should return to the mother country to form an allegiance to the mother church from which so many of their ancestors had fled in disgust and rancor. Never a week passed that Johnson was not invited to dine with some clerical or lay dignitary. Two intimate friends he made were Dr. Francis Astry, Treasurer of St. Paul's Cathedral, and John Berriman, chaplain to the Bishop of London. With both of these he kept up a friendship by letter as long as he lived. On January 3, 1723, Johnson recorded

> This day in the morning we were introduced by Mr. Bridger to wait on Sir William Dawes, the Ld Archbishop of York, who treated us with great kindness and condescension and took notice of our affair. After which I went to Dr. Astry and conferred with him. In the evening Mr. Checkley (just arrived from New England) came to our lodgings to visit us.[23]

The newcomer must have been most welcome. John Checkley was born in Boston in 1680. Whether or not he was a convert the books do not say. He spent some time at Oxford, then returned to Boston and set up as a bookseller. He was a born controversialist, and soon became the arch-enemy of the Puritan establishment in Boston. In 1719 he published an edition of the non-juror Charles Leslie's tract against the Deists, with additions of his own which were a witty assault on the Puritans. This was "the most uncompromising and pungent attack which had yet been made upon the ecclesiastical authority of the Puritan colony."[24] The Boston authorities countered by trying Checkley, not for heresy, but for Jacobitism – a charge that was to haunt him the rest of his life. He had now come to England in search of ordination, but not until a third trip, in 1738, did he attain his purpose. However, in 1723 he proved a welcome addition, with his wit and controversial ardor, to the group.

While most of their time was of necessity spent in London, they were able to see something more of England. Early in May, Cutler and Johnson made a visit of ten days to Oxford, where at Dr. Astry's behest the University made Cutler a Doctor of Divinity and Johnson a Master of Arts. They also visited Windsor and Hampton Court. In June, they went to Cambridge, where they received the same degrees.[25]

All this had been a marvelous experience for Samuel Johnson. He had been received with open arms, wined and dined, honored by the ancient universities. He had formed a number of lasting friendships. And he had fallen in love with England:

> When Johnson discovered the glories of London, the learning of Oxford, and the dignity of the episcopal hierarchy; when, in other words, he became sensible of the values of civilization, or what in New England was known as "worldliness," his puritan prejudices quickly subsided. He became an Englishman and a gentleman.[26]

This was to have an effect in his political views, likewise. He had become, probably unconsciously, one of the first of British imperialists in the colonies. Loyal always to his own Connecticut, he yet tended to think more and more in terms of the empire as a whole, and he likewise linked the interests of royal government with episcopacy in true conservative fashion. In the era of the American Revolution such links were strained until they broke.

One other side of Johnson's character found its opportunity for development in England. No previous writer on Johnson has seemed aware of the fact that his intellectuality – which everyone stresses – was complemented by an equally strong esthetic bent. He loved reason; he also loved beauty. There was not much in colonial Connecticut to minister to this love. There was beauty of nature and of the chaste simplicity that characterized a developing architecture as well as the buildings neatly clustered about village squares. And Johnson was sensitive to such beauty. But in the *Book of Common Prayer* he early discovered a second type of beauty – a the beauty of words. Men are often moved by subtle influences they do not themselves appreciate; it is more than likely that Johnson's conversion to Anglicanism was as much the result of his love affair with Cranmer's prose as it was of his intellectual conviction by the arguments of Archbishop Potter or the evidence of the early Church Fathers. The joy he found in the artistry of the Prayer Book continued to the end of his life. One of the few sermons he found worth printing was one delivered at the opening of Christ Church in his native Guilford, a sermon on the text, "O worship the Lord in the beauty of holiness." This sermon, which was published in 1761, was a prolonged demonstration of beauty in worship. Furthermore, in the Dummer library he had made the acquaintance of Milton and Addison. To these types of beauty his English sojourn added two more. Here he first met beauty in great architecture, and the notes in his travel journal show his appreciation of it. When the time came to build the second Christ Church, Stratford, Johnson took care that it would be the best piece of church architecture erected to that time in Connecticut. Finally, London when Johnson visited it was a notable musical center, and only there could he have acquired that love of music which crops out again and again in his later letters.

As the subtle changes transformed the provincial traveller into a gentleman, Johnson continued his round of sight-seeing. There were innumerable churches to be visited, and his journal was filled with mentions of them: St. Dunstan, St. Andrew Undershaft, of course the Abbey, St. Mary Overie, St. Martin's-in-the-Fields – it would be tedious to enumerate all. But above all there was St. Paul's Cathedral; after service on February 7, 1723, "we took a view of that stupendous fabric, ascended to the top of the dome by five hundred and fifty steps, which with the Cupola and Cross make four hundred feet in height ... It is perhaps one of the finest buildings in the world – an amazing mass of stones," he thought.[27] Over no other church did Johnson, true son of the Enlightenment, grow so rapturous.

7. The Road to Holy Orders

All this was more than pleasant, it was an education in itself, but after all Johnson, Cutler and Browne were in England on serious business which had to go forward. We have noted their meeting with the Archbishop of York on January 3. Two days later they met William Wake, Archbishop of Canterbury, who treated them "like a Father of the Church." But the body the action of which was to be most important for their purpose was the S. P. G. When Dr. Astry introduced them to the Society on January 18, Johnson noted: "Sir William Dawes, Abp. of York, was in the chair, who with the whole body of the clergy present received us with a most benign aspect, and treated us with all imaginable kindness."[28] They met the Bishop of London, in whose jurisdiction they would be after ordination. Everything was proceeding with the utmost smoothness when, on January 22, Cutler fell ill of the small-pox, that scourge of the Eighteenth Century. It was Johnson's first encounter with the dread disease, which was to haunt his whole life. Fortunately Cutler had a very light attack, and in a very few days was about again. On January 25, Dr. Astry and Dr. Berriman again took them before the officials of the S. P. G., "Who granted our requests and made way for our ordination."[29] On February 9, Johnson wrote his ordination sermon. But now a strange scruple seems to have arisen in the minds of Johnson and his colleagues. Were they, who had of course been baptized in the Congregational Church, truly baptized? They ran about consulting with one clergyman after another. By March 9, they had come to a decision. The result was recorded by Johnson in his journal in a Latin note:

> We three, having grave doubts whether Baptism received among the Presbyterians is valid, at 4 o'clock P. M. in the Church of St Sepulchre … received private hypothetical [*i.e.* conditional] baptism. If this be right, may God approve it; and if otherwise than sincerely done, may he pardon it.[30]

On March 20, having received letters dimissory from the Bishop of London, "to whose diocesan care the American colonies were then committed, Johnson, Browne and Cutler "went to wait on the Bishop of Norwich, who examined us in order for ordination, which did also Mr. Ellotson, the gentleman who is to present us; then we signed the Articles."[31] They then proceeded to equip themselves by buying the necessary vestments. Finally, on March 22, "in the morning, 10 of the clock, we waited on the Right Rev'd Thomas, Lord Bishop of Norwich, and at the parish church of St. Martin-in-the-Fields, after Morning Prayer, we were first confirmed and then ordained deacons."[32] On the 31st, at the same church, they were ordained priests. At last they had received that of which they had come in search, the laying on of hands by a bishop in the Apostolic Succession.

Up to this point, everything had proceeded with wonderful smoothness for the pilgrims. They had been cordially received, they had made friends; and they were to be honored by Oxford and Cambridge Universities. Now came tragedy. On April 4, Daniel Browne fell ill. Two days later, the malady was diagnosed as small-pox, and evidently in its most virulent form. On the thirteenth he was dead. Samuel Johnson had lost his oldest and closest friend. On April 16, he noted: "This evening my dear friend, Mr. Brown, was interred in St. Dunstan in the West, attended by about thirty of the clergy of the town."[33]

Saddened, Johnson did not despair. Since he was now a priest in good standing in the Church of England, he was given ample opportunity to exercise his ministry. On April 21, he preached twice, at St. Dionis Back Church in the morning, and at Trinity Chapel in Hanover Square in the afternoon. The following day he read Morning Prayer in St. Ann's. On June 30, he had the honor of preaching in St. Paul's Cathedral. Meantime, in May and June, Johnson and Cutler had visited Oxford and Cambridge.

By July 4, the two men were gladdened by the arrival of James Wetmore, the settlement of whose affairs was apparently expedited by their recent experiences. Wetmore was given conditional baptism the next day, and quickly ordained deacon and then priest. The purpose of their pilgrimage had now been accomplished. Not only were they priested, but the S. P. G. had received them gladly and promised support, and Bishop Edmund Gibson of London, their diocesan, who was deeply interested in the American church, had licensed them to officiate in the colonies. Therefore at the end of July they took ship, only to find themselves windbound at the Isle of Wight until August 8. After a voyage of almost two months, the three missionaries landed at Piscataqua in Maine, and then rode south to Boston.[34] They had been abroad almost a year.

Timothy Cutler, priest, began his ministry at Boston where, possibly by the help of John Checkley, a place was already waiting for him. King's Chapel had become too small to accommodate the rapidly growing number of Episcopalians in that city. And so a new parish was in process of organization, Christ Church, better known to history as "the Old North Church." Here, in the very shadow of the Harvard of which he was a graduate, Cutler remained for the rest of his life, serving faithfully his flock, but often quarreling bitterly with his Puritan neighbors. Cutler liked controversy, and opportunities for it were abundant in Eighteenth Century Boston. James Wetmore assisted at Trinity Church, New York until 1726 and then was assigned by the Venerable Society to Rye, in Westchester County, New York, just over the Connecticut border, where he remained until his death in 1760. He became the founder of a notable family of clerics; a recent Suffragan Bishop of New York was a direct descendant. Johnson was to go to Stratford.

Chapter V

RECTOR OF STRATFORD

1. The Parish

On November 4, 1723, Samuel Johnson, aged twenty-seven, arrived in Stratford. The Reverend George Pigot, who had been awaiting his arrival, promptly departed for his permanent post in Providence, and Johnson was left with his devoted little flock, who were delighted, after all their years of struggle and hopeful waiting, to have at last the kind of clerical leadership they needed, and in some sense deserved. It was Johnson's own idea that he should be sent to Stratford.[1] He had already visited Stratford, and knew, through Pigot and Cutler, of the history of the Anglican underground there. Undoubtedly he already saw it, not only as a parish in itself, but as a strategic point for the future extension of the Church of England in Connecticut. On the day after he reached Stratford, Johnson made an entry in his journal which indicates clearly the spirit in which he approached his new task.

> God having in his merciful Providence spared me another year through so many dangers as I have been exposed unto on my late voyage, and returned me safe to my father's house, and here to my charge, I adore his singular and marvellous goodness… What can I do less than devote my

life thus preserved by Thee to thy service, to do all the good I can for thy glory and the souls of men! And as I am now (for which I adore thy goodness) perfectly well satisfied as to the lawfulness and regularities of my mission (being Episcopally initiated, confirmed, and ordained) so I purpose by thy grace both to adorn my profession by a holy life, as a Christian, and faithfully to fulfil my ministry as a clergyman, by doing all the service I can to the souls committed to my charge.[2]

Stratford lies, as we have noted, at the mouth of the Housatonic River, and a mile and a half from Long Island Sound. Back of it lay gently rolling country, well suited for farming. In 1700, it probably contained two hundred families; the population, then, would have been something just over one thousand people. It was a busy little community, attempting, like all Connecticut villages of the day, to be as far as possible economically self-contained. In 1700 it had two grist mills, two fulling mills, and a sawmill.[3] It was also a minor port; the Housatonic made a bit of a harbor, large enough for coasting vessels. It therefore had a few merchant families like that of William Beach, who was probably the wealthiest of its citizens. The village school had been built in 1670.

The dominant building in the village was the Congregational meeting house, standing on Watch-house Hill, facing the common. Ever since the death of its first pastor, the Reverend Adam Blackman, the history of the congregation had been one of strife. Just about when the second meeting house was built, in 1668, the congregation had split over the acceptance of the Half-way Covenant, and a second organization had been started, which eventually migrated to near-by Woodbury. In 1704 the Reverend John Reed was elected pastor after a sharp contest. His whole tenure of office was one of warfare. He resigned, or was dismissed, in 1707. "No indication as to what was said offensive to Mr. Reed ... has been found, except the intimation that he had made overtures to join the Episcopal Church."[4] In the Stratford of 1707, this was enough. However, Reed never did become an Anglican. He was succeeded by the Reverend Timothy Cutler, whose defection to Anglicanism in 1722 was another blow to the prestige of the Standing Order in Stratford. In 1722 the Reverend Hezekiah Gold, a vigorous Puritan, and the son of Lieutenant Governor Nathan Gold of Fairfield, one of the bitterest enemies of the Anglican Church, became pastor. But again there was a *contretemps*. Young Gold married the widow of John Prynn. Mrs. Gold was as strong an Episcopalian as Gold was a Puritan. She insisted on attending regularly the services at Christ Church, and it is recorded that Gold often had to stand waiting at the door of that building until his wife emerged. The effect of this on the temper of the Reverend Mr. Gold was eventually reflected in his father's warfare with growing Anglicanism.

When Johnson became rector, the Anglicans in Stratford numbered about thirty families – not many, but there were no nominal Churchmen among them. They all meant business. They had long projected a church building, and had gathered some lumber for it, but no actual construction had yet been done. On June 21, 1723, Pigot still being rector, the wardens and vestry petitioned the town selectmen for a parcel of ground on which they might build. Naturally, they got nowhere. But then they proceeded to buy a piece of land right next the Congregational Church. This was too much. The selectmen proceeded to give them in exchange a less offensive site, that still occupied by the old Episcopal burying ground.[5]

In the early spring after Johnson's arrival, construction was at last started, and pushed on rapidly. Christ Church, Stratford, was opened for the worship according to *The Book of Common Prayer* on Christmas Day, 1724. The choice of this day was in itself an act of defiance of the Standing Order. The observance of the Popish festival of Christmas was anathema to all Puritans.

The church was no very imposing structure. Johnson himself described it as a "small, neat wooden building, forty-five and a half [feet] long, thirty and a half wide." It was the bare essential of a church, with no architectural pretensions, and the rudest of furnishings.[6] Possibly, like the first Congregational meeting house in Stratford, it had only a dirt floor, and was seated with rough wooden benches. There was probably a sturdy table covered with a white cloth to serve as an altar, and a reading desk, but there was no organ and no heating system. Here Sunday after Sunday the little congregation assembled, led in worship by their tall young rector, vested in the long surplice and the scarf which he had bought in London. The normal Sunday service was Morning Prayer, Litany, and sermon. The music consisted of metrical Psalms in the Tate and Brady version, sung without accompaniment. But as Johnson was always a stickler for the corporate aspect of worship, the congregation was well trained to make their responses and to sing their Psalms heartily. Had this been a Virginia congregation, the service would have been varied once in a quarter by a celebration of the Holy Communion. But as Johnson was a strong sacramentalist, and in some sense a disciple of the non-jurors, this was not to be the Stratford regime. At least from 1729 on, Holy Communion was always celebrated on the first Sunday of the month and on Christmas Day.[7] This High Church innovation eventually became the New England tradition. The monthly celebration was always preceded by a service of preparation on Saturday. We can be sure that the sermons preached in Christ Church had quality; Johnson had something to say, and habitually prepared his sermons – always written – with great care.

The early parish records of Christ Church are disappointingly meager, but one does get from them some indications of the life of the parish. The vestry elected in 1723 consisted of wardens William Feanes and Nehemiah Loring, and vestrymen Jonathan Pitman, John Johnson, Timothy Titharton, Richard Blacklatch, William Smith, Samuel French, Dr. James Laborie, Daniel Shelton, and John Glover.[8] The name Shelton is of particular interest; Connecticut Sheltons were to be important in the history of the American Episcopal Church for well over a century. One aspect of church life often overlooked by church historians is the vital matter of church support. In missions sponsored by the S. P. G. the Society normally appropriated fifty pounds sterling for the support of the missionary. This was his basic stipend, supplemented by whatever the local congregation could raise. The Stratford records give us tantalizing glimpses of how the vestry attacked this perennial problem. At the parish meeting of 1740 it was "voted that we pay this year toward the support of our minister 4 pence upon the pound of our rateable estates." Year after year, a similar motion was duly voted. In 1738 the financial record shows that the vestry had taken a more drastic action. Collections for church support began to be taken at every service. The Dissenters had long done this in England, but for an Anglican congregation it was revolutionary. In 1741 this weekly collection produced the substantial amount of thirty pounds, eight shillings, and one penny.[9]

It is evident that Johnson went to Stratford with a carefully planned strategy. Vividly aware of the great New England prejudice against prelacy, disliking controversy, though he was often forced to engage in it, he demonstrated, by his own life and actions, that an Anglican priest did not have horns and hoofs, but could be a good citizen and a good neighbor. In the beginning he made no effort to campaign for conversions, but rather cultivated his little flock by careful teaching and assiduous parish visiting. His policy at the time might well be described as one of peaceful co-existence.

2. The Parish Grows

In spite of Johnson's policy of not seeking out converts, the parish in Stratford grew steadily. It was one of the wise requirements of the S. P. G. that its missionaries make semi-annual reports, and from these reports we can trace the continual increase in Stratford Episcopalians. By September 1739, the thirty families Johnson found on his arrival had become seventy-three. There were in that year 105 actual communicants.[10] This is a significant figure. An examination of parish records makes evident the fact that until well into the Nineteenth Century, large numbers of people regularly attended the Episcopal Church, contributed to its support, and considered themselves in every sense Churchmen, but never made their communions. This was not true in Stratford; the proportion of communicants to families was unusually high. This we must attribute to Johnson's strong sacramental teaching. Many years later Johnson wrote to the Archbishop of Canterbury: "I observe one thing happier in those parts than I doubt in most of the King's dominion, which is, that there are sometimes at least as many communicants as families, and in some places many more; and as many men as women."[11]

Every year this growth continued. In 1740 the communicants numbered 121; the following year they had increased to 128; by 1750, the parish (including Ripton) had 192 communicants in 143 church families. Johnson's last report, written in 1754 just before he went to New York to start King's College, was a summing up of

his achievement at Stratford. Since his arrival in 1723 he had baptized 961 adults and children, and had admitted to the communion
443 persons.[12]

Johnson's report of September 1728, gives us a fair picture of the
young priest at work:

> my Church has been considerably fuller this summer than
> ever it was before. Seven entire families are reconciled to
> the church; and though such a number of communicants
> are gone off to the Fairfield parish, yet I have fourscore
> here and in the neighboring town, who constantly, and as
> frequently as may be, attend the communion at Stratford.
> Beside two of the native Indians I have brought within the
> pale of the Church ... there is one large family of English,
> who have heretofore lived like heathens, but are now be-
> come serious Christians, and I have baptised them ... And
> beside the Jew I mentioned before, who is a sincere good
> Christian, and has since been baptised, here is another Jew,
> a very sober sensible young gentleman, whom I have been
> instrumental in bringing over to the Christian faith.... [13]

The reader will note Jews and Indians. Furthermore, there were in
Connecticut, as in practically all the northern colonies in colonial
days, a fair number of Negro slaves. These also were subjects for
Johnson's missionary solicitude. Year after year his reports record his
baptism of from one to four adult Negroes. Many historians have
expressed their opinion that colonial Anglicanism was an exotic
flower, a church of the aristocracy. That may have been true in some
areas. It was not, as the facts given above demonstrate, true in
Johnson's Connecticut. The original Stratford congregation was composed of the poorer people.[14] In fact, a Connecticut person of the
period who "declared for episcopacy" became *declassé*; he forfeited
by that act practically all hope of election to any secular office. It was
Johnson's function to preach the gospel to the poor. What he was
building up in Stratford was not a mutual admiration society of the
respectable elect, but what might be called in the best sense a
"catholic parish."

In 1743, when Johnson had been at work in Stratford for twenty
years, the modest little church of 1724 was no longer adequate for

the steadily growing congregation. Therefore a new church must be built. The new church was a structure of considerable architectural pretensions. Designed by the same Thomas Salmon, who had planned the original church, it was modeled after Christ Church, Boston, where Timothy Cutler was rector. It was sixty feet long, forty-five feet wide, and the walls were twenty-four feet high. But the glory of the exterior was a tower sixteen feet square, terminating in a steeple that rose up one hundred and twenty feet. In 1751 a clock was placed in the tower. The whole town was proud of his handsome church, and Johnson delightedly wrote to the secretary of the S. P. G. that it was "finished in a very neat and elegant manner, the architecture being allowed in some things to excel any thing before done in New England." Unlike most Anglican churches of the period, it had a chancel eight feet deep, flanked on either side by a vestry room and a library. At the head of the center aisle was a pulpit raised on pillars, through which the clergy man would enter the chancel. At one side were the reading desk and the desk for the clerk. "The floor was covered by spacious square pews built at the expense of the occupants." Unlike the Congregational churches of Connecticut, which were built by taxes on all taxable property, this was paid for by voluntary contributions of the congregation. William Beach, a convert, gave the very sizable sum of £3,000. The bell was given by Johnson himself, and eventually the church came to boast an organ.[15]

We get some hint of how Johnson dealt with his parishioners from a letter written by him in June 1748. The Reverend Matthew Graves, English born and trained, was assigned to serve the people of Hebron and New London. He had written Johnson, complaining of the lack of good manners and importunities of his flock. Johnson understood Graves's difficulty in comprehending Americans, and warned him that "the spirit of liberty beats high in their veins, beyond what Europe ever knew...." Therefore they must be handled in a different way from Englishmen:

> For the truth is we can do little or no good to people here unless we do all we can to keep them in a good humor, which if we do we may lead them as we please, and they will think nothing too much in their power to do for us;

otherwise we can neither do nor get any good from them.[16]

3. Founding a Family

For his first two years as rector of Stratford Johnson lived among his people as a bachelor, possibly boarding out with various members of the congregation. But bachelor life was not to Johnson's taste. There is not the slightest evidence that he ever experienced what is usually called romantic love. But he had been brought up in a large and happy family, he was intensely gregarious, and he loved domesticity. On March 25, 1725, he took the first step toward setting up his own domestic establishment. On that date he bought from Stephen Hawley, one of his parishioners, a house for which he paid the considerable sum of £250.[17] One cannot help wondering where he got the money. He had been on salary less than two years, and his stipend was £50 from the S. P. G. and about £5 from the parish. (The difference in sums may have been one between English sterling and Connecticut currency.)

But a house is an empty thing without a housewife. In all probability by the time Johnson bought his house, he had a fair idea of who was to live in it with him. His account of marriage, as he gave it in his brief autobiography, has more than a touch of unconscious humor, and some indication of Johnson's attitude toward matrimony:

> he was apt to be negligent of worldly affairs even to a fault, and therefore, as it was impossible for him to live with any tolerable decency among his poor people without keeping house, it was necessary for him to look out for one to be the partner of his life, who was a person of experienced and noted good economy; and such an one he happily found in the excellent person of Mrs. Charity Nicoll, a daughter of Col. Richard Floyd, and the relict of Benjamin Nicoll Esqr. of Long Island, to whom, being near 29, he was married Sept. 26, 1725....[18]

One would like to know more about this marriage – how and where Johnson met the Widow Nicoll, and how he courted her. But the above quotation is the sum total of our knowledge in the matter. Nor can we form any further picture of what she was like. All of the writers who have dealt with Johnson or his son confess that she remains a shadowy figure, apparently moving on the periphery of Johnson's life rather than in the center. It is significant that all of Johnson's really strong personal attachments seem to have been to men.

But Charity brought Samuel several things besides her talents in practical domestic economy. The Floyds and the Nicolls were families of some standing in the province of New York, and this connection of Johnson with New York was to prove important in the future. Furthermore, Charity had money of her own; it is quite possible that the house in Stratford was really financed by her dowry. Johnson once remarked, "What I have is chiefly owing to my wife's fortune." She also brought to the household two sons and a daughter. "William and Benjamin proved to be very worthy gentlemen and her daughter Gloriana Margaret a very valuable woman."[19] These are Johnson's words, and he proved to be an excellent step-father.

The marriage came just in time to console Johnson, with his strong family affections, for the strain which was to be put upon him. In March 1726, his mother died. She was by now apparently reasonably reconciled to her son's erratic career. On May 8, 1727, Johnson's father also died. Johnson's deep feeling for his father is revealed by the long entry this event occasioned in his diary.

> This day God is pleased to visit me with another terrible dispensation in bereaving me of my dear, tender, and indulgent father. He was a person of sincere and upright devotion towards God, a hearty and zealous lover of His house and ordinances, had a good understanding of the nature of the Christian religion, delighted most in reading the best authors of the Church of England, and was entirely brought off from most of the fanatical and predestinarian principles; entirely reconciled to the Church in point of charity, and would have communicated with us if he had lived, as I have good reason to believe ... had it not been for the bitter and uncharitable tempers of the country....[20]

From this, and various other hints, one gets the impression that Johnson's mother was the dominant personality in the family, and the convinced Puritan.

But as the older generation of Johnsons died out, a new generation came on the stage. On October 7, 1727, Charity was delivered of her first son by the Rector of Stratford. The boy was named William Samuel, thus perpetuating the names of both his grandfather and his great-grandfather. The boy was to prove one of the greatest blessings of his father's life. A little over three years later, on March 9, 1731, a second son, William, was born.[21] The family circle was now complete, with the three step-children, and the two sons of Charity and Samuel.

But the family was seldom left to itself. Thomas Bradbury Chandler, Johnson's favorite pupil, tells us that Johnson rarely sat down to a meal without having invited from one to half a dozen guests. And often so many were invited to stay overnight that all the beds in the house were occupied, and the latest arrived or the youngest in age were forced to sleep on the floor.[22] One feels some sympathy for Mistress Charity. Little as we know about her, we are forced to conclude that she had a serene temper and the virtue of good management of her elastic household. She contributed to the ménage that practicality which Johnson once ruefully confessed neither he nor his father had.

4. The Rectory School

There are people – the authors of these pages are two – who have a positive passion for teaching. They must teach somebody something, even if it is only teaching a cat to sit up. Such a person was Samuel Johnson. From the day he left Saybrook, he was all his life engaged in teaching of one sort or other. Furthermore, it was part of the New England tradition that the minister should also be a teacher. Hardly had Johnson been settled in Stratford, when he received a letter of inquiry from Bishop Gibson of London, concerning Connecticut schools. He at once eagerly replied, recommending Thomas Salmon, vestryman and architect, who already had experience in teaching a school in Stratford, to be appointed and paid by the Society to open a church school there.[23] It is to be assumed that the Society took favorable action, as the school was shortly in operation. Johnson's marriage to Charity provided him with his first pupils; her three children must be suitably educated. Then came his two sons, who must be fitted for entrance to college. Added to the family nucleus were servants, and boarding pupils, mostly coming from New York, where the Nicoll connection was proving valuable. At various times there were in residence at the Stratford rectory four Cuylers, a Roosevelt, a Rutgers, a Van Horn, a Jay, a Cortlandt, and a Stuyvesant. The list reads like a page out of a later New York Social Register. In 1733, the S. P. G. appropriated funds to provide for a second teacher, Joseph Browne. For seventeen years he worked at Stratford in that capacity, receiving a stipend from the Society of £15 per annum – very probably supplemented by tuition from the parents of the pupils. With these assistants and with Johnson's own oversight of the project the rectory school became so renowned that numbers of the Stratford Congregationalists, regardless of the danger of theological contamination, sent their sons to it. The total enrollment rose at times as high as fifty pupils, and in that were to be found, along with the sons of the New York elite, an occasional Indian or Negro pupil. In fact, the school succeeded so well that it killed itself. It was so far superior to the "public" school, that eventually the town selectman were shamed into taking action, and made the community school an improved institution. Therefore in 1751 Johnson reported to the Society that the town schools, supported by the recent sale of public lands, had finally rendered the parochial school unnecessary.[24] After an honorable career, it closed its doors on Lady Day, March 25, 1752.

5. Johnson's Sons

No part of Johnson's life is more attractive than his relations with his two sons. William, the younger, taught by his father in the rectory school, entered Yale and was graduated in 1748. He then read for holy orders with his father, and in 1756, to his father's delight, went to England to be ordained priest in the Church of England. But immediately after his ordination he contracted small pox, and within a few days he was dead. For the second time this scourge had struck down someone near to Samuel Johnson's heart. Not only was this a great grief to his father; it also reinforced that small pox phobia, which was to become something of an obsession to Samuel Johnson.

William Samuel, the elder son, became a person of some importance in history in his own right. Graduated from Yale in 1744, he then lived for a time in Stratford, acting as lay assistant to his father, who hoped he might have a vocation to the priesthood.[25] But William Samuel eventually decided on the law as his profession. He was highly successful in his calling. When the Stamp Act Congress met in New York in 1765, he was chosen by the General Assembly to represent Connecticut in that body, and labored on a committee that considered the rights of the colonies; from its work emerged declarations and petitions to the government in Britain – protests against the unpopular tax. In 1766 William was sent to England as the special agent of the Connecticut Assembly to plead the cause of the colony in regard to a large tract of land, the ownership of which the colony claimed. Here he remained several years, making the acquaintance of his father's namesake, the English lexicographer. When he returned, the American Revolution was brewing. William Samuel held moderately Tory views, but he did not obtrude them, remained in semiretirement during the Revolution, and suffered no injury because of his politics.

The War of Independence over, William Samuel accepted the verdict of war and became a loyal citizen of the United States. He was elected to the Constitutional Convention of 1787, and played a considerable part in inducing Connecticut to ratify that document. He served for a time in the United States Senate, and eventually became president of Columbia College, founded as King's College under the presidency of his father.[26]

Since father and son were frequently separated for long periods of time, their correspondence is full and fascinating. Here were two men, both with better than average minds, and full of affection for each other. More than that – fathers and sons may be normally expected to be affectionate – they respected each other in a way that fathers and sons often do not. There is no better illustration of the nature of their relations than the letter Samuel wrote to his son in June 1747, discussing the son's decision to be a lawyer rather than a clergyman. William Samuel was then twenty – an age at which fathers frequently feel still able to control. The letter is too long to be quoted here in its entirety, but two paragraphs make clear the quality of their relationship:

> You are, my son, and I bless God for it, by genius and abil-

ity equally qualified to shine either in the pulpit, at the bar, or at arms. As to the last, I hope that is now at least in a great measure out of the question. And as to the two former, I shall for my part be entirely easy whichsoever you choose, though I prefer the first, for which you are already so well qualified that you can well afford to spend a year of [sic] two in making a trial of the study of the law, which would by no means be lost time, if you should afterwards quit it for divinity. On the other hand, if you like it you may abide by it.

You say well (as being so young you well may), that you are not for "rushing suddenly into life." And as you can spare yet three or four years to consider and qualify yourself, I doubt not but by that time you may begin in either of those professions with good advantage. Meantime assure yourself it is my daily and earnest prayer both for you and your brother not only that you may be duly qualified, but also directed to such a choice of business for life as may enable you to do God the greatest honor and mankind the greatest good you are capable of, and at the same time, in the best manner to enjoy yourselves here, and be qualified for the most ample reward hereafter. And to my prayers I shall willingly add my best advice and endeavors, and I am glad you have opened the way to a particular and free correspondence and conversation upon these subjects, and would wish you always to converse with me in the freest and most unreserved manner upon any subject that may be of importance to you ... For there is nothing pleases me better than a decent, open, and unreserved freedom.[27]

Less serious, but equally revealing of the intimate relationship between the two men, and also of Samuel's complete domesticity, are the little notices of family life with which the father often concluded his letters to his son in later years, as in this letter, written from New York in 1754:

My tenderest love to my dear daughter and little Charry, and also to Mammy and all the rest, and love to all friends. Your brother Billy has lost his eldest daughter of the throat distemper. He has been here these three days and is returned this morning. He and Benny and Molly give their love and duty. As to me they are exceeding kind and tender, and intent on making my life comfortable, and will not hear of my taking other lodgings. ... And I pray God have you all in his most gracious protection, and remain, Dear Son,

Your most tender and affectionate father and friend, S. Johnson[28]

6. Missionary Center

Caring for his parishioners in Stratford, building a new church, starting the rectory school, founding a family – these activities would seem enough to absorb the energies of one man. But they did not. Johnson also became an active regional missionary.

This process did not start with Johnson. Pigot, during his brief rectorate at Stratford, had already started holding services in neighboring communities. But the initiative did not come from Pigot either. From about the time James I became King of England, there had been a steady flow of people out of the Church of England. Independents, Presbyterians, Baptists, Quakers – all had moved out of Anglicanism to start their separate church organizations. But early in the Eighteenth Century, at least in colonial Connecticut, the tide had begun to turn. All over the colony, there was at this time a movement toward the Church of England, a movement which seems to have been primarily a movement of the laity. And the evidence for this is the petitions which were sent by the laity to the S. P. G. The first of these was dated October 19, 1722, and reads in part as follows:

We, the subscribers, inhabitants of the town of Newton, [Newtown] in the province of Connecticut, being cordially inclined to embrace the articles and liturgy of the Church of England, and to approach her communion, do humbly and earnestly request your honourable Society to send us a lawfully ordained minister ... we intend to set apart for our Episcopal teacher, whenever it shall please God to inspire your venerable body to appoint us one, at least two hundred acres of glebe for the support of a Church minister for ever.[29]

With this there went to England a second petition of a similar nature, from Ripton, dated significantly "All Saints' Day, 1722." Among the signers of this petition were two Sheltons and a Beardslee – names which mean something in the history of the Episcopal Church in Connecticut. In 1730, the laity of New London and Groton likewise petitioned the S. P. G., asking the Society to appoint Samuel Seabury the elder, recently converted, as their minister.[30] Other places followed suit – Reading, Wallingford, Hebron, Simsbury, and Middletown, As the Church began to expand in New England, the dissenting leaders frequently found fault that the S. P. G., a society founded to extend Christianity to the non-Christian, was sending missionaries to already Christianized New England. It was true, on the contrary, at least in Connecticut, that the Society never assumed the offence, but only acted in response to a petition originating from the laity. This early, the Connecticut layman was beginning to manifest that stubborn attachment to the Church which was to distinguish him for well over a century.

This then was the situation, and Samuel Johnson was just the man to respond to it. He had hardly been settled in Stratford for two months after his return from England when he wrote to Bishop Gibson, whom he had met there, describing what he had found:

> The people here are generally rigid Independents and have an inveterate enmity against the established church. But of late the eyes of great multitudes are opened to the great error of such an uncharitable and therefore unchristian spirit. This is come to pass chiefly in six or seven towns of which this of Stratford where I reside is the principal, and though I am unworthy and unmeet to be entrusted with such a charge, yet there is not one clergyman of the Church of England besides myself in this whole colony, and I am obliged to neglect the care at Stratford in a great measure (where there is business enough for one minister) to ride about to the other towns (some ten and some twenty miles off) where in lack of them there is as much necessity of a minister as there is at Stratford, especially at Newtown and Fairfield.[31]

This letter documents the beginning of a process whereby Stratford, under Johnson's vigorous leadership, became, not only the pioneer Anglican parish of Connecticut, but the vital center of a missionary movement which was to continue until the whole colony was dotted with Anglican parishes.

By the end of 1724, Johnson had ridden his horse to Fairfield, Newtown and Ripton, receiving in all three places a hearty welcome. It would appear that he tried to work out a system for a sort of joint vestry, to draw all these places together as a single operation. In 1724 the Stratford records list two wardens each from Ripton, and one each from Fairfield and Newtown, and vestrymen from each place. But the experiment seems not to have worked out, as it was discontinued in 1725.[32]

But Johnson's missionary journeys were not confined to Fairfield County. In June 1724, he reported, "I have since preached at New-London, where I had 60 hearers...."[33] In 1728 he reported another important move:

> I have lately been preaching at New-Haven where the College is, and had a considerable congregation, and among them several of the scholars, who are very inquisitive about the principles of our Church, and after sermon ten of the members of the Church there subscribed £100 towards the building of a Church in that town....[34]

Johnson was well aware of the strategic significance of Yale as a field of work. In 1729 he visited Wethersfield. In 1731 he went outside Connecticut, to Westerly in Rhode Island and Brookhaven on Long Island. There was apparently no end to his missionary zeal.

 Moreover, Johnson's fame for zeal and his abilities prompted the S. P. G. missionary and the churchwardens at Newport, Rhode Island, to invite him to Newport in May 1738, when the Reverend James Honyman despaired of his life and sought a successor. He and the wardens pitched upon Johnson lest "a man of meaner capacity ... be of little service." Willing to serve wherever he might "be thought most advantageous," Johnson visited Newport, but found that Honyman was "considerably mended," and he referred the matter to the S. P. G. for its disposition in the event that Honyman died. Meantime, the Rector of Stratford, grateful for the regard shown him, was content to serve the Church in Connecticut. His only concerns had been that his own people might be well provided for, that he be able to be "in what situation I might be most useful," and that any move not cause a decrease in his livelihood.[35]

The second parish to be firmly established in Connecticut was at Fairfield. Like Stratford, Fairfield had to fight its way to toleration against strong opposition, headed by that mortal foe to episcopacy, Lieutenant Governor Nathan Gold. Gold had once propounded to the General Assembly a law to confine Pigot to the exercise of his ministerial functions within the town limits of Stratford.[36] But in spite of opposition, by the autumn of 1725 the churchmen of Fairfield had built a small church, which Johnson opened for services. However, by this time Johnson was no longer the only missionary in the field. In 1724, Henry Caner, son of the contractor who had built Yale College, a born Churchman and a Yale graduate, came to Stratford to work with Johnson. For three years he lived with Johnson, acting as teacher, lay reader, and catechist, meanwhile studying for holy orders. He was the first of the many whom Johnson was to train. Early in 1727, he went to England for ordination, returned in the autumn of the same year, and was appointed by the S. P. G. as missionary to Fairfield. Caner was a young man of ability, and he soon gathered a congregation of five hundred, packing the church so full that it was necessary to build galleries. North of Fairfield and Stratford lay Newtown; Caner and Johnson took turns holding services there until it was also ready for a resident priest. Caner continued in Fairfield twenty years, until he was called to King's Chapel, Boston. Meantime, ministers of the Standing Order were further unsettled when Episcopal churches sprang up in a dozen scattered towns, some of them led by former Congregationalists like Samuel Seabury, Sr., and John Beach who in 1730 and 1732 joined the missionary endeavors of Johnson and Caner.[37]

Moreover, Caner's Fairfield parishioners advanced the cause of the Church by pressing the Connecticut General Assembly to give them more equitable treatment in the provincial tax laws. Led by Churchwarden Moses Ward, the vestry petitioned for exemption from taxes to support the ministry of the Standing Order. Their influence must have been considerable, or the members of the assembly unusually tractable. Perhaps Ward's argument did the trick; he suggested that Anglicans should no more be compelled to contribute to the Standing Order than should Congregationalists to the Church of England! A law was enacted in May 1727 that exempted Anglicans from paying taxes for the local Congregational minister and church only if they had organized their own "society" and had a resident "person in orders according to the canons of the church of England...."[38] Thus another link was forged in the chain of religious liberty.

Unfortunately, the law proved more impressive in theory than effective in practice. Magistrates interpreted the requirement that a non-Congregational church and its minister must be in "sufficient nearness" for its members to attend services regularly to mean a distance of one or two miles, or five at most. Such interpretation excluded many of Johnson's and Caner's parishioners. As late as 1743, church people in New Milford and New Fairfield were being fined for nonattendance at the Congregational meeting house, they having no resident priest.[39] The only way to make the law effective for the benefit of the Anglican laity was to increase the number of resident Anglican clergy. Clearly, more missionaries were needed, and especially a bishop who might ordain deacons and priests without these persons having to make the long and dangerous voyage to Britain for the laying on of hands.

7. The Great Awakening

The events of 1722 and Johnson's return to Stratford had plainly given a great impulse to the growth of Anglicanism in Connecticut. After about 1740 a new stimulus was given to the growth of the Church of England in Connecticut – a stimulus that was to send hundreds of former Congregationalists into the newly organized parishes of the Church of England. And this stimulus, by one of the ironies of history, came as a result of something never planned to strengthen Anglicanism.

 In October 1740 the Reverend George Whitefield arrived in Connecticut on a preaching tour that was to take him through colonies from Massachusetts to Georgia. This marked an important step in the progress of that movement in American religion known as The Great Awakening. Whitefield was undoubtedly an extraordinary person. Ordained a priest in the Church of England, he continued all his life in that priesthood, in spite of his rigorously Calvinistic doctrines. But he did his own church little service – except by indirection. He was by all accounts one of the greatest rabble-rousers in history, able to make a strong emotional impression even on such a coolheaded person as Benjamin Franklin.[40] It was characteristic of him and of his work that in the American colonies he preached almost exclusively in non-Anglican churches. The essence of his preaching was the necessity of conversion and of "vital religion", and the soul-destroying effect of formal conformity. He denounced Anglican degeneracy. In New England, his dynamic preaching had many results. One result was the tearing asunder of the Standing Order. Even Jonathan Edwards, who was enthusiastic for Whitefield's work, was convinced that though it effected a revival of genuine spirituality, it did so at a great cost. After Whitefield had passed through New England, the congregations of the Standing Order were torn by feuds between Old Lights, who refused to follow Whitefield, and New Lights, who did. Some of the Puritan clergy lost half their congregations; in other cases, pastors were dismissed from their charges because they were found lacking in vital religion. For orthodox Puritanism, the Great Awakening was nothing short of a disaster. In the long run, two religious bodies gained by the revival. The Baptists, who previously to this had hardly existed in New England outside of Rhode Island and who were better fitted than the Standing Order to assimilate the teachings and methods of Whitefield into their system, began now to grow throughout the rest of the New England colonies. To many, their itinerant lay-preaching was horrifying. More surprising, one great gainer by the Awakening was the struggling Church of England in Connecticut. Johnson, whose whole religious temperament was averse to Whitefield's brand of emotionalism, wrote on September 29, 1741, to the Archbishop of Canterbury, describing the progress and effect of the Awakening as he saw it. It was in his opinion

> the most odd and unaccountable enthusiasm that perhaps ever obtained in any age or nation. For not only the minds of many people are at once struck with prodigious distresses upon their hearing the hideous outcries of a set of itinerant preachers that go up and down among us, but

even their bodies are frequently in a moment affected with the strangest convulsions and involuntary agitations, which also have sometimes happened even without their minds being at all affected. The church indeed has not as yet much suffered but has in many instances gained by these strange commotions.[41]

In the following year Caner wrote to the S. P. G. that "Enthusiasm has made no progress at Fairfield, and the effects of it at Stamford, Norwalk, Ridgefield, &c., where it has a large spread, has been the reconciling of many sober, considerate people to the communion of our Church."[42]

Indeed, many historians who have dealt with this episode in American religious history have agreed with Johnson and Caner that especially in Connecticut a large number of Congregationalists, weary of the internal strife that was rending their parishes asunder, turned to the Anglican Church as a haven of refuge in a tempest. Nor was their movement one of mere escapism; many were sincerely concerned about doctrinal issues, which the Awakening had opened to question and serious dispute.[43] And by this time, owing largely to the work of Johnson, the Church of England was strong enough in Connecticut to be prepared to receive them into its bosom. Converts both clerical and lay came, as Johnson put it, because they were as convinced "of the duty of conforming to episcopacy and liturgy as of any other principle of Christianity ... And the same reasons that persuade me, I doubt not, determine the bulk of those that conform to the church in these parts, people ... conscientiously persuaded for themselves (without censuring others) that they could not please God and answer a good conscience if they worshipped him in any other way."[44]

Nor were the Puritans correct in charging that ministerial converts were economically motivated to become priests. Anglican clergy faced the expenses and dangers of travel abroad for ordination; they accepted the hardships of itinerant missionaries, whereas the Congregational ministers usually enjoyed a settled life in one place. Allowing for S. P. G. salaries paid in sterling and for the fluctuation in value of colonial currency, stipends for the Anglicans (paid by the S. P. G.) were not measurably greater than the salaries of Congregational ministers, nor did Anglicans generally have the latter's "fringe benefits" of glebeland attached to their churches.[45]

For Samuel Johnson the Great Awakening resulted in a curious episode, more amusing to us perhaps than to him and the other persons involved. In 1742 the Reverend Theophilus Morris, an S. P. G. missionary of English birth, attacked Johnson. (There is considerable evidence that both in Massachusetts and Connecticut the English-born clergy were at odds with the native American priests of the Church of England.) Morris wrote the Reverend Roger Price of Boston, who as the commissary of the Bishop of London was supposed to exercise a sort of disciplinary control over all the Anglican clergy in New England, accusing Johnson and his son, William Samuel, of a horrible offence. They had actually attended one of the revivals. And so they had; curiosity was one of Johnson's leading traits, and he always wanted to know what was going on. Price despatched him a note of rather gentle reproach, suggesting that he "avoid anything that may show a favorable disposition towards the separation as will obstruct the growth of the Episcopal Church." To this Johnson replied in one of his rare bursts of indignation. After meeting Morris's charge, and explaining just what he had done, he went on to say with justifiable pride:

> I believe I may say without vanity that I have labored as faithfully, and with as good success, as any of my brethren ... I came alone into this colony a few years ago, when there were but 70 to 80 adult Church people in the whole government, and now there are above 2000; there are ten churches actually built and three more building, and seven settled in the ministry. I have nigh 150 communicants, of whom there wanted but four of fourscore together and received the Communion last Sunday, and my people are as regular and rubrical in our worship as any congregation that I know of. Can it then be supposed that I have obstructed its growth? In short I have laboriously studied, and wrote, and rid, and preached, and pleaded, and lived all that was in my power to promote the growth of the best of Churches. I have neither farming nor merchandise, nor do I suffer any other pursuit of either pleasure or profit to embarrass or hinder me in promoting the growth of the

Church, which is the single point that I have in view. If it would not savor of something like vanity, which I hope may be excused on this occasion, I might almost venture to say I have labored more abundantly than they all....[46]

Posterity is indebted to the Reverend Mr. Morris for being the cause of this little outburst, in which Johnson so nobly summed up the accomplishment of his twenty years in the ministry.

8. The Net Result

In 1723, when Samuel Johnson returned from England to take up his work at Stratford, the Stratford congregation was the only organized parish of the Church of England in Connecticut, and it had not yet succeeded in erecting a church building. He died in 1772, substantially fifty years later. When he died, there were in Connecticut forty-three organized congregations, all but three of which had erected buildings. These places were staffed by sixteen priests, many of whom had been trained by Johnson. This notable expansion was the result of many converging forces; it was the work of countless faithful laity, and many devoted missionary priests.[47] But back of it all lies the labor and the genius of Samuel Johnson.

The story is all the more impressive when it includes some comparisons of Connecticut with other parts of New England. When Johnson began his work there were but five other Episcopal churches in Massachusetts and Rhode Island, and only seven other clergymen for all of New England. When Johnson died, Connecticut's 43 Anglican congregations and 16 priests more than matched the rest of New England's. Massachusetts had twenty Episcopal churches (including five in Maine, which lay in Massachusetts's jurisdiction) and fifteen clergy. Rhode Island had but five churches, and New Hampshire one (at Portsmouth). Moreover, the number of Connecticut's Churchmen had risen from less than 100 in 1723 to about 15,000 - 17,200 in 1774, and these accounted for three-fifths of all Churchmen in New England. None of the Anglican clergy in New England were as distinguished as Connecticut's Yale-trained and Johnson-influenced men, and none were as active in the defense and promotion of their Faith as the Johnson coterie of Connecticut.[48]

Chapter VI

The Parson Amidst
Books and Men

1. Johnson Still Reads

It was no exaggeration when Johnson said that he had labored more abundantly than they all. How, in the midst of his productive activity, Johnson found time to read, one has difficulty in imagining. But having the kind of mind, the intellectual curiosity which was one of his leading traits, read he must and did. The list of readings which he had begun in 1719, and from which we have quoted, he continued to keep up until the year 1756. During the Stratford years, he averaged reading over fifty titles per year. He was still within reach of the Yale library, but, as his letters to his English correspondents show, he also built up a library of his own. More than half of the books he read during these years were strictly professional reading, works of piety or controversial divinity. We will not bore the reader by enumerating them. But a look at works of another sort show that his wide-ranging intellectual curiosity was still in evidence. In the field of English literature we observe Addison's notes on *Paradise Lost*. A year or two later he had made his way through *Paradise Regained*. In a lighter vein he turned to Steele's *Conscious Lovers*. In 1725, he read Swift's *Tale of a Tub*; in the following year Pope's translation of *The Iliad*; in 1728, *The Beggar's Opera*; in 1730, *Gulliver's Travels*. In 1726, he discovered a new language to add to his mastery of Latin, Greek, and Hebrew. After completing Boyer's French grammar, he read the New Testament in French for a starter, then plunged into Fenelon and *Le Malade Imaginaire*. In 1728, a new world was opened to his philosophical interest when he read George Berkeley's *Principles of Human Knowledge*. He immediately fell in love with that most readable of English philosophers, and read everything of Berkeley's on which he could lay hands. In 1729, he recorded again going through the whole of Berkeley. And once more he turned to the Church Fathers – Clement of Rome, his old stand-by Ignatius, Origen, Tertullian, and Irenaeus. Apparently he was unafraid of popery, as he read both the *Breviary* and the *Missal*.[1] He was plainly resolute not to let his good mind go to seed.

2. George Berkeley

Early in the year 1729, George Berkeley, then Dean of Derry in Ireland, landed in Rhode Island, full of plans. It was his intention to set up a college in Bermuda, for which he held a royal charter. This was to be not only a place for the instruction of its students in literature and theology, but also a missionary center. For two years Berkeley lived in Bristol, Rhode Island, vainly endeavoring to induce the king's chief minister, Sir Robert Walpole, to provide him the funds that Parliament had voted for this project. In Bristol he bought a tract of land with his own money, and there built a farm-house.

Johnson had already, as we have seen, read Berkeley's writings. As soon as he had heard that the philosopher was in the neighboring province he made a pilgrimage to Bristol. Berkeley welcomed this visit by one of the few men in the colonies capable of discussing philosophy with him, and the two minds made immediate contact. On his return to Stratford, Johnson wrote Berkeley a letter, which makes eight printed pages in the Schneider collection, filled with technical speculations and questionings. Thus began a correspondence that lasted as long as Berkeley lived, and continued after his death with his son, also named George. One fact which strikes the reader about this letter is the pleasing humility with which Johnson approached Berkeley. He was great enough to recognize a superior.[2]

This visit might well be considered as marking the end, or almost the end, of Samuel Johnson's philosophical Odyssey. As William

Ames had given way in Johnson's thinking to Francis Bacon, and Bacon in turn to Locke and Newton, so now they must give place to George Berkeley. The visit left Johnson a complete convert to Berkeleyan idealism. Indeed, he was to become its foremost exponent in the American Colonies during the colonial period. But each of these writers, except possibly Ames, was not wholly discarded. Bacon and Locke and Newton all left their permanent impress on Johnson's mind. One by-product of the visit with Berkeley may have been the publication of Johnson's first work to see the press. In 1731, a little booklet called *An Introduction to the Study of Philosophy* was published in London, bearing Johnson's name on the title page. It had no originality, but is interesting as showing how Johnson still thought of philosophy, not as a technical study in itself, but as the synthesis of all knowledge. It divided the field of philosophy into three parts, rational, natural, and moral, and contained a substantial list of recommended readings in each division of the field.[3] As we shall eventually see, Johnson later expanded this into something more worth while.

The visit to Berkeley had its practical consequences, also. Berkeley had at first intended, when he found out that his project for a college on this side of the Atlantic would never be realized, to make a substantial gift to Harvard College. Johnson, always loyal to Yale, persuaded him rather to give Yale his house and farm in Bristol. These became part of the Yale endowment. After his return to Ireland, Berkeley sent Yale a further gift of about a thousand volumes for its library. These books the trustees accepted with some misgivings, having a vivid remembrance of the disaster wrought by the coming of the Dummer collection of books.

3. Controversy

Unlike many of his New England contemporaries in the ministry, Johnson was not the sort of person to delight in theological controversy. He was basically a friendly man, his temper was amiable, and he would gladly have lived at peace with all mankind. But an Anglican priest at work in Connecticut in the middle of the Eighteenth Century could hardly avoid being drawn into theological polemics. And Johnson was rapidly forging to the front as the intellectual leader of the growing Anglican community in the colony, and indeed in the northern American colonies.

In 1732, the Reverend John Graham, Congregational minister at Woodbury, published what Johnson called "a most scurrilous ballad of verses, misrepresenting the Church in the most ludicrous and abusive manner, objecting sundry things and concluding in these words, 'They that do thus and don't reform these evils, Are these Christ's Church, pray, or be'ent they the devil's' "[4] Quite understandably provoked by this sort of attack, Johnson sat down to pen a reply. This took the form of *A Letter from a Minister of the Church of England to His Dissenting Parishioners*. The letter was published in 1733 in New York by the famous printer, John Peter Zenger.[5] There was nothing new and startling in the subject matter of this pamphlet. It traversed wellworn ground; the Church of England was not Papist; it was not intolerant; it did not reduce religion to mere ceremonial; the use of the surplice, the sign of the cross in baptism were desirable and permissible practices; the Church was not Arminian. Only once, in a brief discussion of predestination did Johnson come to grips with essential doctrine. But the interest of the little book lies in its temper. The opening paragraph indicates clearly the spirit in which Johnson wrote:

> My heart's desire and prayer to God for you and yours, is, that you might be saved. This likewise has been, and is my earnest and constant endeavor; for your souls are very precious, for whom our dear Redeemer spilt his precious blood. I am sorry you will not give me more opportunity to serve the interest of your souls, which I should gladly do with all my heart. But you are taught to keep at a distance from me, and beware of my conversation....[6]

One can only suppose that Johnson sincerely meant this as an irenicon. Actually and understandably, it proved to be nothing of the sort. The very title, with its calm assumption that Johnson, being in apostolic orders, was *The Parson of Stratford*, responsible for the souls of every inhabitant, was more irritating than the usual theological attack.

Graham of course returned to the fray, and Johnson wrote a second letter, which was published in Boston in 1734. It was somewhat sharper in tone than the first. In it he remarked of Graham that he was "indeed sorry, for the poor man's sake that he suffers himself to be so much out of temper and without any provocation; that he should show himself so little of the gentleman, or the Christian; that he should betray so much ill breeding, as well as ill temper...." Such asperity was rare in Johnson. To get himself on his usual higher ground, he took the interesting attitude that Graham was not really representative of the Puritan clergy, asserting that "the generality of your ministers are men of a better spirit, and will not run into the same excess of riot with this stranger in speaking evil of us...."[7] Johnson ended this second letter with a rather eloquent exordium, which struck the same irenic note he had endeavored to keep throughout the dispute:

> Let us not try to magnify and aggravate the differences between us, but rather to make as little of them, and to consider them with as much tenderness, as possible. Let us not dispute which has already most or least charity, but let us strive to see who shall hereafter, really and in fact, most abound in the practice of what heavenly virtue, both towards each other, and towards all men. This is the best course we can take, as far as possible in this imperfect state, to reconcile ourselves to one another, both in judgment and practice; to meet together in truth, and live in peace here, or however to meet at last in that perfect state of truth, and peace, and holiness hereafter, where God and charity alone shall forever reign![8]

There speaks the real Johnson. In 1737 he issued a third brief letter, and then dropped the controversy for writing more to his taste.

4. The Philosopher Writes

We have mentioned above the brief introduction to the study of philosophy which Johnson wrote and which was published in London in 1731. To this text Johnson returned again and again, developing and expanding his thought. In 1744 the introduction was reprinted in London, but in a much enlarged form. Finally, in 1752, it appeared for the third time, renamed *Elementa Philosophica*, and dedicated to Bishop Berkeley. This, which is described as "the first text-book of philosophy published in this country," was printed in Philadelphia by no less a person than Benjamin Franklin.[9] In between the various appearances of the introduction, Johnson brought out two other philosophical works. In 1745, came *A Letter from Aristocles to Authades*, concerning the sovereignty of God, and in 1746, *A New System of Morality*, both published in Boston. By 1755 he was undoubtedly the leading Berkeleyan idealist on the American side of the Atlantic. Partly as a result of his letters to "dissenting parishioners," but still more because of his contribution to the advance of the Church of England in Connecticut, Johnson received the academic recognition he thoroughly deserved. In February 1743, the University of Oxford awarded him the degree of Doctor of Sacred Divinity, and from this time on he was to all his pupils and friends "the Doctor."[10] The more substantial works which followed on the heels of his doctorate, were even greater justification for the honor Oxford did him.

5. He Corresponds

For all his reading, Johnson never was a bookworm. He was too outgoing a person for that, and like every true teacher, he always wanted to share his knowledge and exchange ideas. Although he spent the greater portion of his life within a few miles of New Haven, his English voyage had widened his horizons, and he was always vividly aware of a world beyond the limits of Connecticut, and resolved to keep up communication with that wider world. He had made friends in England, and continually wrote them. And he proceeded to make friends by letter with intellectuals in the colonies.

One such was Governor William Burnet of New York. The Governor came naturally by his intellectual interests, being the son of Gilbert Burnet, Bishop of Salisbury. He and Johnson seem to have made contact some time in 1726; the first letter between them preserved is one from the Governor, dated January 31, 1727, acknowledging the return of books which Burnet had lent Johnson. Both borrowing and correspondence continued until Burnet's death in 1729. Although Johnson admitted the temptation, the

Governor did not persuade him of the rationality of writings like Bishop Hoadly's "on the Trinitarian and Bangorean controversy ... which was then much in vogue."[11]

Longer and more detailed was the correspondence Johnson began in 1744 with Cadwallader Colden, Surveyor General and later Lieutenant Governor of New York. Johnson evidently was trying to sell Colden the ideas of Bishop Berkeley, whose *Principles* he had lent the eminent New Yorker. Locke, Newton, Spinoza, the ultimate nature of matter – the names and the speculations flew back and forth, as these two minds struck sparks from each other. Of more interest to the biographer is the fact here revealed that Colden had been instrumental in sending his De Lancey grandchildren to Johnson for schooling. They were being taught Cornelius Nepos's Roman and Greek biographies of generals and historians, a short history of England, geography, and a short system of universal history and chronology. Of one of the children, Peter, Johnson wrote in 1753 that he had "an excellent turn for learning," and he ventured to hope that "I am educating one who, in God's time, may become a bishop in America."[12] Intellectual though he was, Johnson never forgot that he was first of all a priest.

6. Johnson and Franklin

The first evidence we have of contact between Johnson and Franklin is the fragment of a letter from Johnson to his fellow intellectual, dated May 10, 1750. Johnson had evidently sent Franklin a copy of his *Introduction to Philosophy*, with the hope that it might be printed in America in a revised and enlarged form.[13] Franklin was at once taken by the manifestation of an intelligence in some respects akin to his own. At this time he, with the Reverend Francis Allison, and the Reverend Dr. William Smith, was deeply involved in the foundation of a college in Philadelphia, a college that was eventually to become the University of Pennsylvania. Between the receipt of the letter of May 10 and the following August Franklin, accompanied by the Attorney General of the colony, made the journey to Stratford. On August 9, Franklin wrote Johnson, giving details of his project, and offering Johnson the headship of the institution. He made every effort to entice Johnson. The salary was to be £100 sterling, and he suggested that Johnson's son William might be engaged as tutor. The trustees would pay Johnson's moving expenses. And there was a further bait. Knowing Johnson's strong church principles, Franklin observed that "The Trustees of the Academy are three fourths of them members of the Church of England, and the rest men of moderate principles." They would not be averse to allowing Johnson to start in Philadelphia a second parish of the Church of England, Johnson to be rector, and derive from this a further income. The correspondence was kept up through the year 1751, with Johnson advising on such matters as the course of study in the new college. On Christmas Eve 1751, and again in January, Franklin wrote Johnson, making a last effort to entice him to Philadelphia. He observed that if Johnson could "be thus useful to us at this distance, how much more might you be so if you were present with us, and had the immediate inspection and government of the schools."[14]

Finally, in January 1752, Johnson made his decision. He wrote Franklin that he was clearly aware of his duty to "use what little ability I have ... in the best manner I could, having never been without pupils of one sort or other half a year at a time, and seldom that, for thirty eight years." Grateful that some of his students had come to occupy some of the first places and pulpits in the land, he averred, "But I am now plainly in the decline of life, both as to agility of body and vigor of mind, and must, therefore, consider myself as being an *emeritus*, and unfit for any new situation in the world or to enter on any new business, especially at such a distance from my hitherto sphere of action ... where I have as much duty on my hands as I am capable of...."[15] When Johnson wrote this he was fifty-six years old. He was to have twenty years more of health and activity.

Chapter VII

ONE-MAN SEMINARY

1. Recruiting Begins

The early decades of the Eighteenth Century saw a strong movement toward the Church of England in the colony of Connecticut. We have noted how petitions were sent to the S. P. G. from Fairfield, Newton, Ripton, even distant New London, from groups of laymen eager for the ministrations of the Church. Samuel Johnson, riding the dirt roads on his horse, did his best to satisfy that need. But he was only one man, and he could not begin to cover the ground. If the "best of churches" was to grow in Connecticut, there must be priests to staff it. While the mother church was not as destitute of missionary spirit as some writers on the Eighteenth Century would have us believe, there was little possibility that enough English clergy would leave their comfortable vicarages and fixed endowments to venture into a comparative wilderness. If priests were to be had in Connecticut, they must be made in Connecticut, and Samuel Johnson must make them.

When, in 1724, Henry Caner graduated from Yale and came to Stratford to be Johnson's lay assistant, and later to go to England for ordination, Johnson saw how his problem of staffing might be solved. Yale was only a few miles distant, easily reached on horseback. Perhaps Yale could furnish him with the men he needed. On August 14, 1725, he wrote to the secretary of the Venerable Society: "Sundry of the young candidates for the ministry repair to me frequently for books and conversation upon religious subjects, and many, I hope in time, especially if there were a Bishop here I may enter into the Church's service."[1]

The reader will note that the "young candidates for the ministry" were candidates for the ministry of the Congregational churches. It is a striking fact in American religious history that the ministry of the American Episcopal Church has been, and still is, recruited to considerable extent from the ministries of other churches. Johnson did not begin this process. But the Dark Day gave it a great impulse, and from 1725 on, one of the chief accomplishments of Johnson's years at Stratford was to help keep a steady flow of young men from the ministry of the Standing Order into the ministry of the Church of England.

Part of the strategy by which Johnson did this was to keep in continuous touch with Yale. The events of 1722 had made him notorious, and people flock to hear a notorious preacher. He was young, enthusiastic, attractive, a teacher, and deeply read in religious controversy. His scholarship was unequalled in Connecticut of the period. On February 10, 1727, he wrote to the society:

> A very worthy young gentleman lives with me in my house, who is a scholar, having lately been graduated in a neighboring College, whom I have reconciled to our Church, and indeed, (I may say,) to Christianity, for he never was baptised … Him, therefore, I have baptised and admitted to the communion; and he is a very religious, sober, studious and sensible man … He designs, with Mr. Caner, in due time, to offer himself to the honourable Society's service ….[2]

However, this experiment seems not to have worked out; the young man cannot be placed among the men Johnson was to send to England. From this point on, however, Johnson's reports to the Society made continual mention of his contacts with Yale. In 1728 he wrote:

> I have … lately preached at New-Haven, a large town about fourteen miles eastward, where there is a College … I had near a hundred hearers, and among them several of the College; after service about ten of the members of our Church there subscribed £100 towards building a Church in that town ….[3]

Even more revealing of his method is the statement contained in a report of 1730:

> One thing I have particularly to rejoice in, and that is, that I have a very considerable influence in the College in my neighbourhood; and that a love to the Church gains ground greatly in it. Several young men that are graduates, and some young ministers, I have prevailed with to read and consider the matter so far, that they are very uneasy out of the communion of the Church, and some seem much disposed to come into her service; and those that are best affected to the Church are the brightest and most studious of any that are educated in the country.[4]

Obviously, Johnson was prejudiced in favor of his boys, but we shall see something of the quality of the men he was preparing.

Of course the effects of the Great Awakening on the Yale students also favored Johnson's appeal to them to enter the Church of England. His son, William Samuel, a sophomore in 1741-42, was likewise quick to seize the opportunity to familiarize students and faculty with the dangers of Protestant teachings and the attractiveness of Anglican orthodoxy. Once, for example, he called on his father to forward Daniel Whitby's anti-Calvinist tract, *A Discourse Concerning … Election and Reprobation* (London, 1710).[5] After the Rector of Stratford paid one of his periodic visits to New Haven in the spring of 1745, he informed the Secretary of the S. P. G. that Yale had "ten children of the Church and several sons of dissenting parents, that are much inclined to conform."[6] Included were his youngest son William and Samuel Seabury, Jr., who graduated in 1748. That year ten Anglican students received Yale degrees, and nine Anglican clerics met at commencement time for a conference. Yale's officials grew "deeply alarmed as more and more Anglicans began poaching on their ecclesiastical preserves. They persistently exerted their influence in an attempt to contain the encroachment within and without the college."[7] Samuel Johnson's "poaching" went steadily on, in season and out, and his influence with men entering the priesthood was not confined to the years of the Great Awakening. It both preceded and followed that upheaval.

2. John Beach

John Beach had been a student under Johnson during Johnson's brief career as a teacher at Yale. He was graduated in 1721, and promptly ordained to the Congregational ministry. His intelligence and activity made him from the first one of the outstanding young ministers of the Standing Order. When, therefore, the Congregational parish in Newtown, frightened by the inroads made in their numbers by the work of Johnson and Caner, looked about for a strong leader to stem the tide of advancing Anglicanism, the choice fell on young Beach. But again, the strange and somewhat comic result that followed when Cutler was called to Stratford was repeated. Beach went to Newton to convert the Anglicans; they converted him. In 1732 he dismayed his congregation by "declaring for episcopacy." He was promptly dismissed. He then set out for England, bearing a letter from Johnson to the Bishop of London, recommending him in these terms: "I know, by long experience of him (he having been heretofore my pupil, and ever since my neighbor) to be a very ingenuous and studious person, and a truly serious and conscientious Christian ...."[8] After his ordination the Society sent him back to Newtown. Here his "almost incredible energy and his rare ability to win popular devotion firmly rooted the Church throughout northern Fairfield County."[9] For fifty years he labored, working in close conjunction with Johnson and joining with him in the carrying on of the inevitable controversies of the day. During his long rectorate Newtown became the largest Episcopal parish in Connecticut. In 1781 he wrote to the Society:

> My two congregations are growing; that of Reading being commonly about 300, and at Newtown about 600. I baptize about 130 children in one year, and lately two adults ... I am now in the eighty-second year of my age, yet do

constantly alternately perform service and preach at Newtown and Reading.[10]

Six months later the veteran was dead.

3. Father and Son

Samuel Seabury, the first of the name to find a place in American
church history, entered Yale in 1720, planning to prepare for the
ministry of the Standing Order. He had therefore as teachers both
Cutler and Daniel Browne. Much disturbed by the stirring events of
1722, he transferred to Harvard, where he was graduated in 1724.
He was licensed to officiate in the Congregational Church at North
Groton, near New London, where we have seen Johnson preaching.
Early in 1730, he set out for England in quest of Anglican orders. He
bore with him a letter from Johnson, testifying that he had "led a
sober, virtuous and studious life, and now heartily embraces the
principles of the Church of England ....[11] On Johnson's advice the
Society sent Seabury back to New London, where he took up the
work Johnson had started. He finished his ministry in Hempstead,
on Long Island.

In 1744 Seabury's son, also named Samuel, entered Yale. Leaving in
1748 for England, Samuel Junior carried with him the usual letter
from Johnson, bearing this testimony:

> Seabury had a promising son, and as he designs him for
> the Society's service, he desires me to mention what I
> know of him; and as he has lived four years much under
> my eye, I can truly testify of him that he is a solid, sensi-
> ble, virtuous youth, and, I doubt not, may in due time do
> good service.[12]

How it would have rejoiced the heart of Johnson could he have foreseen that the young man who bore this rather reserved
recommendation would be the first Anglican bishop in America.
And it was to be of the utmost importance for the future of the Diocese of Connecticut, and the whole American Episcopal Church that
its first bishop had in great part learned his theology and his polity
through the influence of Samuel Johnson.

4. Chandler

The number of Yale men who entered the ministry of the Church of England increased considerably in the decade which began with 1740. In 1746, as the following extract testifies, Johnson had not one or two, but a whole batch of prospective priests.

> A love to the Church is still gaining in the College, and four more, whose names are Allen, Lloyd, Sturgeon, and Chandler, have declared themselves candidates for holy orders; and there seems a very growing disposition toward the Church, in the town of New-Haven, as well as in the College, so that I hope there will, 'ere long be a flourishing Church there. I have heretofore desired leave for Messrs. Dibble and Leaming to go for orders, and all now desired to ask the same for Messrs. Mansfield and Allen ....[13]

One of this group stands out for several reasons. Thomas Bradbury Chandler graduated from Yale in 1745. Brought up in the Congregational Church, while at Yale he succumbed to Johnson's wiles, and became an Anglican. After graduation he studied theology under Johnson for several years, and lived under Johnson's roof. Here he became his master's favorite and most intimate pupil. He was ordained in England in 1751, and sent to Elizabeth, New Jersey. (It is significant that the Johnsonian influence was being extended outside New England.) Here he was highly successful; under his leadership the parish became one of the largest in the province. Until the outbreak of the Revolutionary War he was the leading Anglican priest in New Jersey, and a foremost figure in the abortive attempt made in the 1760s to secure the episcopate for the colonial church. Like many of Johnson's pupils, the Revolution drove him into the Loyalist camp. During the war, he lived in England, but like the younger Seabury and William Samuel Johnson, having accepted the verdict of arms, he became a loyal American. And in 1785, he returned to New Jersey. He demonstrated his Johnsonian principles by campaigning vigorously against the *Proposed Book of Common Prayer*, a document slanted in the Unitarian direction. He was also vigorously opposed to William White's tentative proposal for ordination by presbyters, if episcopal ordination could not be had.

During these "critical years" New Jersey stood fast with New England in the various constitutional conventions of the Church, holding out for the rights of the episcopate. Chandler very likely had a hand in this. He was of sufficient repute in England to be considered as a possible bishop for Nova Scotia. Important in his own right, he was perhaps still more important as a link between two greater men. In his last years he wrote the first life of Johnson, but he died before it was printed. The small volume was therefore seen through the press by Chandler's son-in-law. The son-in-law was John Henry Hobart. Hobart had been educated at Presbyterian Princeton, and had read theology with the Latitudinarian William White. But from neither of these sources did he acquire the theological principles he was to advocate with surpassing skill and energy. Hobart became the greatest American bishop of his day, the acknowledged leader of the High Church party, who followed in the wake of Seabury in revolutionizing the concept of the office and work of a bishop, not only in the United States, but throughout the Anglican Communion. It was by way of Seabury and Hobart that the idea spread that a bishop was the first missionary of the diocese. By his personal contacts during his trip to England in 1823-24 it is very probable that Hobart stimulated the writers of the *Tracts for the Times*. In all this one can see, though at one remove, the pervasive influence of Samuel Johnson.

5. Leaming

Jeremiah Leaming, of the class of '45 at Yale, was converted to Anglicanism while in college. After graduation he studied theology under Johnson's direction, and for two years functioned as lay reader at Norwalk – near enough to be under Johnson's thumb. Ordained in England in 1748, he eventually returned to Norwalk as rector, and there built up another of Connecticut's strong parishes. In 1776 he was arrested as a Loyalist, and so mistreated that he was permanently crippled. Nevertheless, he was one of the ten Connecticut clergy who persevered and who met at the glebe house in Woodbury on Lady Day 1783, to elect a bishop. Leaming was himself the first choice of the meeting for the office, but he declined because of his age and physical disability. He served as rector of Stratford from 1784 to 1790, was given an honorary doctorate by Columbia University in 1789, and died in 1804.

6. Jarvis

One of the last of the men trained by Johnson was Abraham Jarvis, who graduated from Yale in 1761, read theology with Johnson for two years, and in 1763 went to England for ordination. On his return he became rector of the church at Middletown, Connecticut. During the Revolution he was forced to suspend services, but he was one of the first clergy in the state to resume them after the signing of the Treaty of Paris. He was secretary of the clergy meeting which elected Seabury bishop. In 1787, when it looked for a time as if the Episcopal churches in the various colonies might not be united in one church, and Connecticut was seriously considering establishing in the United States a complete episcopal succession derived from Scotland, Jarvis was designated by his fellow Connecticut clergy to be the second member of that succession. When Samuel Seabury died in 1796, Jarvis was elected to succeed him. As the election was not unanimous, he declined the office. In the following year he was again elected without a dissenting vote. Consecrated in 1797, he continued in office until his death in 1813.

7. Lesser Lights

We do not wish to bore the reader, but it is only by continuing our survey of Johnson's pupils that the breadth of his influence can be made clear.[14] Roger Viets graduated from Yale in 1758. He had become an Anglican during his college days. Immediately after he graduated he served as lay reader at Simsbury, Connecticut, meanwhile studying under Johnson's direction. As we have seen, as far back as the days of Henry Caner, Johnson had used this combination of study and field work to train his men. After ordination Viets returned to Simsbury as priest in charge. The stipend here was so small that Viets had to supplement his income by teaching and even farming. (The worker-priest is not a modern invention.) In spite of this, his work was very successful. "For twenty years he ranged over a vast territory, from Hartford, Windsor and Suffield to Litchfield County, and northward to Hartland and Berkshire County, Massachusetts ... the mission prospered and in 1774 had about nine hundred people in Simsbury alone."[15] Fined and imprisoned as a Loyalist during the Revolution, he removed with many other churchmen to Nova Scotia, where he ministered until 1811.

Henry Barclay was not a convert, but the son of a priest in the colony of New York. He came under Johnson's influence while at Yale, where he graduated in 1734. He immediately went to the Mohawk mission at Fort Hunter, where he functioned as lay reader and catechist. Here his work was highly successful. After his ordination he became rector of St. Peter's Church, Albany, but continued to minister to the Mohawks. In 1738 he reported to the Society that five hundred of the Indians at Fort Hunter – which must have been nearly all who lived there – were Christianized, and fifty were communicants.[16] He eventually became rector of Trinity Church, New York City.

Gideon Bostwick was one of the last in this long list. He was converted to Anglicanism while at Yale, graduated in 1762, and ordained in 1770. The S. P. G. stationed him in a new location, at Great Barrington, Massachusetts, Although he was a known Loyalist, he managed to keep his church open during the Revolution, After the war, using the Johnson technique, he made it a missionary center, journeying up into Vermont, and over the Berkshire Hills into Columbia County, New York, where he was instrumental in the founding of Christ Church, Hudson, When he died in 1793, it was calculated that he had baptized 2,274 people. Johnson was well aware of the importance of what he was doing as a teacher of incipient clergymen. Writing to Benjamin Franklin in January 1752, he expressed pride in "having never been without pupils of one sort or other half a year at a time, and seldom that, for thirty-eight years. And thank God, I have the great satisfaction to see some of them in the first pulpits, not only in Connecticut, but also in Boston and New York...."[17]

In the spring of 1754, Johnson left Stratford to become the first president of King's College. Although he was far removed from Yale, Yale graduates still resorted to him for direction in their theological studies, In 1763 he resigned the presidency and returned again to Stratford, planning to spend his days there in retirement. But he wrote to Archbishop Secker in August of that year, to indicate that he would not be entirely useless in his retirement. It was his hope that he might "live here to some good purpose, by directing candidates and others to their studies ...."[18] This hope proved to be well founded. In 1768 he wrote to Archbishop Secker once more:

> The bearer hereof is Mr. John Tyler, whom I humbly beg leave to introduce to your Grace's favarable notice. He has been educated and graduated at New Haven College, admitted *ad eundem* at the College at New York, and has for above a year diligently pursued his studies, chiefly in divinity here at Stratford. He often read service in my absence to very good acceptance, and always behaved well, and he now goes recommended for orders and a mission and I make no doubt will be a worthy and useful missionary.[19]

In 1770 Johnson was seventy-four years old, and had only two more years to live. But he was still able to think about the future, and to make plans for it. On June 11 of that year he wrote to the secretary of the S. P. G., outlining a scheme:

> I am extremely obliged to the Society for ordering Mr. So-masters to be placed here at Stratford. This happily falls in with a design I have entertained of holding here a little Academy, or resource for young students of Divinity, to prepare them for Holy Orders; the design of which is chiefly to improve them in classical learning, Latin and Greek, to teach them Hebrew, and direct and assist them in studying Divinity; and before they go, if not graduated otherwise, I would procure them the degree of M. A. at the College at New York. [I have several times directed one or more in their studies, and have now four here, whose names are Marshall, Fingley, Perry and Jones ...] This I shall continue while I live, with the assistance of Mr. Kneeland, who is very well qualified to continue it when l am gone.[20]

Here, probably for the first time in the history of the Anglican Communion, the old man was projecting something revolutionary – the establishment of a full-fledged seminary. Johnson did not live to see his design carried out, but the idea was picked up and developed, fifty years later, by John Henry Hobart, whom we have seen to be in the Johnson tradition.

There is much one would like to know about Johnson's method of operation in thus making Anglican priests – how he made contact with Yale students beyond his occasional preaching in New Haven; by what arguments he won them over to the Church of England; how he trained them after their conversions; what books they studied – but we have only the barest hints derived from references in his letters, many of which we have quoted. But if the process is largely hidden, the product is not. Between 1722 and Johnson's death forty-four Yale graduates offered themselves for the ministry of the Church of England. Thirty of these were converts. Twelve had been either licensed or ordained to the ministry of the Standing Order. Not only did these Yale graduates constitute a major part of the ministry in the rapidly growing Church of England in Connecticut. By the outbreak of the Revolution, Yale graduates were also ministering to Anglican congregations in Vermont, New York, Massachusetts, New Jersey, Delaware, and even in South Carolina. Now it is not maintained that this process of recruitment to the Anglican ministry was entirely the work of Samuel Johnson. As we have noted, there was throughout New England in the Eighteenth Century a drift from Puritanism and from the Puritan ministry back to the mother Church of England. However, it is possible to measure roughly the Johnson influence in advancing this drift.

Both Yale and Harvard were Puritan colleges in Puritan colonies. During the period from 1700 to 1760 Harvard graduated a little more than twice as many men as Yale.[21] Furthermore, the Church of England was in a far stronger position at Harvard than it was at Yale. The first Church of England parish in Boston, King's Chapel, dates from 1686. By the middle of the Eighteenth Century, Boston contained three strong Anglican parishes; New Haven had but one, and that relatively weak. In Boston lived a royal governor, almost always a nominal Anglican, at least, with his entourage of royal – and Anglican – officials. In New Haven the governor was a native son, and invariably a Puritan. All this would lead one to expect that Harvard would have produced at least twice as many recruits for the ministry of the Church of England as Yale. As a matter of fact, during the period under consideration, thirty-five Harvard men entered the ministry of the Church of England. Yale sent thirty-nine. This gives us some measure of the influence of Samuel Johnson and his one-man seminary.

Chapter VIII

WRITER AND THINKER

Samuel Johnson's ideas may be conveniently examined under four heads – politics, education, philosophy and theology. None save philosophy was ever summed up by Johnson himself in any particular body of writing, but they may be gathered from bits of reference in his letters and other manuscripts.

1. Political Views

Johnson's political attitudes seem especially scattered, for politics was not his chief concern except where it bore upon academic and ecclesiastical issues. But from first to last, his positions were singularly consistent. One of his cardinal principles was a rooted objection to "democracy." This may seem startling to a modern reader, as now-a-days to label anything democratic is to give it the highest possible sanction. This was not so in the Eighteenth Century; democracy was in many circles as much a naughty word as communist was to the adherents of the late Senator Joseph McCarthy. Johnson and his contemporaries of course thought in classical terms in which democracy was equated with mobocracy and its natural tendency which was toward dictatorship. Just as monarchy tended toward tyranny, and aristocracy toward oligarchy, so democracy was supposed to degenerate into one of the greatest of evils. The one great alternative to all these dangers was thought to be a "mixed" government in which all three elements (monarchy, aristocracy and democracy) were properly balanced so that each was checked by the others, and none should gain a pre-eminence. Thus all interests might be represented, and each might contribute its best advantages for the well-being of the whole.

Twice Johnson offered serious objections to the government of Connecticut as being excessively democratic. Around the year 1748 he set down several pages of "Proposals Regarding the Government of this Colony," which were transmitted to the Archbishop of Canterbury. Here he stated:

With regard to our government it is by much too popular.

> The persons in place absolutely depending on the annual election of the people for their posts, popularity and a servile compliance with all their humors and schemes however so extravagant or unreasonable, is the greatest virtue. Whoever honestly and steadily adheres to his principles and schemes, if they happen not to hit the taste of the populace is sure to be excluded from all posts ... liberty here is licentiousness ....[1]

Johnson suggested that the common law ought to be established in Connecticut, that the governor should have "a negative," and that the council be "not so absolutely dependent upon the people."[2] Ten years later, the worst thing he could say about the government of Connecticut was that it was still "little more than a democracy."[3] And when, almost at the end of Johnson's life, American politicians were making more and more use of the mob, Johnson's reaction was immediate and sharp. In 1767, for example, he denounced "those factious people that falsely call themselves Sons of Liberty."[4] He was not, therefore, sympathetic with much of the American Revolution which became even more menacing after Johnson died.

But it must not be thought that Johnson was a mere reactionary bigot. Like many colonial Anglicans, his political views were in part the result of a profound tension in his thinking – and his emotions. He loved his home, his family, and his colony. Writing to Archbishop Secker in 1760, he made the flat statement that Connecticut was "the best of all His Majesty's provinces in America." The disadvantages under which it labored, however, were "owing to its constitution being a little more than a mere democracy and the prevalency of rigid enthusiastical conceited notions and practices in religion and republican mobbish principles and practices in policy ... Everything is managed by profound hypocrisy and dissimulation."[5] Johnson's trip to England, and his generous reception there, had given him a broader vision and second loyalty – to Britain, "that dear island, and its grand metropolis...."[6] His loyalty to England found its focus in the person of the king. He objected to his dissenting neighbors because they were "generally people of antimonarchical as well as antiepiscopal principles ...."[7] It was difficult for the most devoted monarchist to find much to admire in George II, but when he was succeeded by George III, religious and respectable, Johnson's letters of the period manifest an outburst of genuine loyalty. It is hardly too much to say that Johnson was an imperialist and royalist *par excellence*. In some respects he was ahead of his time. In others, Johnson was a man who fell out of step with colonial thinking which was veering away from monarchy and empire.

As early as 1737 we find him saying that "the most effectual method to secure our dependence on the Crown of Great Britain would be to render our constitution here, both in church and state, as near as possible conformable to that of our mother-country ...." And in the same letter he suggested the appointment of a "Viceroy" – in other words, a governor-general to "represent his most sacred Majesty in the affairs of civil government."[8]

In 1760, Johnson proposed that *The London Magazine* publish a paper in which he set forth most fully his views on colonial government. These were stated in fourteen propositions, which may, however, be summed up in a lesser number. First of all, he felt that the existing diversity of colonial governments was wrong. The proprietary governments he viewed as out-moded, and advised that they should be abolished. In this, he was in line with the whole trend of the times. As we have seen, he had no use for the substantially republican charters of Rhode Island and Connecticut; they should likewise cease to be. The best type of colonial government seemed to him to be that of Massachusetts; therefore this should be the model for all the rest. Vividly aware of the inefficiency that the Great War for the Empire of 1754-1763 had so clearly demonstrated, the impossibility of making the various colonies cooperate for a common aim, he returned to his earlier idea of a viceroy, appointed by the king, to act as an organ of unity. This official had best be located in New York. And he should be assisted by an inter-colonial assembly, consisting of two members from each province (one chosen by each provincial council and one from each assembly) to meet once a year "to attend on the Lord Lt. and under his presidency, to represent and consult whatever may contribute to the union, stability, and good of the whole ...." Here it is not hard to see the influence of Franklin, whose Plan of Union had been presented to an intercolonial gathering in 1754, but had failed of adoption. Johnson's last suggestion was the very practical one that there should be a uniform colonial currency, established under the authority of Parliament.

Of course, religion had its place in this scheme of things. Johnson was quite aware of an underground swell toward complete colonial independence, and was completely opposed to it. He therefore concluded that one preventative of this was better Christianity, as there was "the strongest connection between fearing God and honoring the king." Frankly accepting the religious pluralism of the colonies, he included a strong plea for genuine toleration and "a spirit of harmony, mutual indulgence and forbearance ... avoiding everything unkind and invidious." Of course, the Church of England, "an essential part of the British constitution," should have American bishops, but they should have no "superiority, or authority over other denominations ...."[9]

The last decade of Johnson's life was one of growing tension between colonies and mother country. It is interesting, in view of his general principles, to see how he reacted to the events of the day. Like practically all Americans of whatever party, he viewed the Stamp Act as a grave error. When it was repealed, he wrote Archbishop Secker that all America was "overflowing with joy for the repeal of the Stamp Act ...."[10] When this repeal was followed by the Declaratory Act, he foresaw further trouble.

On February 9, 1769, Parliament passed several resolves. They asserted that: acts of the Massachusetts legislature, denying the power of Parliament to pass certain measures, were illegal; the attempt of the Massachusetts legislature to get other colonies to join its stance was subversive of the constitution of Great Britain; Boston was condemned for acts of violence against the officers of customs revenue; a military force was therefore to be placed in Boston to enforce the laws; elections held in Massachusetts in September 1768 were in effect an assertion of independence (by reason of their tenor). In March, writing to William Samuel, who was still in England, Johnson expressed a fear of the outbreak of actual war. His apprehensions were clearly stated:

> I thank you for sending the Resolves, etc. What dreadful things they are! They are like so many thunder-bolts upon poor Boston, and it is well if they do not actually turn into great guns and bombs before they have done, for these Oliverians begin to think themselves Corsicans, and I suspect will resist unto blood. But if it should come to this, I doubt Old England and New will fall together, and both become a prey to the House of Bourbon.[11]

How shrewdly the old man anticipated in part the future course of American history. It was perhaps well for his happiness that he died before the tension ended in civil war.

2. *Noetica* and *Raphael*: His Educational Views

The publication of Johnson's *Elementa Philosophica* in 1752 included a section called *Noetica*, a discussion of the first principles of knowledge and the progress of the human mind towards its highest perfection.[12] Here was an appropriate beginning for Johnson's presidency of King's College, but *Noetica* was obviously the result of his long pedagogical interests and activities. Benjamin Franklin noted in 1754 that the demand for *Noetica* "in this part of the world has not yet been equal to the merit of the work," but that it was being reprinted in England "where good judges being more plenty than with us, it will, I doubt not, acquire a reputation that may not only make it extensively useful there, but bring it more into notice in its native America."[13] The work evidently did not enjoy the popularity or acclaim it may have deserved, but it remains an illustration of Johnson's educational views and of the advanced stage of his thought and practice in comparison with contemporary ideas and practices.[14]

Johnson wished to help students "direct and methodize their thoughts" as they began their work of learning and teaching. And he clearly announced and adhered to his intention to follow "that excellent philosopher" Bishop Berkeley.[15] A brief portion of the work will suffice to indicate how he conceived the mind progressed in knowledge and will suggest how he worked as a teacher. The "first notices" of the mind, he wrote,

> are doubtless those of sense, but directly joined with a consciousness of its perceptions ... and every fresh notice of sense and consciousness, goes on to excite its admiration, and engage its attention ... [thus] by degrees, having a great number of feelings, tastes, odors, sounds, and visible objects, frequently repeating their several impressions, its conscious memory still enlarging, it begins, by means of the intellectual light ... gradually to collect and recollect the several relations and connections it observes to obtain among its various ideas ... all visible objects or ideas are only in the mind; so ... [in] the case of infants, [who] can have at first no notion of distance, nor of any connection between things visible and tangible ... both distance and that connection must be learned by long trial and experience ... And, at the same time that it hath these things to learn ... it is also learning the names of things, and the connection and use of words, which is another language. And, as if all these were not task enough, it hath all this while, to be learning how to use its limbs ... tongue ... and its whole body in all its exertions, and particularly ... the poise of its center of gravity, and the use of its feet in walking.

> All these things require a great deal of earnest application and the exercise of much thought and experience. So that it seems evident that those little creatures [children], from the beginning, do consider, reflect and think a prodigious deal more than we are commonly apt to imagine ... the reason why there appear so many little, low, weak and childish things in them, which we are apt to despise and think them beneath our notice, is not for want of good

sense and capacity, but merely for want of experience and opportunity for intellectual improvements. Hence also it appears, that we ought to think little children to be persons of much more importance than we usually apprehend them to be; and how indulgent we should be to their inquisitive curiosity as being strangers; with how much candor, patience and care, we ought to bear with them and instruct them; with how much decency, honor and integrity, we ought to treat them; and how careful it concerns us to be, not to say or do any thing to them, or before them, that savors of falsehood or deceit, or that is any kind … indecent or vicious.[16]

As one scholar has put it, "This respect for childhood is one of the strongest notes in Johnson's educational doctrine. It seems very remarkable to find such a principle so clearly expressed at a time when Jonathan Edwards could publicly assert that children were 'like little vipers.' The prominence Johnson gave to this humanitarian principle did not grow out of the Puritan attitude toward life, but was, we believe, an original contribution from the man himself."[17] Nor is it too much to say that it stemmed from the Stratford parson's basic theology.

Johnson further explained that while children gained a general knowledge of the world about them, they developed a "very quick sense of justice and injury …."[18] Education must encourage and assist them to cultivate "that inward, intuitive, intellectual light, which … perpetually shines … from the Deity."[19] Children must be taught to curb their appetites and passions, to value mutual good will, and behave with kindness and honesty in order to promote the common weal. Meantime, they should be taught grammar and language (at six or seven years of age), to understand "the most interesting and engaging things in history, poetry, and morality, and especially the most instructive and useful things in the Holy Scriptures." Moreover, "care should be taken; as far as can consist with good government, to contrive to put them and keep them always in a good humor, which will make every thing take the better effect."[20] Here Johnson was also ahead of his age, for not many teachers of his century thought in terms of making study a pleasure.[21]

From these beginnings Johnson proceeded to layout a general course of education: music and numbers turned as much as possible to facts and practical uses; at ten or twelve children should be taught a general notion of geography, history, and of nature on earth and in the heavens. From an earlier introduction to reading and writing they should be instructed in the connection of their own and other languages: English, Latin and French, and then Greek and Hebrew. By age sixteen or eighteen they should have also studied rhetoric, poetry, and mythology, as well as history. And then "it will be time for them to have their minds closely turned inward upon themselves, to take an exact view of their intellectual powers, and the objects of them, by the studies of metaphysics and logics," higher mathematics, the fine arts, natural science, moral philosophy, ethics, theology, economics and politics. The end of all these arduous efforts was not to learn "precise philosophical notions and verities, as matters of mere speculation," but to "promote in us pure and holy affections and all manner of virtuous dispositions and practices … that we may learn to love and delight in Him, who is all in all, our chief and sovereign good … our highest perfection and happiness, both intellectual and moral …" By such devotion toward and imitation of God, men must practice the "holy discipline of christianity" until "qualified to quit this our present station, and enter upon that eternal life … our highest perfection and everlasting happiness in the future state of our existence."[22]

Some time after his return to Stratford after his presidency of King's College Johnson sat down to write a piece which he called *Raphael or The Genius of the English America: A Rhapsody*. This was never published until the Schneiders found it among the Johnson papers, and printed it in full in their four volume edition of Johnson's works.[23] It is cast as an account addressed to a friend, Crito, of a dialogue between Aristocles-Johnson and the archangel Raphael, whom he made the guardian angel of the American colonies. It begins with a religiophilosophical introduction, in which one finds many of Johnson's leading ideas – his profound belief in the goodness of God, his conviction that God desires human happiness, and that such happiness is obtained when man, a free and rational being, conforms himself to the will of God. Its particular interest lies in the fact that it contains the writer's mature reflections on education. Johnson had been a teacher all his adult life. His teaching experience had ranged from the bringing up of his own children at pre-school age, through all the gradations from primary school to graduate studies in theology. And he had always been something of an educational reformer since the distant days when he introduced his students at Yale to the Copernican astronomy, and fed them with Newton and Locke.

He held the basic American notion that education is vital. In his opinion "that which should naturally employ every man's first and tenderest concern, and one of the chiefest things that should demand the care of those that would study the public good of mankind" was "the education of youth."[24]

Johnson began his consideration of education with the preschool child, under the tutelage of parents. He firmly believed in discipline, but the discipline must be reasonable. His comment here is shrewd and practical:

> The first and principal care in the education of a child should be to establish your authority over him by inflexibly insisting on reverence and obedience and therefore it is best never to require anything of him but when you intend to be peremptorily obeyed, for if you are lax and negligent in some things and at some times, he will soon expect you should be so on other occasions ... You should therefore take care to command nothing rashly and unadvisedly, nothing but what is reasonable, fit, and just, but when you have declared your will see that it be ever immediately and punctually obeyed ....[25]

Johnson obviously had a profound respect for the minds of children: "They come into the world ... with an eager curiosity to know things; their curiosity is to be indulged, and their little questions should be carefully and distinctly answered," he wrote.[26]

Basic to all education, in his opinion, was religious education. He believed in the catechetical method, but had little use for the catechisms then current, and offered in their place samples of a catechism framed in "the plainest and most familiar method and in a language adapted to their little capacities ...." And he proceeded to give illustrations of the Nicene theology in simple terms. One of these was that God "is kind and good, righteous true and faithful, and therefore ... his creatures and children ... must love and serve Him, and learn to be like Him, and be kind and just, true and faithful one to another and never hate and abuse one another, nor quarrel, nor lie, nor steal, etc."[27]

As a good New Englander, Johnson firmly believed in education as a function of the secular state, at least up to the college level. With an eye to the Connecticut General Assembly, with its perpetual urge for economy, he exclaimed:

> For God's sake therefore let the people of this country re-solve to be more generous and public spirited and freely open their hearts and purses for the creditable and honor-able support of their public officers both of religion and learning, which are so highly necessary for the public weal. And let him never be deemed a friend to his country, much less a patriot, who under the plausible pretense of being frugal ... is stingy and narrow spirited with respect to the public good ...."[28]

As a practical teacher he had long since learned that students vary greatly in their capacities. He therefore urged that in place of making the curriculum a Procrustean bed, whereby the student was fitted to the curriculum, the attempt be made to fit the curriculum to the student. Under the system as it existed, he was convinced that too fre-quently it happened that "one who might have made a very handsome figure in the capacity of a husbandman, a merchant or a mechanic, has made but a very poor scholar, and a contemptible fig-ure in the quality of a divine, a lawyer, or a physician."[29] He was ob-viously feeling toward the notion of a vocational education.

Finally, he dealt with college education. If this was to be effective, first of all admission requirements must be tightened. He had always deplored that students entered college too young. Furthermore, he insisted that college education should not be confined to mere read-ing and retaining. He held that "it is necessary in order to ripen and improve the minds of young men, that the manner of their instruc-tion be so contrived as to make them exert their own geniuses as well as read the works of others." They must learn to summarize accurately what they have read; they must make exercises and compositions of their own, which should be both elaborate and original.[30] Johnson was not only the "first American to formulate a system of ethics; he was one of the first to give to education that thought and attention which his countrymen have continued to devote to it" – sometimes, perhaps, with less precision and good sense than did the Connecticut parson. His educational principles may be neatly summarized in a sentence: "proceed from the general to the particular; from the concrete to the abstract; respect the personality of the child; make his work pleasant for him if possible, and give primary emphasis to the development of the moral side of his character."[31]

3. The Philosopher

Ezra Stiles once remarked of Johnson that he took his ideas from the last person he talked to. In general this was both unkind and untrue, but Stiles was a shrewd observer and knew Johnson rather well, and he did put his finger on one of Johnson's traits. His was not so much one of those powerful minds that blazes new trails in the world of thought as he was a reader, an explorer, and a follower. But Johnson was not merely an echo; he could develop what he learned. We have seen him a devotee of Bacon, of Locke, of Newton, and finally of Berkeley. His admiration for Berkeley and Berkeley's philosophical system lasted as long as he lived, and it is generally agreed that he became the foremost exponent of the idealism of the Irish bishop outside of Great Britain.

"Accepting the essential soundness of Berkeley's immaterialism, Johnson ... proceeded to raise objections to certain details...." And he was not only "a thinker of some originality who went to other men for the main building blocks of his philosophical structure," for he was a traditional systematist who treated logic, epistemology, metaphysics, psychology and ethics in a "form conventional to" the type of literature represented by his *Elementa Philosophica*. Although Johnson has been ranked with Jonathan Edwards, Cadwallader Colden and John Witherspoon as one of the "four colonial philosophers who deserve the title in its full meaning," he has largely been left on the shelf. And Edwards has received far more attention than is warranted, when the volume of scholarly work on him is compared with the scholars' neglect of Johnson. Also, Johnson was important no less than Edwards in fields other than philosophy, for like Edwards and other philosophers, he took a leading part "in the affairs of church or state or both."[32] But in order to appreciate Johnson the philosopher, one must begin with George Berkeley.

Berkeley's theory of idealism attracted Johnson because it squared with his interest in religion. Risking the dangers of oversimplification and brevity, we may say that Berkeley was a Christian Neoplatonist; he believed the real world consisted of God's thoughts. Material objects are but wavering images of truth which transcends them. Nothing exists independently of mind, and the word "matter" is used to designate what is supposed to be an "independent existent." To Berkeley, atheism not only relied on an allegation that material substance exists, but also appealed to those who found it difficult to understand how material substance could be created out of nothing but God's fiat. Therefore, atheists must be combatted by depriving them of the bases of their impiety. But the problem lay in how to get rid of matter without denying the validity of scientific enterprise.

Like Locke, Berkeley thought the objects of human knowledge are ideas imprinted on the senses, or ideas perceived by attending to the passions and operations of the mind, or ideas formed by help of memory and imagination. The danger of rationalism was that in using it, men departed from sense and instinct and tended to think in words instead of about the things the words signify. In order to meet this danger, Berkeley argued that matter is an abstract idea. If one sought the "original" of the idea of matter, all he could find was particular men, trees, chairs. Upon analysis, anyone of these did not reveal matter, but only certain qualities; so that "material substance" or "matter" were abstract ideas.

Berkeley realized that "on the premises of the historical plain method you can never show that any idea implies the existence of its object. Like a good empiricist, he therefore tried to argue that observed facts can only be explained on the hypothesis of a divine cause."[33] He proceeded to argue toward man's knowledge of God from a distinction between man's notions and ideas. According to Berkeley, the self exists, and I know that it exists. But since I cannot have an *idea* of the self (we cannot know spiritual activity, but only ideas which are inert and passive), it must be that I have a *notion* of existence as an indivisible, incorporeal and immortal soul. This is an intuitive certainty, and from it I know that God exists, and I can come to understand His nature by reflecting on my own activities as a spirit. Samuel Johnson sharpened the distinction, and therefore clarified, Berkeley's terms. "Idea", he explained, should be confined to immediate objects of sense and imagination, and "notion" (or conception) signified the objects of consciousness and pure intellect.[34]

The foregoing is perhaps adequate to demonstrate the Berkeleyian stance against materialism. It hardly suggests the scope or detail of his philosophy, which Johnson basically accepted and then improved upon. With emphasis upon the physical world as consisting of God's thoughts, Berkeley's idealism attracted Johnson as a strong defence against the scepticism of his age. A scholar in theology and philosophy, and interested in science and literature, Johnson was also basically a religious man who sought the unity of all knowledge. A careful and independent thinker, he "came to new questions with an openness of mind and a candor that was remarkable at a time when prejudice was unusually predominant."[35]

In 1730, shortly after his visit to Berkeley in Rhode Island, Johnson began to work out his exposition of Berkeley's idealism – a process at which he was to labor at intervals for years. He drew up a little *Outline of Philosophy*, sketching in the divisions of the subject as he then saw them. He divided the field into three parts, Rational Philosophy, Natural Philosophy, and Moral Philosophy.[36] By these divisions he meant briefly communication, science, and conduct, with conduct as the climax of the whole. Thus his approach was a pragmatic one; the value of philosophy was not that of a system of pure thinking; it must lead to right conduct.

In the following year, 1731, he expanded this into a booklet of thirty-six pages, which was published in London under the title *An Introduction to the Study of Philosophy*. This was basically a textbook for the use of college students, built on the tripartite division sketched above. These three fields he again subdivided, and made a portentous list of authors who might be consulted under each sub-heading. In 1744 this was again published in London in a revised form. Its full title indicates clearly what Johnson was trying to accomplish in this work. It is called *An Introduction to the Study of Philosophy Exhibiting a General View of all the Arts and Sciences, For the Use of Pupils*.[37] In 1746 appeared, printed in Boston, a seventy page booklet entitled *A New System of Morality*. This is in large part an expansion of the third part of the *Introduction*.

In 1752, the work which had gone through so many variations took its final shape. Printed in Philadelphia by Benjamin Franklin, it was now entitled *Elementa Philosophica*. It was divided into two parts, *Noetica*, or things relating to the mind or understanding, and *Ethica*, or things relating to the moral behavior. It was by now a sizable volume. By it Johnson's reputation as a philosopher stands or falls.

It is not our purpose here to attempt a critique of the work. That is a task better suited for the historian of American philosophy.[38] But certain general observations on the book are relevant. It indicates Johnson's consistent desire to organize all knowledge into a coherent system. It was the first textbook of philosophy published in America, and it was actually used as a textbook for a number of years in the college at Philadelphia, and also in King's College. It established Johnson's position as the foremost exponent in America of the philosophy of Bishop Berkeley. Indeed, to James Truslow Adams, who wrote the sketch of Johnson in the *Dictionary of American Biography*, this is Johnson's chief title to fame. But it must be noted that Johnson's concern with philosophy was in a sense a severely practical one. He was not in love with philosophical insights for their own sake. A child of the Enlightenment, he viewed with apprehension the tendency of the thinkers of that movement to wander off into Deism, and he welcomed Berkeleyan idealism as a buttress for classical Christian belief. And it is significant that *Noetica* leads to *Ethica*; philosophy must teach morals, or it is useless.

It is also worth noting that two of the historians of American philosophy are in agreement that in one respect Johnson went beyond his teacher, Berkeley. In his doctrine of the self-activity of the mind, and the human mind as a creative cause, he anticipated the thought of Immanuel Kant.[39] Moreover, he "added to Descartes' first principle; not *I perceive*, but *I perceive and act*, therefore I am; and this brings us to another doctrine in which Johnson did much original thinking" – a doctrine we have already considered in his educational theory.

This is the idea of self-activity, "a central principle in modern educational theories" which owes much of its "importance to the German philosophy and especially to Hegel ...."[40]

4. The Theologian

It is a great pity that Johnson, with his philosophical training and his gift for organizing knowledge into a coherent whole, never attempted to do for theology what he tried to do for philosophy – write a complete synthesis. He had a theology, but it must be gathered bit by bit from sermons and controversial tracts. Most of the theological writing of the period took the form of such tracts, and to the modern reader they seem to be largely confined to skirmishes on the periphery of theology – to deal with episcopal versus presbyterian ordination, sitting or kneeling to receive Holy Communion, sponsors in baptism. We have already discussed Johnson's *Three Letters to his Dissenting Parishioners*, which are almost entirely concerned with such matters.

But because Johnson did have a philosophical mind, he early perceived that the real issue between Anglican and Puritan was something far more fundamental than these things. The essential core of any theology, any religion, is its doctrine of God; or to put it more bluntly, the kind of God that religion worships. On July 4, 1731, Johnson preached a sermon before a clergy meeting at Newport, Rhode Island. George Berkeley was among those present. Johnson preached from Job XXVIII:28 On "True Philosophy, or The Wisdom of Religion and Virtue." The essence of the sermon is as follows:

> In the Mosaic dispensation, God found it necessary in order to awaken the minds of that stupid nation [Israel] to discover himself chiefly under the character of a terrible being, that they might learn to fear his great and fearful name ... But in the Christian dispensation, it was his design to discover [reveal] himself chiefly under the character of a most amiable and benevolent being, that those who under the former dispensation, had feared him in a manner that was only slavish and mercenary, might now no longer fear him as servants, but as children (having their

fear tempered with love) and their obedience accordingly not servile but filial, not slavish but ingenuous, not forced but voluntary.[41]

This brief passage is packed full of meat. In the first place, to Johnson, unlike many of his contemporaries of the Enlightenment, man's knowledge of God is not a product of human thought, but a revealed knowledge. This Johnson insisted on time after time. In the second place, he has gone to the heart of the real difference between Anglican and Calvinist. They worshiped different gods, and he here pointed out the difference. Thirdly, he carefully distinguished between the conception of God in Old and New Testaments, and in some sense anticipated the modern approach to the Bible as the history of an evolution of the doctrine of God. Also by implication he pointed out that Puritans laid far too much emphasis on the Old Testament, sometimes seeming to forget that there was a New Testament.

Johnson also had a doctrine of man, and it proceeded logically from his doctrine of a loving God. The fullest expression of this is to be found in the pamphlet, published in Boston in 1745, entitled *A Letter From Aristocles to Authades. Concerning the Sovereignty And the Promises of God.*[42] This is an all out attack on the cardinal Calvinistic doctrine of predestination, and a defense of the Catholic doctrine of man's free will. As we have seen, in the first of his *Three Letters* Johnson had dealt with this crucial matter, but in a brief and perfunctory manner. Now he gave it a complete expression. His problem was to preserve two things, the sovereignty of God, and the freedom and accountability of man. He did it in an ingenious fashion.

God is ... confessedly sovereign and arbitrary in the various distribution of his talents and favors to his creatures, and the several conditions in which he places them, as proper means and occasions of probation. It is from his mere sovereign good pleasure that he allots to one creature the nature and condition of a man, to another that of an angel; to one man a healthy, to another a sickly constitution; to one poverty, to another riches; to one small abilities and mean advantages, to another large powers and great opportunities for learning and improvement; to one man or number or men, one talent, *viz.*, the light of nature; to another two talents, *viz.*, Judaism; to another five, *viz.*, Christianity ... But this is but a temporary and probationary state; whereas in the state of retribution after this life, the condition of men will be decided for all eternity ... according to what use and improvement they shall have made of what they had received....[43]

The reader will note that Johnson was a realist; he recognized that men are not born equal. And whereas, in the reaction against predestination that was characteristic of the period, a number of liberal thinkers moved over into what would eventually be tagged Universalism, Johnson, ever a moralist, maintained that God was a God of justice and judgment, as well as of love and mercy.

There are other interesting insights in the pamphlet. Well aware that there are New Testament texts, which seem to express predestination, he took the modern attitude that argument from isolated proof-texts is not fair argument; that it is the total sense of the Scriptures that we must follow. The whole teaching of the *Letter From Aristocles to Authades* is well summed up in this passage:

I cannot think of a greater dishonor that can be done to Almighty God, than to represent him as arbitrary, considered as a governor and a judge, when he has taken abundant care throughout the whole Scripture, from the beginning of Genesis to the end of the Revelation, to represent himself, not as arbitrary, but as a moral governor of the world; proceeding upon stipulations with his reasonable creatures; treating them, not as machines or stocks and stones, but as rational and moral agents ... and rewarding or punishing them according as they shall be found to have conducted themselves.[44]

It is interesting to see how, in the following passage from one of his sermons, Johnson used his idealistic philosophy to reinforce scriptural teachings about free will:

Some understanding these and the like expressions of Holy Scriptures too literally, have gathered from them, that in having this change wrought in us we are entirely passive ... It would be contrary to the nature of things, because we are intuitively certain that we are free active creatures ... It would be also contrary to many plain texts of Holy Scripture, which always supposes, and frequently requires a vigorous activity on our parts in turning from sin to God.[45]

Holding such beliefs of the essential nature of God and of man, Johnson early in his career had asked himself, "Why did God create Man?" To this question, his answer was, "The end of our being is our true and endless happiness." This sentence comes from a sermon on the reasonableness, usefulness and duty of prayer, printed in 1760.[46] But we find the same idea in a sermon he preached in 1715. And through all the sermons which came between the two, the same idea continued to pop up. The very word "happiness" recurs again and again. That God made man to be happy, that God desires human happiness was fundamental in Johnson's personal religion. This does not mean that Johnson was a religious Polyanna. He had seen too much of life, he was too intelligent, to be unaware of human sinfulness. He was, as his diary shows, quite aware of his own imperfections. But because of his conviction of the sovereignty of a God who is primarily a loving God, he managed to escape from that morbid pre-occupation with sin that meets us in so much of Puritan thinking. This was also the result of his happy temperament.

We have already seen how, in the first sermon he ever preached, young Samuel had arrived, from his reading in the Church Fathers, at a balanced and Catholic Christology – the assertion that Jesus of Nazareth was true God and true man. In this, as in so many other respects, Johnson here parted company with many of those who shared with him in the ideas of the Enlightenment. For others, the Enlightenment led from Calvinism to Unitarianism. But Johnson held fast his Trinitarian faith. In 1765, probably as a practical educator impatient with the imperfections of the Prayer Book catechism, he published a catechism of his own, in which we find this question and answer: "Q. 17. Who is Jesus Christ? A. The only begotten Son of

God, very God and very man, and sent by him to be the savior of the world."[47] From this position he never varied.

We have said that Johnson was a sacramentalist. Naturally, being a man of his time, he recognized two sacraments only, as generally necessary for salvation, baptism and the Lord's Supper. In the same catechism which we have quoted, he emphasized the necessity of frequent communion, but never defined the word "frequent." He did, as far as Connecticut was concerned, increase that frequency to once a month and at the greater feasts. His Eucharistic doctrine seems weak to the modern High Churchman. He thus defined the meaning of the Eucharist in his short catechism: "It is a public, solemn, and religious eating bread, and drinking wine, in remembrance of the sacrifice of the death of Christ, Wherein the bread represents his body, and the wine his blood." His explanation of the "ordinance" was that it implied "The receiving of Christ and all the spiritual blessings he purchased by his death, namely, pardon, grace and eternal life."[48] But far more clear cut than this is a statement found in one of his sermons, never published.

> By dwelling in the tabernacle of his body he hath united himself to us, and dwelleth in all mankind, especially in all the faithful who are made members of his body by baptism and are partakers of his blessed Body and Blood in the Holy Eucharist. As he offered himself a sacrifice and intercedes for us in virtue of it, so he hath ordered a constant commemoration of it to be offered by his ministers and received by his people, in the sacramental bread and wine as symbols of his body and blood, so that the transaction may be represented on earth, while it is performed in heaven.[49]

Here, then, is a profession that the sacrament was not merely a memorial but a re-presentation of and participation in the original Eucharistic sacrifice.

The death of his son William in England caused Johnson to think seriously about the state of the departed. In a letter to William Samuel he justified the practice of offered prayers for the dead, at the same time carefully distinguishing this practice from Roman doctrine. "This custom of this commemorating our departed friends obtained in the best and earliest times of Christianity, and by degrees degenerated to praying for them out of purgatory."[50] But in another letter to William Samuel on the same subject, he indulged in a bit of speculation: "I am inclined to imagine that our progress will be thus gradual, and not by such a sudden change to our highest state of perfection as some apprehend."[51] Johnson was plainly feeling his way toward some doctrine of an intermediate state between heaven and hell, as implied by the Prayer Book of 1928.

Johnson's political views were those of his time and the events of the decade following his death made them obsolete. Many of his educational views remain valid. His philosophy is interesting historically, but very few students of philosophy today would endorse Berkeleyan idealism as Johnson expounded it.But his theology, rooted in the Scriptures and the Church Fathers, is still held by millions of Christians. Here he transcended his age and spoke for all time.

Chapter IX

CLERICAL MAN OF BUSINESS

1. The Commissary System

One of the handicaps under which Samuel Johnson and the Anglican Church in colonial America had to function was the lack of a resident bishop. The commissary system was an attempt to alleviate this disadvantage. As early as 1633 William Laud, then in his last year as Bishop of London, began to exercise a sort of jurisdiction over parishes or missions of the Church of England outside the British Isles. Translated to the Archbishopric of Canterbury in that year, Laud planned an American episcopate, but the outbreak of the civil war in England put a stop to his efforts in that direction. In 1673, the Committee of Trade and Plantations of the King's Privy Council regularized this jurisdiction by ordering that any clergy sent out to function in the colonies must be licensed by the Bishop of London. Henry Compton, then bishop, was a strong man, who proceeded to try to make his control over the colonial churches amount to something.

Shortly after the Glorious Revolution of 1688, Compton began to appoint officials called commissaries to act in his name in the colonies.[1] They were to exercise discipline over the colonial clergy, and to take measures for the general welfare of the Church. The effectiveness of these commissaries depended largely on their own character and ability. Two of them stand out – James Blair of Virginia, and Alexander Garden of South Carolina – who really functioned as leaders in their respective colonies. Thomas Bray's short tenure of office in Maryland resulted, as we have seen, in the formation of the S. P. G. But most of the commissaries were superiors in name only, resented by the clergy whom they were supposed to control, and by the colonial governors who were always jealous of their prerogatives. Virginia, where the church was established, had a continuous succession of commissaries until the outbreak of the War of Independence. But New England had but one throughout its colonial history. This was the Reverend Roger Price, who served from 1730 to 1748, combining the office with the rectorate of King's Chapel, Boston. English born and trained, he never seemed to be able to fit himself comfortably into the new world, quarreled frequently with the vestry of the chapel, and seems to have made little impact on the Church either in Massachusetts or Connecticut. When, in 1748, Bishop Gibson died, Price's commission expired with the bishop who gave it, and no successor was ever appointed. Thus, there was in New England Anglicanism in the mid-eighteenth century what can best be described as a power vacuum.

2. Johnson Begins to Advise

The pressure of events practically pushed Johnson into this vacuum. As we have noted, all the missionaries of the Venerable Society were required to make half-yearly reports of their cures. From the very beginning of his Stratford ministry, Johnson's reports became much more than an accounting for his stewardship in his parish. He had met Bishop Gibson in London just as that prelate was taking over the see, and Gibson quickly showed that he valued Johnson's advice – and not merely on affairs in Connecticut. Thus, on October 10, 1724, at Boston he wrote the bishop in defense of his friend Timothy Cutler. Cutler had been accused of heresy, of even the horrible sin of Papistry, by the Reverend Henry Harris – an English born colleague. Johnson, well informed, told the bishop that Harris's real trouble was that he had hoped to be made rector of the new parish of Christ Church, and because Cutler got the job, Harris was taking this method of revenge.[2] Johnson improved the occasion by pointing out that such things happened because of the lack of proper ecclesiastical authority on the spot.

Fortunately, most of Johnson's advice to the Society and the bishops was concerned with more important matters than this tea-pot tempest. As we have seen in a previous chapter, as soon as Johnson had settled in Stratford he began to use this as a center of missionary work to the surrounding communities. But he soon began to look farther, and to recommend the opening of such work in places beyond his own immediate reach. By August 1725 his preaching at New London had produced results, and he could report that he had procured land and raised funds to start a building there.[3]

This was no mere presumption on Johnson's part. In May and June of 1727 he received two letters from the Society, asking for full information about certain aspects of the Society's opportunities. In reply, he wrote on September 20, 1727, a long letter in which he gave a brief history of the Church in Stratford. He mentioned what was going on at Fairfield. He again stressed the case of New London, making the significant comment that the Churchmen there "have desired me to recommend their case to the honourable Society, that they may be supplied as soon as may be...."[4] Already the Churchmen of Connecticut were looking up to Johnson as their best means of making contact with the S. P. G.

Directly across the Sound from Stratford lay Long Island, the eastern part of which had been settled largely from Connecticut; indeed it had almost come to consider itself a part of that colony. In September 1727, Johnson had this to observe to the S. P. G. secretary: "directly over against us, southward on Long Island, lies Brook Haven, about twenty miles over the water, where I have often preached ... to a considerable congregation, who are building a handsome Church, and have also desired me to intercede for their speedy supply."[5] All through the following decades, this process continued. Laity repeatedly asked for the help of clergy.[6] In almost every one of his reports, Johnson made suggestions of importance. As we have noted in a previous chapter, he was well aware of the strategic importance of New Haven, and in April 1728 he brought it to the attention of the Society. In the same letter he advised that a mission be established at Norwalk.[7] In June 1731, he stated that he had "laboured much to promote the Church at Westerly Narragansett" in Rhode Island.[8] His interests were never confined merely to Connecticut. Among other places which he brought to the attention of the Society in succeeding years were Guilford, Middletown, Wethersfield, Waterbury, Ridgefield, Ripton, Simsbury and Hebron, all in Connecticut.[9]

His letter to the Society of October 1, 1746, is worth quoting entire, for it illustrates beautifully the range of Johnson's interests, and the detailed advice he gave the S. P. G. Even his heading of the letter, "Stratford, in New-England," was characteristic of Johnson's identification with the center of his life – a life, which for all its energies restricted in time and space, yet reached out with broad visions and toward distant horizons.

> Since my last, I have received the Bible and Common Prayer-Books safe, for which we are all very thankful. My son continues to read and instruct the youth at Ripton with good success, and the Church there flourishes. I continue to visit them, and administer the Sacraments to them once in two or three months, and they are going on to finish their Church. My Church also flourishes in this parish, where two new families are added, and I have baptised twenty-four, and admitted eight communicants since last March, whereof one is a negro man. I have also visited Middletown and Guilford, where the Church keeps its ground, though I cannot say it much increases for want of ministers. A love to the Church is still gaining in the College, and four more, whose names are Allen, Lloyd, Sturgeon and Chandler, have declared themselves candidates for holy orders; and there seems a very growing disposition toward the Church, in the town of New-Haven, as well as in the College, so that I hope there will, 'ere long, be a flourishing Church there. I have heretofore desired leave for Messrs. Dibble and Leaming to go for orders, and am now desired to ask the same for Messrs. Mansfield and Allen, as soon as the Society can be in a disposition to receive them. Mr. Cole, for whom I wrote long since, is, I doubt, discouraged, having heard nothing from him in a great while. I presume it probable, that leave was given

him to go home, by Mr. Dean; but as we have not heard a word of him since he left London, we have too much reason to fear he is lost.[10] If this should prove to be the case, (as Mr. Lyons is said to be removed, and Mr. Dean to have been appointed to succeed him at Derby,) the people there are very desirous that Mr. Mansfield may have leave to go for them, where they are providing a glebe; and Waterbury having also provided one, begs to have a minister for themselves, with Northbury and Litchfield, and that Mr. Cole may have leave to go for them, or one other of the candidates, if Mr. Cole be otherwise provided for. New-London is also providing a house, and Mr. Cole or Mr. Lloyd would do well for them.[11]

During his years as president of King's College, Johnson's attention was largely engrossed with the affairs of that institution, though he was ever the missionary. But on his return to Stratford in 1763, his flow of advice to the Society was resumed. In May 1763, he suggested a mission at Hartford.[12] In 1764, his roving eye began to look farther afield. In that year he opened relations by letter with Sir William Johnson, whose successful furthering of Christianity among the Mohawk Indians of upper New York interested him. In the same year he became concerned with work in the Berkshire Hills of western Massachusetts. On December 26 he wrote to the secretary of the Society:

> I have lately been applied to by some of the people of Great Barrington, a town at the frontier of the province of Massachusetts, adjoining to New York Province, within about 20 miles of Hudson River, who join with a number of people on the New York side of the line, in desiring the Society's favour. They are both pretty numerous, and are building a Church which they model by ours at Stratford....[13]

It is of particular significance that once again the initiative came from the laity, and that Johnson was their chosen agent for dealing with the Society. The result of this application was both the founding of the parish at Great Barrington, and also the start of Christ Church, Hudson, New York, now one of the strong parishes of the Diocese of Albany.

3. Clergy Placement

Johnson not only advised the Society about places where missionary work should be initiated; he was also deeply concerned with the placing of proper men to do the work. This was natural, for a large number of the men available were his own students. But his concern with the strategy of clergy placement and clerical relations with their parishioners was not confined to his own product. From the very beginning of his ministry at Stratford, he advised both the Society, the Bishops of London, and the successive Archbishops of Canterbury on matters of personnel. We have already seen his action in getting the Society to place Henry Caner in Fairfield, and its excellent results. In 1726, though expressing "the greatest submission and deference" to the S. P. G., he strongly recommended sending his associate in the trip to England, James Wetmore, from New York City to Rye, just over the Connecticut border. The upshot was Wetmore's long and successful ministry in that New York community.[14] Another side of Johnson's numerous interventions in placement is evidenced by his letter of September 30, 1743. The elder Samuel Seabury had recently left New London, and had been succeeded by the Reverend Theophilus Morris. The latter was from Dublin University, and there was considerable tension both in Massachusetts and in Connecticut between clergy of British origins and the home grown article. Johnson wrote:

> I am in much concern for the great damage I fear the Church in these parts will sustain by Mr. Seabury's removal, and Mr. Morris' succeeding him at New-London. This gentleman had the misfortune to have but little esteem among the people where he had officiated, and to be much despised by many others. I have faithfully laboured, both with him and them, to prevent this misfortune, but so the event has proved, which put the people of New-London into a terrible consternation ... so that they were unwilling to admit him into their Church till his character should be cleared up ... They were advised by the Clergy here, in the mean time, out of duty and gratitude to the Society, to admit him ... which ... they immediately did, but yet depend upon the Commissary to take cognizance

of the affair … I should not have said this much, but that I have been earnestly solicited by that people to mention something of it....[15]

Johnson suggested that another priest be sent to New London. Morris left, and New London remained without a resident missionary for several years.[16]

At times Johnson must have felt lonely as well as dismayed about the difficulty in providing enough clergy for the churches of Connecticut. In April 1747, for example, he reported to the Bishop of London that the S. P. G. had forbidden "anyone to go home for orders without leave first obtained." This, he understood, applied to clergy for new missions. But what of deaths and removals? The Society seemed to apply its order even to these cases, and Johnson felt it a very great discouragement to the Church in these parts, especially under our present circumstances. The death of the Reverend Mr. Commissary Vesey, Mr. Davenport, Mr. Richard Caner, and his removal from Norwalk before his death, and that of Mr. Lyons and Mr. Morris, and the resignation of Mr. Commissary Price, have occasioned a number of vacancies, four of which are in this colony, so that I am now alone here on the seacoast ... for more than one hundred miles; in which compass there is business enough for six or seven ministers ... nor have we yet leave for any to go home, though there are five or six valuable candidates [for ordination].[17]

Another example of Johnson's work with clergy placement and with troublesome people in general is the case of Matthew Graves. In 1751, Graves, missionary at New London whose circuit included Hebron, objected to the ordination of Jonathan Colton who served the Hebron church as lay reader. He complained to the Bishop of London that Colton had not only contested Graves's authority, but also that he was otherwise unfit for the priesthood; Graves insisted that Colton had pursued the business of merchant and apothecary instead of study for the ministry, and even accused him of extortion. But what he seemed to resent most of all was that his Hebron parishioners, thirty miles from New London, wished to escape his oversight and enjoy the benefits of a resident clergyman. Once Colton was ordained, they expected him to return to Hebron. So Samuel Johnson explained to Bishop Sherlock in October, when he reported that there had been sharp contention between Graves and his flock. True, a few of the laity may have treated Graves indecently, but Johnson judiciously observed that Graves may have carried his resentment against his people too far by attacking Colton's fitness for holy orders. Johnson was joined by his Connecticut colleagues, Ebenezer Punderson and Richard Mansfield, and Henry Caner of Boston, in recommending Colton for ordination and for stationing him at Hebron. They won the case for both, but Colton was one of the many travellers who never survived the Atlantic crossing and its hardships; he died of smallpox on his voyage home.[18]

Writing to Archbishop Secker in 1760, Johnson again demonstrated his concern for and oversight of the Church, this time in New Haven, which was not doing as well as Johnson had hoped. He informed Secker that the Church in Connecticut was generally flourishing, but there were difficulties:

> Mr. Punderson seems a very honest and laborious man; yet the Church at New-Haven appears uneasy, and rather declining under his ministry, occasioned, I believe, partly by his want of politeness, and partly by his being absent so much, having five or six places under his care. I wish he was again at Groton and some politer person in his place, and another at Guildford and Branford[19]

Writing from his King's College residence, Johnson continued a long report to the Archbishop about parochial needs in New York and in Connecticut, where he had recently visited. Connecticut had thirty churches but only fourteen ministers. Prayerbooks and tracts were needed. Middletown and Wallingford were without a priest, and they needed the help of the S. P. G. to support one. Several men were preparing for holy orders. Westchester and New Rochelle, New York, had lost their priests "who had been disabled for some considerable time before, and Rye hath lately suffered a grievous loss by the death of good Mr. Wetmore, of the small-pox, so that there is not one Clergyman in all that county or the county above."[20]

And from time to time there were other problems. In 1763, for example, when the Reverend James Lyon of Brookhaven, Long Island, was in trouble with his parishioners because of his short temper, Johnson summoned him to Stratford, and "expostulated on the decaying state of the Church there, [Brookhaven] and persuaded him to go and begin the world anew to better purpose in Virginia or Maryland, where are vacancies. This he agreed to do," Johnson reported to the S. P. G.[21] The Lyons case illustrates Johnson's influence in pushing unworthy clerics out of place. Here he was using the tactics of many modern American bishops.

4. Ritual Adjustment

At least twice Johnson found it necessary to discuss with either the S. P. G. or the Bishop of London certain details of ritual. In the baptismal office, the priest is required to exhort the godparents to see that the baptized child be brought to the bishop for confirmation. But without bishops in the colonies, this was an unlikely prospect for the colonial Church, and some clergy omitted to conform. Johnson submitted the matter to Bishop Gibson for judgment, but obviously felt that the omission was the right thing. Use of the exhortation sometimes prompted "our adversaries [to] object to it as a mere jest, to order the godfathers to bring the child to the Bishop, when there is none within a thousand leagues of us, which is a reproach that we cannot answer." In the same letter, he defended his practice of making extensive use of candidates for the ministry as lay readers – the only way in which services could be maintained in some places.[22] Evidently, Churchmen in England made no fuss about such necessary colonial deviations.

In 1750, some officious person complained to the Society that the Connecticut clergy were *"presuming to vary from the established form of Prayer...."* Johnson sprang to the defense of his brother priests, pointing out how much they had suffered for the faith, hazarding their very lives to go "a thousand leagues for Episcopal orders" and suffering disease, sickness and expense in their work. They were not to be blamed if in the New England climate, and in unheated churches, they omitted "Perhaps the first lesson, or some of the latter part of the liturgy ... on some extreme cold day...."[23] Devoted as he was to the *Book of Common Prayer*, he was plainly convinced that rubrics must sometimes yield to common sense.

5. The Taxation Controversy

When Johnson arrived in Stratford in 1723, the Standing Order was operating under the law of 1708, which formally established the Congregational system. While this law allowed that persons who differed from the Standing Order might now worship in their own way – a concession to the struggles of the Stratford laity, it required all taxable persons to pay toward the support of the minister of the Congregational Church in their town. It became one of Johnson's constant subjects, in his letters to both the Society and the English bishops, to protest against the injustices this brought about. On June 23, 1724, writing to the Bishop of London, he offered his complaint:

> My Lord, the poor people here are very much discouraged on account of the unreasonable demands of the government in exacting taxes from them to the support of the Independent teachers, for which sundry people, and those of both sexes, have been unmercifully imprisoned, contrary to the indulgence granted to them in government, by their charter, which forbid them to do anything contrary to the laws of England, and we humbly beg your Lordship's protection. I have complained of this grievance to the governor here, but can get no relief....[24]

He suggested that a letter be sent to the governor to remedy the situation. It is apparent, from a letter written by Johnson in the following year, that Bishop Gibson wrote in protest to Governor Joseph Talcott. Talcott's reply, dated July 27, 1726, stated that "there is but one Church of England minister in this colony, and the Church with him have the same protection as the rest of our Churches, and are under no constraint to contribute to the support of any other minister." The governor flatly lied, and he accused a few persons of declaring themselves Anglicans in order to escape ecclesiastical taxes for the Standing Order.[25]

But the threat of English intervention did produce a result. In answer to a petition of May 1727, from the wardens and vestrymen of the newly organized church in Fairfield, in which they noted that ten of their people had been imprisoned for failing to pay taxes, the assembly acted. A new law was passed which provided that where there was a society of the Church of England, with a resident minister, the church taxes of his membership should go to his support. Anglican parishioners were also excused from paying taxes to build Congregational meetinghouses.[26]

This seemed fair enough, but there was a fly in the ointment. For years, there were more congregations of the Church of England in Connecticut than there were clergy, and Anglican priests were forced to supply several parishes. The local authorities therefore interpreted the law to mean that it only applied to places where the clergyman was resident. Time after time, in his letters to England, Johnson had to point out that this led to the imprisonment of Anglican laymen. Mention of this topic occurs in Johnson's letters as late as 1751. Vestries and other clergy joined in the protest, but Johnson had to be the leader. It is interesting to note that in a letter of 1751, one of the last in which he dealt with this matter, Johnson raised the typical American cry, though he did not use the actual words, that the Connecticut law constituted "taxation without representation."[27]

5. Clergy Meetings

As Johnson's one-man seminary came into operation, the number of Anglican clergy in Connecticut steadily increased. If they were to function effectively as leaders of a minority group which was subject to continual persecution, they must learn an important lesson. They must drop some of the excessive individualism so characteristic of the pioneer American, and begin to act together as a corporate body. It was one of Johnson's principal achievements that as a leader of the Connecticut clergy he was able to weld them together for common action with other New England priests.

The first of these regional clergy meetings of which we have any record took place at Newport on July 21, 1725. The priests present were Timothy Cutler, James Honeyman, James McSparran, Samuel Myles, Matthias Plant, George Pigot, John Usher, and Johnson. The occasion for the meeting was the disturbance created by the appearance in New England of John Talbot and Robert Welton, the two non-juring bishops. In view of this, the conference petitioned the king, citing the dangerous situation caused by these men, and using this as a reason for the immediate appointment of a conforming bishop for the colonies. This petition only Usher refused to sign, and he abruptly left the conference.[28] The same men again petitioned for a bishop in May 1726 when they met at Boston, this time to the Bishop of London, but Usher was conspicuous by the absence of his signature.[29]

The New England clergy probably continued to hold annual conventions until 1748. From 1725 until then, fifteen of them are indicated although there are gaps in the record for 1728-30, 1732, and 1734-37.[30]

Unfortunately, there were no such things as convention journals in those days, and we can only reconstruct something of their history from the scattered documents extant. Here we find the first mention of a convention of the clergy of Connecticut only. It took place at Fairfield on March 14, 1733/4. There were but four clergy present, Johnson, James Wetmore, Henry Caner, and Isaac Browne. This group addressed a letter to Bishop Gibson, recommending Ebenezer Punderson for ordination. Punderson was one of several "dissenting teachers" who were converting to the Church. The four clerics also expressed cheer at "the good disposition toward the excellent constitution of our Church, growing up among the people wherever the honourable Society have established their missions." It is notable that Johnson signed the address first. This was probably an indication that he was the presiding officer.[31]

The second of these Connecticut clergy conventions, as far as our evidence goes, again took place in Fairfield on March 29, 1739. This was attended by the elder Seabury, Punderson, Jonathan Arnold, Wetmore, Caner, John Beach, and Johnson. The purpose of this meeting was solely to petition the S. P. G. about financial matters and grievances. Their petition cited the Connecticut Act of 1727, and stated that while this pretended to free Episcopalians from taxation for the Standing Order, it was frequently evaded or interpreted to the disadvantage of the Church. The petition went on to cite the situation in Fairfield, where certain lands belonging to the whole community had been sold, and the entire proceeds appropriated to the Congregational Church. An even worse case of unjust discrimination had arisen when seven whole townships in the northern part of the colony, the ownership of which had long been in dispute between Massachusetts and Connecticut, had been sold:

> and the money arising from the sale of these lands they have appropriated either to the schools, or to what they call the established ministry of this government, at the election of the several towns so that, according to the sense of their law, we of the Church of England are excluded from any benefit of that sale.[32]

Another complaint concerned the Connecticut Assembly's proposal "to appropriate the loan of their last commission of £50,000 of bills of credit to that purpose." In response over 630 laymen petitioned the assembly for a proportion of the funds to support their own clergy, but to no avail.[33]

The New London meeting of the clergy in May 1740, was attended by ten priests, including Commissary Price and James McSparran of Rhode Island. The purpose of this affair was to petition the Society for the establishment of a mission at Hopkinston, in which Price took a special interest.[34] The highly important gathering of August 1742 we shall deal with later.

The Stratford meeting in September 1750 was notable for one incident. This meeting dealt once more with the vexing matter of church taxes; as in 1749, the clergy asked that the Church be allowed to collect its own share of the church tax, rather than having it pass through the hands of the normal tax collector. But the Reverend Matthew Graves, the English-born priest who had followed the elder Seabury at New London, refused to concur in 1749, and took the rather extreme step of writing some of the members of the colonial assembly, urging them not to grant the request. Graves also appeared before the assembly to protest his fellow priests' "spurious address" and refused even to attend their conference in 1750. He evidently felt the clergy's request would create unnecessary local difficulties, whereas Johnson and the others were not only annoyed at the system of collecting taxes but also at the law which forbade "us a vote in raising them, with which many of our people were very uneasy."[35] Graves was the one priest in Connecticut who persistently refused to follow Johnson's leadership.

During Johnson's absence from Connecticut, while he was President of King's College, we know of but one convention of the Connecticut clergy, that held in 1760 at New Haven. The preacher was the Reverend John Beach, one of the best of Johnson's pupils. The Reverend Edward Winslow, who informed the S. P. G. of this meeting, wrote that the sermon was published as a testimony against erroneous teachings and that a copy of it would be forwarded by Dr. Johnson – an indication that Johnson was keeping in close touch with what was going on in the Connecticut Church.[36]

The example of clergy meetings thus set by the New England clergy was taken up elsewhere. In November 1758, while Johnson was living in New York, the clergy of New York and New Jersey met, and determined henceforth to hold annual clergy conventions.[37] At the meeting of May 21, 1766, attended by "the principal rectors and missionaries of New York, New Jersey, and Connecticut," organization was carried a step further, when a standing committee was set up. Dr. Johnson was elected president, and Samuel Seabury, Jr., secretary.[38]

The importance of all these clergy meetings was not their actual accomplishment, which was small, but their promise for the future. Here was slowly emerging a new feature in the life of the Anglican Church. Without bishops, without commissaries – for Roger Price seems to have played an extremely small part in the movement – without state action or state authorization, the Anglican clergy in the colonies from New Jersey northward were learning a most important lesson. They were learning to look beyond the bounds of the parish or the mission, to organize themselves on a purely voluntary basis, to act corporately. They were even learning one of the hardest lessons the colonial American ever had to learn; to look beyond the limits of the individual colony. Out of their cooperation sprang much of the movement to obtain bishops for America – an attempt which failed in its immediate object but which nevertheless provided some of the experience on which ultimate national union and organization of the Church was based.[39] When finally the War of Independence cut the umbilical cord, when neither the S. P. G. or the Bishop of London had anything further to say to the Church in America, they had precedents to follow, a method of work. From these colonial meetings sprang the diocesan convention and the General Convention. And the leadership in this whole movement for corporate activity came in large measure from Samuel Johnson.

7. The President of King's versus the President of Yale

In 1740 the Reverend Thomas Clap became Rector of Yale College. He was well fitted for the position. He was a competent scholar, a stern disciplinarian, and resolved to make the rector a controlling figure in college policy. He was the strongest rector Yale had since the brief tenure of Timothy Cutler. But he was also a rock-ribbed Puritan, who carried on a steady warfare against modern tendencies, such as the alarming growth of Deism. Armed with a new college charter in 1745, Clap was given the title of president. "As president of Yale, he stood as the ceremonial head, as the high priest, of Connecticut Congregationalism."[40] Naturally, he was much perturbed by the steady growth of Anglicanism in the institution which he headed; one out of every ten Yale graduates during his term of office entered the Anglican ministry. For over a decade, his policy was one of moderate toleration. Anglican students were allowed to attend Sunday services in the church at West Haven, provided this did not interfere with the regular collegiate routine. Johnson's son William, for example, was permitted to serve as lay reader and catechist for neighboring Anglican parishes while he was a student at Yale.[41]

But when, in 1753, Trinity Church, New Haven, came into being, within a stone's throw of the Yale campus, Clap went into a tail-spin. This was too much. Therefore, in October 1753, he made "the most fateful administrative decision of his presidential career."[42] He announced that all Yale students must receive religious instruction and must worship within the college and under the supervision of approved ministers. This meant that the two sons of Ebenezer Punderson, Anglican rector of Trinity, who were students at Yale, could no longer attend their father's church. Punderson protested, but to no avail. Clap defended his position on several grounds. Every student must conform to the religion, rules and order of the college; there could be no exceptions. It was the business of the college to provide sufficient spiritual training for its students; "sufficient" of course meant Calvinistic. And if the students were allowed to go outside of the college for Sunday worship, they might simply play hooky. Finally, he affirmed that in Yale, as in all societies, the majority must rule – a principle that would have closed every Dissenting chapel in England. He did make one concession; Anglicans might attend their own churches when the Sacrament was celebrated, "and at Christmas, and such other Times as shall not be an Infraction upon the general Order and standing Rules of the College...."[43]

Anglicans insisted that the concession was insufficient. Arguing that Yale's purposes were not as narrow as Clap suggested, they reminded him that Churchmen contributed to the support of the college and that it was not the agency of the Standing Order because non-Congregationalists aided it through annual legislative grants. Punderson ordered his sons to attend Anglican services and to pay no mind to Clap's rules.

We now must jump to an undocumented conclusion. Punderson found that he was no match for the stern and authoritative Clap, backed by the whole power of the Standing Order. He must therefore have appealed to the one man who could act with effect – Samuel Johnson. The beginning of the Clap-Johnson correspondence on this matter has not been preserved. On January 30, 1754, Clap wrote to Johnson, referring to previous letters which had passed between them. It is apparent that Johnson had been appealing to liberty of conscience. Clap's position was completely clear:

> There is a law of college obliging all the students to attend worship in one place....

> Mr. Punderson orders his sons to break this law....

> Now the part which the founders and governors of a college are to act is to found and give regulations for it. The part which others are to act is to send their children there or not, according as they approve the constitution or not.[44]

Clap's position was clear-cut, logical, and well stated. As to the Anglicans' claim that Yale must be non-sectarian because non-Congregationalists' tax monies were voted to support the college, Clap reminded them that Yale compensated them by educating many of their clergy![45]

Johnson replied almost immediately, on February 5. His letter was long, and meant to be conciliatory; Johnson did not enjoy quarrels. He noted that the statutes of King's College, which he was just then nursing into existence, allowed parents to state where their sons could go to church on Sunday – this in spite of the fact that Anglicans formed the majority of the college governing board. Clap had appealed to the intention of the founders and benefactors of Yale, which was only to provide ministers for the Standing Order. In reply Johnson asked, "why may not our church also be provided for with ministers from one common College as well as your churches?" He also pointed out that one of the college benefactors had been Bishop Berkeley, and that Johnson had been the "principal ... in effect the only" instrument in securing that benefaction. He reminded Clap that it would be his duty to report all this to the S. P. G. – a step which "I abhor and dread to be brought to; and, therefore, by the love of our dear country (in which we desire to live, only upon a par with you, in all Christian Charity), I do beseech you … not to insist upon it." And he shrewdly observed:

> let Dissenters never more complain of their heretofore persecutions or hardships in England, unless they have us tempted to think it their principle, that they ought to be tolerated, in order at length to be established, that they may have the sole privilege of persecuting others.[46]

Never was the weakness of the Puritan position in regard to freedom of religion more neatly stated.

So far, Johnson's approach to Clap had been one of sweet reasonableness. He had always believed that people would respond to reason. But now he proceeded to show the ace he had up his sleeve. The colony of Connecticut was a corporation, owing its very existence to the charter of Charles II. This charter gave the corporation no right to create a secondary corporation. The politicians of the colony were very well aware of this defect. When the Collegiate School was first formed, they had been very slow to have it incorporated by the provincial assembly, but eventually that had been done. In his letter of February 5, Johnson further observed:

> It may also deserve to be considered that the Government at home would probably be so far from going into the for-

mality of repealing this law [Clap's rule for compulsory attendance at service in the college chapel] that they would declare it a nullity in itself; and not only so, but even the corporation that hath enacted it; inasmuch as it seems a principle in law that a corporation cannot make a corporation, nor can one be made without his Majesty's act.[47]

In his next letter, that of February 19, Johnson after remarking that he had "always been very tender of the charter privileges of this government," and that he had tried to make Anglicans loyal citizens, repeated his attack on the Yale charter, and advised that the assembly should consider the validity of that document before it was questioned in England.[48]

Clap was no fool. "Better to concede a point than risk the possible fate of dissolution by royal decree. For Clap, interference by the Crown was a terrifying specter."[49] Without any fanfare the rule about Sunday church attendance was quietly dropped, and Anglicans were free to go on Sunday where they would. By June 1754, William Samuel wrote his father that "Brother Billy" had reported how Clap "seems to have yielded the point as to the Church scholars, that as many as ask leave to attend, have it, but the scholars are negligent and but few of them trouble their heads about it."[50] Johnson immediately suggested that Ebenezer Punderson "take some pains with those wicked scholars ... and put something into their hands to read that may animate and indoctrinate them better. What! are they so mean and abject that having been so long under restraint, they now are come even to hug their chains ...?"[51]

Whatever the lack of Anglican students' zeal, at least from this point on there was a general disposition on the part of the Yale authorities to treat Anglicans with greater respect. Some persecution was over; Johnson had won his battle.

8. A Commissary for Connecticut

In August 1742 a clergy conference was held at Fairfield, attended by Henry Caner, Samuel Seabury the elder, John Beach, Ebenezer Punderson, Richard Caner, and of course Johnson, They addressed an important letter to Bishop Gibson of London, who had always showed himself an active friend of the colonial Church. They deplored the want of a colonial bishop, and thanked Gibson for his attempts to attain that necessity. And they thanked him also "for the kind provision your Lordship has made for us, as some remedy to this inconvenience, by appointing Commissaries among us under your Lordship's special direction.[52] This was by way of prelude. Then the convention proceeded to serious business – a practical complaint:

> But as the number of Clergy within this district is considerably increased, since the appointment of a Commissary at Boston, we humbly hope your Lordship will excuse us if we presume to suggest, with great submission, whether it might not be highly expedient for your Lordship to appoint a Commissary in this colony; our distances from the Commissary at Boston is such as makes it impractacable for us to attend upon the yearly Convention, and, consequently, to receive the benefit of that appointment. There are now fourteen Churches built and building, and seven Clergymen within this colony, and other daily called for; the nearest of us about one hundred and twenty, and the most of us upward of two hundred miles from Boston....

> We would not be thought to prescribe, and therefore bespeak your Lordship's candour, when we presume to mention the Reverend Mr. Johnson, of Stratford, as a person from whose ability, virtue and integrity we might hope all the advantages which such an authority would enable him to derive to us, if your Lordship should think proper to bestow this honour upon him.[53]

Johnson did not sign this letter, but sent with it in September one of his own. He joined his brother clergy in recommending the appointment of such a commissary, noting that the Connecticut laity now numbered five or six thousand. He concluded:

> My brethren have, indeed, done me the honour to mention my name to your Lordship. As to this, I beg leave to assure your Lordship that it is from their own motion, and not in the least owing to any influence of mine, that they have so

done; and that if your Lordship shall think it fit, at all, to appoint a Commissary in this colony, I shall be very well satisfied to submit to any other person whom your Lordship shall think proper to appoint to preside over us.[54]

We do not, unfortunately, have the bishop's answer to these letters; but nothing came of them. There the matter rested for some eight years.

In December 1748 Thomas Sherlock succeeded to the See of London which he held until July 1761. From the very beginning of his term of office, he was doubtful of the legality and the practicality of his jurisdiction over the Church of England in the colonies. Even if it were legal, he felt that it was impractical for a bishop three thousand miles away to exercise effective control over the colonial Church. He therefore became the most active of the English bishops in the old struggle for a colonial episcopate. Time after time he approached the ministry, the Lords of Trade, or the Privy Council, in the matter. He encouraged the colonists to keep up their petitions for the episcopate. But always he came up against two stone walls. The English ministry was supremely indifferent or hesitant to grasp such a political nettle, and the English and colonial Dissenters continued their pressure. Partly because of his disbelief in the effectiveness of commissaries, partly perhaps to force the ministry to take action, Sherlock adopted a new policy. Except for Virginia, where the commissary was also the president of William and Mary College, he never appointed a commissary; thus in effect the office practically ceased to exist.

Meantime the idea would not down, nor the idea that Johnson was the ideal commissary for Connecticut. On December 7, 1747, Henry Barclay of New York wrote Johnson a most interesting letter. The Reverend William Sturgeon, Yale graduate who had just returned from being ordained in England, brought great news. Sturgeon had seen Philip Bearcroft, the secretary of the S. P. G. "He tells me farther," Barclay wrote, "that you are to be appointed Commissary of Connecticut and Dr. Cutler of Boston, so that upon the whole I believe you may be well satisfied your interest is as good as ever it was...." And the postscript to this letter indicates clearly that Barclay also expected a commission as Commissary for New York.[55]

It is just possible that Gibson did make these appointments. But if he did – and there is no other evidence in the matter – within a few months he was dead, and all commissions emanating from him automatically ceased. There are two other little echoes of this rather mysterious affair. Among the Fulham papers is a letter from Johnson to Bishop Sherlock, thanking the bishop for his "favourable Thoughts & Intentions with regard to me."[56] It is doubtful that Sherlock appointed Johnson a commissary, but evidently some rumor of the prospect got around to the Reverend Matthew Graves of New London, whom we have already met. Whereupon in July 1750 Graves wrote to Sherlock to protest:

> 'Tis reported, my Lord, that you intend to appoint a new Commissary in these parts, and that a native of the place is to discharge that office; but I hope your Lordship (for God's sake pardon my well-intended freedom) will be pleased to consider that, as an American is Commissary in the western, so to condescend that a European may be impowered in the eastern part of this continent; for my part, I am not at all fit for that honourable post, but will be bold to say, that Dr. McSparran is every way qualified for it. All Europeans, especially ministers, meet with a very ungracious reception here....[57]

The animus of this is obvious.

But although, as seems most probable, Johnson never had the formal title of commissary, he had something better – the actuality. In September 1750, for example, Bishop Sherlock sent Johnson "an account how matters stand here [London] with respect to the ecclesiastical state of the churches abroad" – a copy of which had been sent to the commissaries of the late Bishop Gibson. Sherlock would be obliged to him for any news that Johnson could supply. Although the Stratford parson was not armed with a commissary's commission, he was considered to be as valuable a source of information and advice as any of the men who were so equipped.[58] For nearly fifty years he was the constant advisor of the S. P. G. He was frequently consulted by Gibson and Sherlock. He was in steady communication with Archbishop Secker. No other priest in the northern colonies had a tithe of his real effectiveness, and "he wielded more power in ecclesiastical matters than any American commissary ever did."[59]

As a clerical man of business, Johnson faced no more challenging task than the struggle to establish an American episcopate. But the story of these efforts deserves separate and more particular attention, not only because they illuminate another corner of Johnson's career, but also because they were a significant part of the American Revolution.

Chapter X

CHAMPION OF AN EPISCOPATE

1. The Need for Bishops

"So great, so prodigious is the detriment it is to the church and religion that we cannot be favored with a resident bishop!"[1] Thus Samuel Johnson anguished in 1754 as he did countless times before and afterwards. Such was the ecclesiastical situation when he espoused the Anglican cause in 1722, and such it remained until after his death in 1772. Despite the phenomenal growth of the Church in the northern colonies, and especially in Connecticut, it owed none of this success to the benefits of a well-rounded organization, for in polity it suffered from a strange anomaly – it was an episcopal church without bishops, or at least none but those in far off England.

This is not the place to pass in review the whole long struggle to remedy this condition – a struggle that began with Archbishop Laud in 1638. Our purpose here is to see clearly the part Samuel Johnson played in this attempt. By the time he was a mere boy the S. P. G. revived the episcopal project, and it enlisted the support of pious Queen Anne. But the queen died before anything could be accomplished, and her Hanoverian successors showed no interest in an American episcopate. In order to appreciate Johnson's efforts to obtain one, we must remember several facts about his era. For two decades Sir Robert Walpole, the king's first minister (1721-1742) avoided measures that threatened to stir up powerful or embarrassing opposition. His successors, especially Henry Pelham and the Duke of Newcastle, likewise tended to shy away from the issue for the same reason. And opposition there was – an alliance of New England Puritans with English Dissenters who went into action at the slightest mention of bishops for America.[2]

The story of Samuel Johnson's labors to obtain bishops for his beloved Church suggests that he, perhaps above all others, deserves the title of champion or advocate of an American episcopate. These efforts began even before he set out for England in 1722 on his quest for holy orders. In December 1719 he set down his "Thoughts of Episcopacy" with what he conceived might justify him in accepting presbyterial ordination. Although, as we have seen, he followed expediency for the moment, and was ordained a minister of the Standing Order, he reasoned from the unity of the Church and deduced the need for the historic episcopate as the center of visible unity for all Christians.[3] More reading and deliberation finally led him to risk the expense and dangers of a 3,000 mile voyage to obtain priesthood in apostolic succession – a step which he would probably have taken three years earlier had there been a bishop in America to confer orders. But by October 1722, he had decided that "There may be more souls damnified for want of Episcopal government in the country and that by far at length than by making this appearance" of declaring for the Church of England.[4] Never thereafter did he waver in his conviction of the importance of the episcopate to the Church, and doubtless he astonished more than one person by ranking it so high as a fundamental of Christian religion – of the *esse*, not merely the *bene esse*, of the Church.[5]

Nor is it difficult to see why Johnson and others were so concerned for their lack of a capstone to the three-fold order of the sacred ministry – deacons, priests, and bishops. Bishops were not merely the chief officers of government in the Church. Upon them the entire sacramental system depended. Without them the laity could not receive the sacrament of confirmation. Without them neither deacons nor priests could be ordained. And without a priest in this succession there could be no valid celebration of the Holy Communion. In the

American colonies the dissenting bodies had organizations complete for self-government and self-perpetuation. Churchmen insisted that they were entitled to similar rights.

To appreciate the quality of Johnson's efforts to settle bishops in the colonies we must keep three questions in mind. First, what were the basic features of his campaign? Second, how could he advocate conformity to the English ecclesiastical system and still propose an autonomous episcopal government in America without state support? Third, how did other colonial developments affect the episcopal scheme? In essence, Johnson's campaign consisted of appeals to English prelates, to the S. P. G., and to political leaders on both sides of the Atlantic. He did his best to draw his fellow missionaries into the contest, some of whom he induced not only to petition, but also to pamphleteer for the cause. Johnson also maintained that there was no inconsistency between the English ecclesiastical system and his desire for a colonial episcopate free from the Erastianism of England. Finally, the impact of his appeals, reasonable and moderate though they were, was affected by events which always interfered with winning the fight: the Great Awakening, wars, political and fiscal measures like the Stamp Act, the efforts of Dissenters, English and American, to frustrate the Church, and in general the American Revolution, which prevented the British government from allowing an American episcopate.

The contest for bishops also revealed a kind of paradox in Johnson's religious and political outlook. Despite the bitter animosity of the Dissenters toward episcopacy, Johnson remained both a High Churchman and an advocate of toleration. He never attempted to make episcopacy the only accepted religion of the colonists. Convinced though he was of the authenticity, holiness, and apostolic origins of the Church of England, he was no rabid proselytizer, but a teacher of Christianity to everyone, and of Anglicanism to those who wished to learn about it and accept it. No religious body, he argued, need be favored over the others. And yet he believed that the Church promoted the sociopolitical stability that supporters of royal-and-Parliamentary sovereignty had uppermost in their minds.

2. Johnson Begins His Campaign

As soon as he returned to Stratford in 1723, Johnson began his long years of correspondence with the S. P. G. and with prelates like Bishop Gibson, immediately and unfailingly urging the necessity of bishops for the colonies. At first he did so without more than a general notion of how to provide for them, but in time his proposals became more specific and more varied. In January 1724, he wrote Bishop Gibson that he knew of five or six young men who might soon be ordained but for their unwillingness to risk the dangers of travel to England: "the fountain of all our misery is the want of a bishop, for whom there are many thousands of souls in this country do impatiently long and for want, do extremely suffer."[6]

As the only priest in Connecticut, Johnson immediately faced not only the responsibility for his Stratford parish, but also the challenge of missionary work in towns close by. More clergy were urgently needed, and one way to get them was to make it easier and more attractive to obtain ordination from bishops who were more accessible. Writing to General Francis Nicholson, royal governor of several colonies in succession and an avid founder of Episcopal churches, Johnson revealed a slight variation on the theme: "our chief misfortune [in Connecticut] is the want of a King's governor and a bishop," he said.[7] Thus Johnson was showing not only a Whiggish spirit of toleration, but also a Tory conviction that solid respect for royal government and an orderly, mixed society under a balanced constitution would be promoted by a flourishing Episcopal church. Here were echoes of the old dictum of Stuart times: no Bishop, no King! This Johnson repeated, as tensions between mother country and colonies approached their final explosion into war and independence.

In the autumn of 1724, John Talbot and Robert Welton were moving about New England. Both had been consecrated bishop in England by non-juring bishops. Johnson, knowing nothing of this, invited Talbot to preach for him in Stratford. When Talbot revealed his status as a non-juring bishop, Johnson was horrified, and promptly disassociated himself from Talbot. Early in 1725 Johnson reported to both the S. P. G. and the bishop of London that there was a real danger that Talbot would be asked to ordain priests. This would set up a schism, and the danger was real. As he explained to Gibson, this showed "how unhappy our case is, that for want of a bishop ... people are in danger of running out of one schism into another and withal into a state of disaffection to His Majesty King George."[8] Non-jurors were, after all, tainted with loyalty to the Stuart line and less than enthusiastic supporters of the Hanoverian kings. This was another argument "to move the government to send us such [bishops] as will be acceptable both there and here...."[9]

In July 1725, Johnson attended what was evidently the first general meeting of New England Anglican clergy at Newport, Rhode Island. There the assembled clergy noted the need for a bishop, partly to counteract the non-juring threat. They accordingly submitted a petition to the Crown. In August, Johnson also wrote one of his London correspondents, John Berriman, that Dean George Berkeley might do more good on the continent than in Bermuda, if only he could be sent over as a bishop.[10]

In the next five years conditions improved somewhat. The Bishop of London seemed increasingly sympathetic and interested in the plight of the Church in Connecticut. In 1727, Johnson welcomed the return of Henry Caner in holy orders, so that Fairfield as well as Stratford had a resident priest. Churchmen managed to persuade the Connecticut Assembly to amend the law so as to allow them to have their religious taxes paid to their own clergy under stipulated conditions. The Church was growing. Johnson was grateful to Bishop Gibson for his "powerful interest and influence," especially in "so good a work as that of sending Bishops into America."[11] But by the end of Gibson's episcopate in 1748 the American Church was no closer to obtaining its own bishops. Yet despite this disadvantage and other adversities, the efforts of Johnson and his fellow missionaries were bearing fruit.

In 1736, Matthew Hutton, Bishop of Gloucester, responded to Johnson's complaint that America needed a bishop by explaining why the English Church had failed to provide one. "My own interest to be sure," he said, "is inconsiderable, but the united interest of the Bishops here is not powerful enough to effect so reasonable and right a thing...."[12] The Whig supremacy and the regime of Walpole were insurmountable obstacles, especially when buttressed by an Erastian and Latitudinarian establishment. But Johnson kept trying. With the accession of John Potter to the Archbishopric of Canterbury in 1737, he immediately introduced himself to the new primate with congratulations and thanks for Potter's book *Of the Government of the Church*, which had been one of the instruments of his own conversion, and seemed to afford a salutary counterweight to the Low Church influence. He assured Potter that an American episcopate would not, as had been suggested, promote colonial "independency." Quite the contrary. In his opinion, it was the Dissenters who were guilty both of anti-Episcopalian and antimonarchical tendencies. Begging the Archbishop to lend his aid to the cause of American episcopacy, he insisted that "the most effectual method to secure our dependence on the Crown ... would be to render our constitution here, both in church and state, as near as possible conformable to that of our mother-country...." And so he urged the provision of wise and good bishops and governors, and even a viceroy.[13] When Bishop Gibson confessed a lack of influence in persuading the government to provide bishops, Johnson repeated much of what he had written Potter, and expressed a suspicion that opponents of the Church had deliberately discouraged the scheme for an episcopate by talk of colonial independence – a "most unaccountable way of reasoning," he thought; "yet since it is thus ... we must patiently submit and wait upon Providence till it shall please God to enlighten the minds of men, and send us better times."[14]

Notwithstanding his melancholy profession of resignation and patience, Johnson did not sit on his hands. In November 1738, he and his fellow clergy addressed the Bishop of London, the Archbishop of Canterbury, and the S. P. G. with a statement of the depressed condition of the Church in Connecticut, praying for its relief. Their complaints included charges that Connecticut had an established religion despite the lack of authority under its charter to provide such an organization. The law exempting Anglicans from tax support of the Standing Order was evaded. Johnson's Stratford school was denied public funds, although Connecticut law authorized them. The civil authorities refused to defend the Reverend Jonathan Arnold's claim to land at New Haven, which a Londoner had given for an Anglican church there. A riot had prevented Arnold and his servants from possessing or using the ground. Such were the evidences that the Connecticut government wished to prevent the Church's growth and "utterly to destroy it."[15] A resident bishop might well be able to prevent or moderate such injurious treatment. Perhaps an appeal to the King in Council would remedy the situation. A petition to the Connecticut Assembly for an equitable share of the revenue raised from the sale of public lands and allocated to churches of the Standing Order and schools was rejected. And in October 1740 the assembly also repealed the 1727 tax exemption law.[16]

The Church faced renewed perils and fresh opportunities as the Congregationalists continued their attacks, the provincial government remained discriminatory, and no prospect of a resident bishop seemed imminent. The coming of the Great Awakening, signalled by Jonathan Edwards's Northampton revival in 1734 and carried to its peak of enthusiasm in 1740-1742 by George Whitefield's itinerant preaching, opened a new phase in Samuel Johnson's efforts to acquire an American episcopate. In England the Bishop of Oxford, Thomas Secker, fired a salvo in 1740 with an address to the S. P. G., urging it to renew efforts for an American episcopate. This prompted the Reverend Andrew Eliot to reply with "Remarks upon the Bishop of Oxford's Sermon." Eliot's polemics illustrate the Dissenters' old fears, now aggravated by the religious revival and especially by Whitefield's rantings against his own Communion. An episcopate would lead to colonial tax support by the assemblies or Parliament's action. Bishops could not confine themselves to purely spiritual affairs; an Erastian Church suggested quite otherwise. And it was feared that bishops must seek additional power even to execute a spiritual discipline or to make it effective.[17]

We have seen how Johnson was repelled by the enthusiasm of the Awakening and by the renewed furor against the Church. Yet many Dissenters despaired of the controversy and turned to the Anglican way. How much more effective the Church might be if she had a resident bishop as well as more clergy and the benefits of local self-government! In a letter "To the Archbishop of Canterbury, and not Much Otherwise to the Bishops of Gloucester and London" in September 1741, Johnson ruminated on the "great progress of the most odd and unaccountable enthusiasm that perhaps ever obtained in any age or nation." He found that "The church indeed has not as yet much suffered but has in many instances gained by these strange commotions." If growth was to continue, the clergy would have to "take much care and pains among the people," and there should "be more laborers sent into the harvest."[18]

By 1742, Connecticut had fourteen Anglican churches built and building, seven priests, and over 2,000 people – a great increase from Johnson's solitary beginning in 1723 with 100 adults in one church. But more clergy were needed. A resident bishop could more readily supply them than could dozens of prelates across the wide Atlantic. Even one or two English bishops traveling at intervals through all the colonies would encourage more men to seek holy orders, so that more laborers for the harvest could deal with the opportunities given by the reaction against the extravagances of the Great Awakening.[19] As the decade ended Thomas Sherlock succeeded to the See of London, which he held from December 1748, to July 1761. Johnson's appeals to him increased in strength, and Sherlock replied that he emphatically preferred an American episcopate to commissaries; he urged the King in Council to take action.

3. Another Proposal

In 1750, two of the strongest bishops in England, Joseph Butler of Durham and Thomas Secker of Oxford, offered a plan for an American episcopate. To avoid obvious criticisms, this plan provided that such bishops should have no coercive power over the laity, that they should in no way interfere with civil officers, that they should not be supported by colonial taxes, nor would they even be settled where Dissenters were in control of the provincial governments. In other words, this was a proposal for a purely spiritual episcopate – such an episcopate as the American Church eventually obtained.[20] On November 28 of the same year, the episcopal clergy of Massachusetts, under the leadership of Timothy Cutler, addressed a letter to the S. P. G. setting forth identical proposals.[21] Perhaps after all Johnson's labors were about to bear fruit.

Writing to Bishop Sherlock in September 1750, Johnson assured the bishop of the clergy's happiness under his jurisdiction, but he wished that it might be exercised by suffragan bishops instead of commissaries. Was it not unfair, he asked, to be without bishops when the

French and Spanish provided Roman bishops for their overseas possessions?[22] Almost at the same time Sherlock was writing Johnson to solicit information such as he sought from the commissaries named by his predecessor. The prelate revealed that he was asking the government for "one or two bishops to reside in proper parts of the plantations," but that his petition was laid over until the King returned from Hanover.[23] When the Dissenters lobbied against the plan, they persuaded the government to drop it for fear of additional colonial trouble. The arguments of the Anglican clergy in Massachusetts and Connecticut evidently were either submitted too late or were too unconvincing to the government. Johnson indicated the possibility of an alternative. "Indeed," he wrote, "it is beyond imagination to conceive how much weight an Episcopal visitation would have to promote the true interest of both religion and government even if it were but one in five or seven years."[24] What he was here suggesting was that an English bishop might occasionally itinerate in the colonies if a resident one could not be provided.

By 1752, Sherlock had reconciled himself to the exercise of his American jurisdiction by the use of commissaries, although he and his three successors all favored an American episcopate because their jurisdiction was of questionable legality, and the commissary system was a poor substitute. Meanwhile one secular crisis followed another: King George's War, the Great War for the Empire, and then the controversial programs of successive British ministries of which sought to grapple with the American revolutionary outbursts of the 1760's. After the Stamp Act crisis, the scheme for an episcopate had less chance than ever of succeeding. And independency in religion was, as Churchmen had feared, leading to republicanism in state affairs.[25] Whether an American episcopate would have had a salutary effect is debatable. At any rate the British government, fearful of the consequences, tried to keep the issue out of the public eye.

In the midst of these shifting circumstances, Samuel Johnson became more critical of the apparent lack of concern of the Church of England for her colonial children, more dismayed by the inability of her leaders to influence the government. He could hardly believe that anyone could be so insensitive and unresponsive to so great a need. A man with such strong convictions and such steadfast loyalty to his cause might well have despaired and given up the fight. But Johnson's devotion and inner strength saved him from disappointment that could easily have led to disgust and resentment. Instead, he persevered.

In 1751 and 1752, Johnson continued to beg for a resident bishop, or failing that for one sent to visit the colonies at least every seven years. He felt it shocking that his own son would have to travel a thousand leagues for his ordination, pointing out that of twenty-nine candidates whom he had personally known to go "home" for ordination, six had been lost by shipwreck or disease. The Bishop of Oxford could "give no encouraging prospect. We must endeavor again when we see opportunity," he wrote. John Berriman wrote similarly that such was the opposition "to the proposal for sending over bishops as leaves no room for the present, to expect them." And Bishop Sherlock feared "that others who have more power and influence, do not see the thing in the light that we do...." To Francis Astry, Bishop Secker, and Philip Bearcroft, Secretary of the S. P. G., Johnson replied with melancholy dismay: "May God in mercy yet incline the hearts of those whose province it is to have compassion upon us."[26]

4. Johnson and Secker

In 1754, appeared the third edition of Johnson's *Elementa Philosophica.* In it appeared a letter which opened the issue of an episcopate to a wider public. Johnson had written, in the form of a letter to Thomas Bradbury Chandler, "Some Impartial Thoughts;" which offered a summary of his position on the controversy as of July 1753. William Smith of Philadelphia, who was seeing the *Elementa* through the English press, had inserted this without Johnson's consent, and also had taken liberties with Johnson's text. The document was a compendium of specific details which had emerged from the years of advocating an episcopate.[27] First, Johnson noted the distress of the American Church for want of proper discipline of the clergy. Also, the colonies could and would furnish more of their own clergy if there were but a bishop in America to ordain them. It was unfair that the various sects enjoyed their own autonomous systems while the Church did not. Bishops would merely put the Church on an equal footing with them, and would no more damage the colonies' consti-

In 1754, Johnson accepted the presidency of King's College, and from then until he returned to Stratford in 1763 as retired president, he was largely preoccupied with the management of the college. He did not lose sight of the need for an episcopate, but his correspondence slackened somewhat on that subject. He evidently realized that the years of war between Britain and France – 1754-1763 – were not the times when the scheme could be furthered. Not only was warfare diverting, but the British government's efforts to enlist the aid of the colonists in the great imperial struggle made the ministry even more unwilling to push any program that was not essential to the war effort and that would aggravate colonial balkiness. Interestingly, Johnson's correspondence with his son William, then in England, does not reflect much interest in the old issue – until March 1756.[31]

At that point William wrote of rumors of "some very grand design" of the S. P. G. which some said was "the affair of sending bishops over to America...."[32] Indeed, a year earlier, Thomas Bradbury Chandler had relayed news from England that Bishop Sherlock had offered the King in Council to give £10,000 to support an American bishop if one were sent while he remained Bishop of London.[33] And now Johnson's son reported that "there is not above one or two in the ministry now who oppose it and they are more favorable than they were...."[34] At Oxford he met "fellows of several of the colleges, Hutchinsonians, and truly primitive Christians" who spoke "with much tenderness of our unhappiness in the want of bishops and do all they can to promote such a design...."[35] What must the colonial champion of an American episcopate have thought to such tantalizing suggestion? When his son, having just been priested, died of smallpox, Johnson was almost embittered that a seventh precious life had been sacrificed to the "atheistical politics of this abandoned age." His son's death should have awakened the stupid age to the need for "bishops (at least one good one) to take care of the Church in these vastly wide extended regions." Writing thus in grief to George Berkeley, Jr., son of his old friend the Bishop of Cloyne, Johnson yet evinced more sorrow than anger.[36] But he did not omit using the example of his son's death to press his case with the S. P. G. In 1757, he wrote, "Would to God this unhappy event could prove some occasion of procuring for us so great a blessing! In this case I should hardly think my son's life ill bestowed."[37]

In 1758, events occurred which once again raised the hopes of Johnson and his fellow priests that their great cause might at last be won. In April, Thomas Secker was translated from Oxford to the primatial See of Canterbury. Johnson, as did other clergy, expressed his delight – and his longings – through congratulations. Secker responded to Johnson, whom he recognized as standing justly at the head of the northern clergy. He promised that he would use his new rank to promote the work of the S. P. G., and said that he would depend on the advice of the missionaries, but especially on that of Johnson. Yet Secker was cautious in his salutation to the "Good Dr.," and he warned that the virulence of Dissenters must be moderated before an episcopal scheme could succeed. In view of the charges that Anglicans were proselytizing other Christians instead of converting unbelievers, he felt that the Society must be careful where it established new missions. Facts must be marshalled to deal with the stern opposition stemming from the English Dissenters, who worked in close alliance with their American brethren. Though Secker promised an undying interest in winning an American episcopate, he felt that the time had not yet come. He urged friendly and "accidental" discourse with opponents to assure them that no plan was then under way, and that there was no intention to harm anyone in his existing liberties. No unnecessary offense must be given, and Anglicans must be as obliging as possible without betraying the doctrines, interests, and honor of the Church. Although the Archbishop invited Johnson's counsel, he urged him that where they were agreed, "you will have the goodness to lead others" into the same way of thinking and acting. "Thus let us each be doing the best we can, and leave the event to God."[38]

Neither the temper of Secker's letter nor Johnson's reply in March 1759, reveals the slightest reason for suspecting these Anglican leaders of "aggression" – unless one insists on believing the worst, and interpreting their cautious strategy as mere deception. Johnson expressed the gratitude of his fellow clergy for Secker's directions, and quite agreed with them. He reported new attacks on the Church, the S. P. G. and King's College. These were the work of William Smith, Jr., of New York in his *History of New York* and of Smith's cohorts writing in the *Independent Reflector*. As to the charge that the S. P. G. was proselytizing among Dissenters, Johnson repeated his assertion that converts to Anglicanism had been "accidental" save for the way in which Anglican laymen familiarized their neighbors with the Church, and led them from curiosity to conviction. "I never once tried to proselyte [sic] dissenters," he said, "nor do I believe any of the other ministers did; we never concerned ourselves with them till they came to us, and when they did, we could do no other than give them the best instructions and assistance we could...." Johnson did not meekly submit to Secker's admonitions of caution and patience. He remonstrated that he and others had always tried to assure their opponents that they "never pretended to desire any episcopate that should have any jurisdiction over them or indeed any concern with them...." It was a "miserable pass indeed" that the Church could not be on a par with its rivals, and Johnson wished a legal judgment could be issued to determine whether colonial charters authorized the Dissenters "to establish themselves and make dissenters of us." An American bishop need not be settled in hostile parts; perhaps one in Virginia, where the Church was accepted and established, could visit New England periodically. (Johnson knew very little about the Virginia laity.) And "may we not hope," Johnson asked, "that the great minister who now so gloriously conducts the public affairs [Pitt] is a friend of religion" and that with the return of peace he would be asked to assist in providing an episcopate? Meanwhile, Johnson begged, the Archbishop might use his influence "that such might be appointed our governors as are friends to religion and will countenance and encourage the Church and set an example of constant or at least frequent attendance on the public worship, which has not always been the case...." In New York since 1743 governors, except for Sir Charles Hardy, had rarely been seen in church.[39] Thus far, Johnson carried his notions of church-state connections, but they were scarcely exceptional in his age.

Thomas Secker's tenure as Primate of All England (1758-1768) marked the peak in the campaign for an American episcopate, and it is no accident that Samuel Johnson's strongest urgings coincided with it. It was also the period when Dissenters' opposition to the plan attained a new virulence. The cause for this is not hard to find. In 1685, there had been no organized work of the Church of England north of Maryland; not a single parish existed. By 1760, there were over one hundred and eighty flourishing centers of Anglican work, notably in New England. Many of these had appeared in only the most recent decades. Anglicanism in the northern colonies had become a force to be feared. In 1759, Secker, in spite of his caution, petitioned the King in Council to allow colonists to have bishops wherever they might be well received; commissaries in America had already exercised a similar jurisdiction that was not claimed to be burdensome, and there had been little objection to them except from royal governors. To replace them with suffragan bishops would necessitate no alteration in civil government. The colonial Church should be free to enjoy what Protestant Dissenters had – a succession for their ministry but without taxes or crown funds. A bishop could be supported by annexing some preferments and allowing him to receive "benefactions."[40] Evidently the Archbishop was willing to allow his petition to remain on the table for a more propitious time. But in 1760, he proceeded to enlist the support of prominent politicians against a more favorable day in the future.

In 1760, Johnson wrote East Apthorp, first rector of the new church in Cambridge, Massachusetts, urging him to follow Secker's advice about caution, but expressing a hope that the time was not a great way off when the episcopate would come to America. He went on to pray that Apthorp might "be the first that may serve your country in that capacity."[41] It speaks volumes for Johnson's unselfishness and complete devotion to the cause of the Church that he, the acknowledged leader of the New England clergy, and the trusted confidant of the English hierarchy, should make this suggestion.

In July 1760, Johnson submitted to Secker's scrutiny a proposed essay on episcopacy and colonial government. Written the previous winter and intended for publication in the *London Magazine*, the essay he suggested might be submitted to the Earl of Halifax and to William Pitt for review, if Secker cared to do so. Framed as a series of questions, and signed "Philanglus Americanus," it provoked Secker to rebuke Johnson for so untimely and inexpedient a proposal. At least the Archbishop was grateful that Johnson had referred the paper to his judgment rather than offering it directly for publication. The Archbishop assured Johnson that Lord Halifax was "very earnest for bishops in America," and that their efforts might be crowned with success "when it shall please God to bless us with a peace."[42]

Secker's rebuke to Johnson is explicable because of the prelate's strategy of caution. But the parson's essay was untimely not only because of its strategy, but also because of its contents. It proposed measures that ran counter to colonial tendencies, as the postwar events all too vividly demonstrated. The opening query was not unreasonable: should not the British government prepare plans for the post-war period? But what followed was a remarkable statement of High Church royalism. Should not colonial governments be more similar to one another and to that of the mother country? Would it not be good for Parliament to legislate a model government for all provinces and to change the excessive republicanism of the charter colonies? Should not all colonies be royalized (with governors named by the crown) and combined into an inter-colonial union headed by a viceroy or lord lieutenant? Could not each colony send an assemblyman and council member to meet with the lord lieutenant and to approve or veto the acts of each colony before they were submitted to the crown? Because of the confusions of currencies, should not Parliament establish one medium of exchange for all the colonies? Should not something be done for the better regulation of religion so that the fear of God and honor of the King might be joined to foster Christian principles and intercolonial cooperation? There should be no discouragements to religious diversity, but the Church should be placed on an equal footing with the dissenting sects, and it should be provided with bishops to "ordain and govern the clergy, and instruct and confirm their laity. It is not proposed that the episcopal government should have any superiority, or authority over other denominations, or make any alterations relating to, or interfering with any civil matters as they now stand."[43] On this latter point Johnson's Whig libertarianism continued to moderate his otherwise Tory inclinations. When Secker objected to the publication of this remarkable document, Secker was undoubtedly right; it would have furnished excellent ammunition for the anti-Anglicans of New York and New England.

Johnson did not receive the Archbishop's rebuke of November 1760, nor his missive of December 1761, until April 1762. By then he was nearing retirement as President of King's College, and Secker had continued his policy of restraint. He had declined to present a petition for bishops from the Massachusetts clergy, dated January 1761, to the King on the grounds that it was as premature and controversial as Johnson's paper of questions.[44] Although he had referred a similar address from the New York clergy to George III, he advised Johnson that the time for action was not yet ripe. Indeed, he said, this "was a matter of which you in America cannot judge, and therefore I beg you will attempt nothing without the advice of the Society, or of the bishops."[45]

Everything seemed now to hinge upon the peace concluding the Great War for the Empire. Johnson assured Secker that he was content to follow the Archbishop's advice, and that he had merely intended Secker to use his essay as he best saw fit. But he was more hopeful than ever. "Blessed be God for the happy unanimity of the nation and the good disposition of Lord Halifax towards our being in due time provided for with Bishops," he wrote, "and your good hopes relating to that affair."[46] But as the months slipped by, and colonial petitions such as the New York clergy sent to the Bishop of London in September 1762, continued to roll in, Secker never found an opportune moment to accomplish what Johnson so much desired.[47] The difficulty was reflected in Secker's letter of October 6, 1762 to the Connecticut parson. Having received a pamphlet from America, entitled "The real Advantages which Ministers and People may enjoy by conforming to the Church of England," a sarcastic attack on Anglicanism, the primate expressed disbelief that Dissenters in general would seriously approve such a "ludicrous manner" of writing against the Church. He felt that "Some good persons, who are not of our church" might be persuaded to "take part with us" if the pamphlet were answered "by the prudent use of very mild and friendly remonstrances, setting forth the uncharitableness of such treatment, and the injustice of such representations." He also wisely observed that "whereinsoever we are justly accused we should own it, and mend; which is the only good answer in such cases."[48] Paradoxically, in some ecclesiastical matters requiring mending, as in the discipline of the clergy, a bishop was practically the only guarantee of reformation other than the personal repentance and amendment of life in deficient clergymen.

5. The Apthorp - Mayhew Controversy

Secker's suggestion of an answer to "The real Advantages" pamphlet marked another stage in the struggle – renewed ecclesiastical warfare in the colonial press. This conflict extended beyond Secker's archepiscopate, first in the Apthorp-Mayhew controversy of 1763-1765, and then in the Chandler-Chauncey contest of 1767-1771, which included some particularly spirited exchanges in the *New-York Gazette* and the *Pennsylvania Journal* during 1768 and 1769.

In one sense the Apthorp-Mayhew controversy was a renewal of earlier struggles. But in this case it was the Anglican East Apthorp's tract that set off the fireworks, whereas previously the Dissenters had been the aggressors. In March 1763, Apthorp published *Considerations on the Institution and Conduct of the Society for the Propagation of the Gospel in Foreign Parts* to vindicate the missionary work of the S. P. G. in New England.[49] The following month Jonathan Mayhew, Congregationalist minister of West Church, Boston, poured contempt on Apthorp's argument with his *Observations on the Charter and Conduct of the Society for the Propagation of the Gospel in Foreign Parts*.[50] Mayhew charged Anglicans with plotting to root out Presbyterianism and to establish episcopacy. The issue of bishops was raised with the more general questions of Anglican missionary activity. The Reverends Henry Caner of King's Chapel, Boston, and Arthur Browne of Portsmouth offered rebuttals.[51] Browne's *Remarks* boldly admitted the S. P. G.'s desire for bishops and neatly parried the Dissenters' charge that Anglican clergy needed discipline by observing that bishops would provide it! Johnson also entered the fray with a letter vindicating the S. P. G. and published as an appendix to Caner's *Candid Examination of Dr. Mayhew's Observations*.[52] He observed that the time-worn Dissenter technique of raising all the clamor that was possible was again being used, but he thought that the Church really benefitted from the furor because Mayhew's malignant attack was so venomous that it could hardly affect the Dissenters except in an adverse manner. Mayhew, of course, expected that the Peace of Paris would be followed by the introduction of bishops to America, and it was well known that efforts to do so were being made.[53]

One proof of the justice of Mayhew's suspicions was Secker's letter to Johnson at the end of March 1763. He expected the ministry would plan measures for the colonies that summer, and "then we must try our utmost for bishops." English Dissenters, he noted, were raising the alarm, suspicious that the ministry had already been approached about the issue.[54] When Johnson answered Secker's letter on August 10, he reported that he had attended and preached at a Connecticut clergy conference in June, and had reminded his brethren to follow the Archbishop's admonition to exercise caution and precision in their epistolary campaigns for the Church. At this point East Apthorp had declined to answer Mayhew's *Observations*, but Arthur Browne had done so, and Johnson had prepared a statement of his own. "Now must be the time, if ever," he said, "to be in earnest for bishops ... The Dissenters also, and our newspapers, are full of the talk; and indeed they know the thing is so reasonable, that we should and ought to be complete in our kind, as well as they in theirs, that they seem to expect nothing else; and I believe if it was once done, they would generally soon be easy enough."[55]

Grateful as he was, and approving too, for Johnson's intended answer to Mayhew, Archbishop Secker was unable to seize the opportunity for providing American bishops. He was too cautious. And as he explained the situation to Johnson in September 1763, he revealed both his deficiency and the difficult circumstances in which he found himself. The public, he feared, might think that the S. P. G. had established too many missions in New York and New England. He suggested that rather than justify them it would be best "to excuse ourselves in that respect, as being prevailed on by entreaties [from the laity] hard to be resisted, ... and resolved to be hereafter more sparing in the admission of them, instead of making it our business to *Episcopize* New England, as Dr. Mayhew expresses himself." In this, as we have seen, Secker was wholly correct; the initiative in new work had come from the laity. What the government would do about the episcopate he could not guess. The Earl of Egremont, Secretary of State for the Southern Department (which included American colonial jurisdiction), died before he could report a recommendation to the ministry. Lord Halifax, who as President of the Board of Trade had frequently been mentioned as strong for the church, had now succeeded Egremont. But although Halifax was friendly to the notion of an episcopate, Secker doubted that he would dare act, lest he rouse opposition to an already unstable ministry.[56] And so the old difficulty remained – a ministry too shaky and too lethargic in church matters to risk an unpopular stand.

In January 1764, Secker published anonymously "An Answer to Dr. Mayhew's Observations," containing much of what Johnson and others had argued for some years. Anglicans in America could not enjoy the benefits of the Church, "having no ... Bishops within three thousand miles of them – a case which never had its parallel before in the Christian world. Therefore it is desired that two or more Bishops may be appointed for them ... to ordain ministers ... confirm their children ... This is the real and only scheme that has been planned for Bishops in America; and whoever has heard of any other, has been misinformed through mistake or design." Secker's answer was conciliatory and reasonable, for he argued that the Church should merely enjoy toleration among Dissenters, who had won toleration for themselves.[57] Exchanges followed, with Mayhew making rejoinders and Anglican advocates offering rebuttals. Mayhew insisted that prelates would never be content without temporal powers, and that Churchmen would increase in numbers until they could gain control of colonial legislatures and affect an Anglican establishment. East Apthorp replied that such fears were groundless. And to Johnson he wrote that if Anglicans could but join hands across the Atlantic, as the Dissenters so regularly did through their corresponding societies, they might very well succeed.[58] Pure fear of Anglicanism played a large part in the whole controversy. Years later John Adams wrote that the alarm had grown considerably; Americans feared that if Parliament acted to provide bishops, it might very well proceed to prohibit the existence of other religious bodies.[59]

The events of 1765 onward, repeatedly interfered with Anglican hopes and efforts. One ministerial debacle seemed to follow the other, from the Stamp Act to the Townshend duties, and successive ministries led by George Grenville, the Marquis of Rockingham, the ailing Pitt, the Duke of Grafton, and Lord North vacillated between stern measures and conciliatory gestures. Colonial leaders, incensed by Britain's attempts at tighter controls, tended to see bishops as merely another part of some grand design to destroy their liberties. Samuel Johnson viewed the home government as better affected toward the Dissenters than to the Church. In 1765, he told Richard

Terrick, the Bishop of London, that the government was "even dis-affected to it, otherwise it would doubtless establish episcopacy here as it is there."[60] In September he complained to Archbishop Secker that "nothing in favor of religion in any shape, especially the Church of England" was to be expected. "Would to God," he exclaimed, "now that England gives laws to America, that there was a law ... obliging all denominations to pay a sufficient tax to the support of religion and schools (since there must be a toleration) and requiring whatever denomination prevails in each district, that at what time fifty families or more of any other denomination appear to embody [organize] themselves, they be exempt from paying to the prevailing denomination, and that the tax arising from them be paid to the support of their own way of worship." This of course was the old cry of Connecticut Anglicans. Johnson was uneasy lest the clamor prevent another attempt at providing bishops. And he observed that had the measure been effected "last spring (when the dissenters themselves expected nothing else) and the Stamp Act postponed till the next [1766], it would have been but a nine days wonder...." Another opportunity had been missed, and "both the Bible and the episcopate" were "fast sinking together in this apostatizing age...." He feared that unless the whole Church roused itself, there was "a greater probability that the episcopate will in not many years be demolished in England than established in America. May God forbid it and protect our land and his church."[61] It was not often that Johnson reached this extreme of pessimism.

6. Chandler Takes the Lead

From the autumn of 1765 until late summer in 1766, leadership in the battle for bishops shifted from New England and from Samuel Johnson's hands to the clergy of New York and New Jersey, who were headed by Thomas Bradbury Chandler of Elizabethtown, Johnson's closest disciple. In October 1765, the New York and New Jersey clergy met to petition the King, the two archbishops, and Bishop of London, and the S. P. G. for the episcopate. Myles Cooper, Johnson's successor at King's College, was assigned the work of addressing the Universities of Cambridge and Oxford. Chandler quickly informed Johnson of their activity, for he and his fellows regarded the old man as "Father of the Clergy." Chandler and the others were tired of the strategy of prudence and caution, for it had produced nothing. Honesty and forthrightness they felt were the best policy, if patrons of the Church were to be forced out of their apparent lethargy. Chandler believed the Church suffered less from persecution from without than from irresolution and pusillanimity within.[62]

By March 1766, the Bishop of London approached the Board of Trade with a recommendation for an episcopate. The Stamp Act crisis, he noted, had shown that Anglican clerics deserved to be granted their petition in view of their support of the government. But if a colonial episcopate could not be provided at once, Terrick urged that it be duly offered on the basis of cool deliberation, true policy, and freedom from all reasonable objection as far as conscience and religious liberty were concerned.[63] The best that can be said of the government was that it was nothing if not cool in its deliberations. That it was so responsive to the Dissenters' lobbying, so steady in avoiding the extension of episcopacy, so averse to trouble-making, and so hesitant to aid Churchmen, hardly bespeaks an imperial tyranny, whether royal or Parliamentary!

On May 20, 1766, Johnson attended the commencement at King's College. The next day he presided at a convention of fourteen priests from New York, New Jersey, and Connecticut, who decided to continue their appeals to the S. P. G. The clericus noted with sorrow and dismay that two more priests had recently been lost by shipwreck near Cape Henlopen on their return from ordination in England. These made a total of ten men lost out of fifty-one who had gone on the dangerous quest. Johnson noted this in his letter to Secker earlier in the month, bemoaning the fact that such a loss to the colonial Church was proportionately greater than the Church had suffered during "the popish persecution in England...."[64]

With the repeal of the Stamp Act in March 1766, and "all America over-flowing with joy," Johnson thought that the time was ripe for action, for he believed that the colonists "would rather 20 bishops were sent than that act enforced."[65] But in June, Samuel Auchmuty of New York saw the situation in a different light. Writing to Johnson with news from England, he reported that the clergy request for bishops was "thought to be ill timed," and that it was doubtful whether such a desirable event will soon take place," although the

King was strongly in favor of it. Auchmuty was somewhat out of patience with the English hierarchy, and thought Secker should be more like Laud! But the S. P. G., by way of a sort of consolation prize, rewarded Johnson's son William Samuel, Auchmuty, Henry Caner, and Chandler by persuading the University of Oxford to give them honorary doctorates.[66]

The last five years of Johnson's life were dominated by fresh blasts of disputation between his pupil Chandler and Charles Chauncey, an ally of Mayhew. Each of the two combatants had their supporters. That Chandler became the most prominent – and perhaps most no-torious-public defender of the Church was due in large part to John-son's encouragement and advice. Johnson, although he had to spend much of his life as an Anglican in controversy, never really enjoyed that sort of writing, and he believed Chandler to be better equipped for the task than he, especially since the old man felt the weight of his seventy-one years.[67] Doubting whether anything would "take ef-fect in this stupid age," he yet believed that if ought could be done to promote a general acceptance of an Anglican episcopate, Chandler was the best qualified to explain the cause.[68]

As early as September 1766, Chandler heard that Johnson believed he should write something for the campaign. He knew the task would be difficult, because it was then very unlikely that the English government would act, and also because the southern clergy showed few signs of interest in supporting the scheme.[69] That au-tumn the Connecticut, New York, and New Jersey clergy conven-tions again requested the help of the English Church authorities, and complained of the refusal of the S. P. G. to establish more mis-sions in New England. The New Jersey clergy, meeting at Shrews-bury, decided to draught an address to the public, and when Chandler agreed to write it, he asked Johnson's suggestions for the arguments he was to use.[70]

7. Johnson's Last Efforts

In the meantime, Johnson had made by letter a new and interesting contact. Sir William Johnson, landed magnate of the Mohawk Valley, and imperial superintendent of Indian affairs in the northern colonies, was an enthusiastic Churchman. On October 31, 1766, the old priest wrote the baronet that at least three American bishops were desirable: one for the northeastern colonies, to be stationed at Albany; one for the south, stationed in Virginia; and one for the West Indies. He begged Sir William to use his influence with the government to further this far-reaching scheme.[71] In November the New York clergy also wrote Sir William, asking his advice, and reminding him that his own difficulty in staffing the Mohawk mission was due to the lack of an American bishop. For several years Sir William continued to correspond with his Connecticut namesake, discussing not only the episcopal issue but also missions and schools for the Iroquois.[72] Thus Johnson had enlisted powerful clerical and lay voices in the battle for his dream.

In November 1766, while Chandler was at work on his appeal to the public, Johnson revealed a new line of thought concerning the episcopate in a letter to Archbishop Secker. In its own way it was a typically American proposal for cutting through the red tape of the establishment. If the state would take no action to provide the American Church with the vital ministry of bishops, it was the Church's "duty to provide for herself be the consequences what it [sic] will." If the English prelates would not unite to insist upon government action, or if they did and the government refused, then the Church should herself act, and send over two or three bishops. This might mean government persecution, but the Church should accept the suffering rather than permit the disappearance of bishops or their dwindling "into mere worldly political creatures, instead of truly spiritual persons." This was a drastic suggestion for an eighteenth-century Churchman, and points the way to the Oxford Movement of half a century later. Johnson's investigations had convinced him that all Anglican clerics "northward of Philadelphia" except one were faithful men, and that most of the laity were united in the cause. Being honest, he had to admit that the southerners were generally lukewarm about episcopacy, and that some of the southern clergy stood in need of discipline. He repeated to Secker the idea he had suggested to Sir William of the three American bishops. He did not reveal that Chandler was preparing his famous *Appeal*.[73]

Chandler had promised that Johnson should examine his intended pamphlet before it was published, and in January 1767, he submitted the proposed title page of the work. It read, "An Appeal to the Public, concerning the *Reasonableness, Usefulness*, and *Necessity* of an AMERICAN EPISCOPATE: in which the *Plan*, on which it is proposed, is *fairly stated*, and the *Objections* against it are *candidly refuted*." Already Johnson had sent for Chandler's consideration a plan of the pamphlet and a copy of an address to the Bishop of London.[74]

The press of other business as well as the careful work of writing prevented Chandler from publishing his *Appeal* until November 1767. Meanwhile he labored over Johnson's suggestions for improving the draught; in March he told the Connecticut patriarch that he wished he were closer to Elizabethtown so that the New York and New Jersey clergy might have "the advantage of being under your immediate influence and direction ... and ... could inspect every paper drawn up by us relating to the Church, and preside in every convention held by us on the affairs of it...."[75] In April, Johnson endeavored to extend his influence in a new direction and enlist support for Chandler's forthcoming paper by writing the Reverend John Camm of Virginia. He asked Camm to rouse the southern clergy, and confessed great wonderment that they had never indicated an interest in obtaining an episcopate. Johnson argued that if the claims of the Dissenters that "19-20ths of Americans are utterly against receiving bishops" were to be refuted, the southerners must help.[76] There is no evidence that Camm ever replied. The Virginians did not bestir themselves until May 1771, when they acted with great caution, as we shall see. Johnson had great hopes for Chandler's work. He wrote William Samuel that it would be "the best thing ever done in America," that it should be reprinted in London, and be placed into everybody's hands. William Samuel did not share his father's enthusiasm. In June 1767 he wrote that Lord Shelburne, now Secretary of State for the Southern Department, did not believe an episcopate was needed in the colonies. He expected no good effects in England from the pamphlet; "Perhaps the more you stir about this matter at present," he warned, "the worse it will be."[77]

Even before Johnson received his son's missive, he had heard of Shelburne's views, and he urged William Samuel to convince the Earl to the contrary. The opportunity must not be lost again. Johnson further wondered why the king and bishops should not proceed to act.

"Pray inform yourself," he urged, "whether it is not possible by the King' s supremacy to do without" troubling "these great people that will hate and give no attention to it."[78]

Finally, in November 1767, Chandler's *Appeal* came off the press. Anglicans were of course delighted. Sir William Johnson judged it an excellent piece, judiciously written, modest, clear, and dispassionate; and he thought it would surely help the cause. The baronet had already offered to arrange a New York land grant to support an American bishop, and promised other such aid for missionaries in the Mohawk Valley. Furthermore, he had made all this known to the British Secretary of State.[79]

But opponents quickly entered the lists, and a battle royal followed, which raged in pamphlets and newspaper essays until 1771. First of the assailants of Chandler was Charles Chauncey, whose open letter of December 1767, in response to the Bishop of Landaff's S. P. G. sermon, had argued that bishops were not really needed for missionary work among the heathen, but were intended to convert colonial Dissenters. William Livingston of New York wrote similarly. Anglican Charles Inglis furnished a rejoinder, vindicating the Bishop of Landaff's sermon. In 1768 Chauncey issued *The Appeal Answered ...,* and Chandler replied in 1769 with *The Appeal Defended....* Chauncey responded in 1770 with *A Reply to Dr. Chandler's "Appeal Defended ...,"* and in 1771 Chandler issued *The Appeal Farther Defended.* In the New York and Philadelphia newspapers a parallel debate was conducted in 1768-1769 between William Livingston and William Smith, Jr., the American Whig, and Francis Allison, the Sentinel, on the one side, and Samuel Seabury the younger, Charles Inglis, and Myles Cooper on the other. The latter, writing under the pseudonym "Timothy Tickle," produced "A Whip for the American Whig," and Dr. William Smith as "the Anatomist" answered "the Sentinel."[80] The voluminous details of these exchanges may be omitted here. The Anglican arguments were basically the same as Johnson and others had presented since 1723. The opposition likewise rehearsed its old fears of hierarchy, privilege and intolerance.[81] Unfortunately for the Anglicans, the renewed controversy came at a time of colonial opposition to the unpopular Townshend Acts, which threatened new taxes, and took other measures unpopular with the colonists. Thus American resistance to civil measures discouraged the ministry from risking more trouble in the ecclesiastical sphere.

Johnson noted that the Dissenters' time-worn tactics were all too successful; they gained their point "by meer dint of Clamour," as he wrote to Sir William Johnson in March 1768. And to William Samuel he reported in the following April that the "wicked Triumvirate of N. Y." had "beset Chandler most furiously, and without any more regard to the truth and right of the case, than the people of Newgate and Bedlam...." Those who so violently claimed "civil liberty for themselves, as violently plead the cause of tyranny against ecclesiastical liberty to others," he said. Such madness and malice might only be overridden by good sense and good-natured perseverance in answering them, and by men who would continue steadfastly to plead the Anglican cause to the home government. This, for the generally charitable Johnson, was strong language. He was convinced that the government's reluctance to act "seems to forbid all hopes for this century and probably till the millenium."[82]

Johnson himself did little in the way of writing polemics for the press, although he kept up his correspondence with friends and officials in Britain and supplied one of the answers to "the American Whig." To Archbishop Secker he observed in May 1768 that the furor was such that only God knew "What will be the end of these things ... May he overrule these untoward and unruly tempers to bring about the best good of the best of churches...."[83]

Aside from the political controversy and the mounting attack by Dissenters, the episcopal cause suffered other disadvantages. Sir William Johnson, for example, believed that the government had not seriously considered providing a bishop because the value of his offer of lands was not "justly known" in England. In August 1768 both Johnson and the American Church suffered a great loss. Secker, who in spite of his caution had been a real friend to the colonial Church, died, and was succeeded by Frederick Cornwallis, whose chief title to fame was his ostentatious social life.[84] In October of that year Johnson asked the Bishop of Oxford to help fill the gap by using his influence "to prepare as many as may be among the great and good to insist strongly, as soon as there can be any probability of success, that we may be provided for with bishops without which sacred order the Church in these parts must soon sink and become the contempt and triumph of her enemies."[85] A few days later he wrote to introduce himself to the new archbishop as "the oldest clergyman of the Church in America (now in my 73rd year) and extremely solicitous for its welfare and prosperity here...."[86] Johnson of course asked Cornwallis for his influence in the episcopal campaign, but he did not establish the kind of extensive connection with Cornwallis that he had enjoyed with Thomas Secker or other bishops and archbishops.

As we have seen, Chandler, Inglis, and Myles Cooper had now succeeded to a larger role in laboring for an American episcopate. They "planned and maneuvered, scribbled and pleaded, moving towards their goal by every available approach."[87] Again during 1770 and 1771 they tried to persuade the Maryland, Virginia, and Carolina clergy to support their efforts, as Johnson had so often insisted was necessary if the plan was ever to succeed – and with the usual lack of result. With Samuel Seabury, Jr., these three men became the most active leaders in the unending struggle, gradually eclipsing the leadership of Johnson and Connecticut Churchmen. Yet the Connecticut influence never disappeared entirely, for Johnson was constantly consulted.[88]

During the final year of Johnson's life the campaign slowly wound down, though a few moves were still made. Announcing that his latest defense against Charles Chauncey's attacks was ready for the press, Chandler wrote to Johnson in March 1771 that he expected the Virginia and Carolina clergy to concur in the appeal for bishops. If they would, Chandler believed it "impossible that our scheme should be longer frustrated," especially because "there never was an instance, in any age of the world ... in which such a reasonable and moderate request would have been refused to such a body of people, in such a situation, and in such a relation to the national establishment." But he also detected another note of the difficulty when he expressed sorrow that his writings had apparently met "with no better encouragement in Connecticut, where our friends used to be fond of reading every defense of the Church; but I suppose they are tired of the controversy," he said.[89]

In May 1771, the Connecticut clergy convention made another appeal for the episcopate to the Bishop of London. Reviewing the history of their labors, and expressing doubts whether any bishops would ever be sent to the colonies, they pledged to continue the campaign with an affirmation expressive of Samuel Johnson's perseverance:

> Should our application be judged unreasonable, we doubt not it will be remembered that necessity has no law. We believe Episcopacy to be of divine origin. We judge an American Episcopate to be essential, at least to the well-being of religion here. We therefore think it our duty to exert ourselves, in every proper way, to bring it into effect: and as we know of no way more harmless, nor any more likely to insure success, than importunate prayer to our God, to our King, and to our superiors, we believe it our duty to pray without ceasing, and hope our request will be answered in due time, if we faint not.[90]

By contrast, the Virginia clergy, meeting in June 1771, made a much feebler gesture. They rejected the idea of requesting the crown for a bishop, but agreed to ask the Bishop of London's advice about what to do, and established a committee to determine whether a majority of Virginia's clergy favored a petition to the king. Only about a dozen priests had attended the session, and they would not risk further action without a majority's support *and* Bishop Terrick's approval. The bishop had, however, already sanctioned such procedures. But the Virginia House of Burgesses was opposed. And when the New York and New Jersey clericus addressed the southerners, the Reverend Thomas Gwaitkin, professor of mathematics at the College of William and Mary, finally summarized the arguments of the Anglican opposition in 1772. The southerners professed no "aversion to Episcopacy in general, to the mode of it established in England, or even to an American Episcopate, introduced, at a proper time, by proper authority, and in a proper manner." But Gwaitkin, and too many others like him, opposed an "immediate establishment, from a prudential regard to the practicable, a desire to preserve peace, heal divisions, and calm the angry divisions of an enraged people."[91] The times never seemed right nor the manner proper enough to the uninterested or the faint-hearted. But the Dissenters suffered from no such division as they repeatedly succeeded in squelching every move that Anglicans made.

In October 1771, Auchmuty, Ogilvie, Inglis, and Chandler added the New York and New Jersey clergy's support to what their Connecticut brethren had done in May by writing Lord Hillsborough, now Secretary of State for the American colonies. They rehearsed the old reasons for the need of bishops with no jurisdiction over any but Anglicans. And they also warned against what was rapidly proving to be all too true. "Independency in Religion will naturally produce Republicanism in the State...."[92] Johnson had said this many times.

Writing what may have been his last letter to his old mentor in October 1771, Chandler indicated that Anglican efforts were still being made. Myles Cooper was going to England "partly as a missionary ... in order to convert the guardians of the Church from the errors of their ways." Chandler had written another pamphlet. It was an address from the New York and New Jersey clericus to their Virginia brethren to urge their support. Chandler wanted the names of the ten men (of sixty) who for want of bishops in America had crossed the Atlantic for ordination, only to be lost to disease and shipwreck. Such solid facts were strong arguments for the episcopal cause. As he had not heard from Johnson since early spring, Chandler wondered what the parson of Stratford thought of his "farther defense;" suspecting that Johnson's silence indicated that it was "not according to your mind," he regretted that his Elizabethtown residence rendered him unable to consult Johnson "about my papers before their publication...."[93] The latter statement suggests how much the center of activity had shifted from Connecticut, but it also reveals that the Connecticut influence could never be completely separated from the New York-New Jersey axis.

What may have been Samuel Johnson's last letter to England on the subject of episcopacy was written on November 1, 1771, to the Reverend John Parkhurst of Epsom, Surrey. An author of Hebrew and Greek grammars, Parkhurst shared with Johnson a common interest in the promotion of the study of ancient languages. Johnson had previously sent a manuscript of a Hebrew grammar to Parkhurst, who was to arrange for its publication. In this letter he commented that the bearer of the manuscript had been one of two candidates for holy orders who had recently perished at sea on their return voyage. Bemoaning their fate and that of his son William years earlier, Johnson observed how greatly American Churchmen had "suffered for want of bishops, and yet," he added, they could not "prevail for the removal of such a monstrous absurdity of being obliged to go a 1000 leagues for every ordination. Pray, Sir, pity and pray for us, and use all the influence as you have opportunity, towards our being relieved of this distress."[94] Two months later the great Connecticut champion of episcopacy was dead.

Johnson's struggle for the episcopate then ended in apparent failure. Three years after his death came the War of Independence – a war that Johnson, with his strong loyalty to the British Empire, would have opposed and hated. But this very catastrophe, as it seemed at the time, brought with it the result he desired. On the Feast of the Annunciation, March 25, 1783, ten Connecticut clergymen, all stalwart Johnsonians, met at Woodbury to elect the first American bishop. And that bishop was Samuel Seabury, Yale graduate, whom Johnson had sent to England with a letter of recommendation for ordination. The Diocese of Connecticut, Johnson's child, was thus the first American diocese to complete its organization. In June 1785, Seabury landed in America, a bishop in the apostolic succession. Johnson was dead, but his spirit lived on in Seabury and others who shared his convictions and who had directly benefitted from his good influences. Samuel Johnson had succeeded in his fight for an American episcopate.

Chapter XI

FOUNDING OF KING'S COLLEGE

1. The College in Embryo

The reputation of Columbia University as an illustrious center of learning reaches back to its beginning as King's College. Based in part on its boast of the services of a long succession of distinguished scholars, that renown originated with the man who began the school – without campus, buildings, endowment, or even much of a library. As first president of King's College, the mother of Columbia, Samuel Johnson was of the calibre required to create a good school and to set it on the road to greatness. Just as a college "acquires life through the lives of its members," so the "character of its vitality depends upon past generations."[1] Despite the apparently limited success of his presidency, Johnson's life gave life to King's College. The tracing of the influence of the generations after him is beyond our present concern; we are here trying to assess his actual contribution as a midwife at the birth of King's.

First, however, we must look briefly at the colony in which King's College was born. The colony of New York, unlike its bordering sisters of Massachusetts and Connecticut, made no pretense of being a theocracy. From the time of its formal erection into an English province in 1664 New York was, what it remains today, a kind of melting pot *par excellence*. Dutch, English, Jews, Huguenot French, Negroes, with their varying and often conflicting religions, made up its polyglot population. We have seen how, in New England, Anglicans were forced to fight for the barest toleration. In New York, on the contrary, Anglicans fought for something like control; sometimes, it must be admitted, their methods were not the most straightforward. There is just this much of truth in historians' allegations of "Anglican aggression."

By the middle of the eighteenth century, there were in New York two so-called political parties, usually designated "Anglican" and "Presbyterian." Better styled "factions," these colonial ruling groups were little more than loosely knit cliques of individuals in pursuit of political advantage, land grants and lucrative offices. The Names are somewhat misleading, and they were in no real sense religious groups. It happened that the De Lanceys were Anglicans and the heads of one faction, while the Livingstons, who led the opposition, were mostly Presbyterians. And both coteries used religious issues to conceal what was at bottom simply a struggle for power.[2] As we shall see, this partisan strife played a large part in the beginnings of King's College.

Long before Johnson came on the scene, other men had demonstrated interest in a college for New York. One was proposed as early as 1702 by Lewis Morris, lord of the manor of Morrisiana and vestryman of Trinity Church, New York. The vestry were interested, and the governor was asked for the use of part of the Queen's Farm for a college, but nothing came of this proposition. Dean Berkeley during his sojourn in Rhode Island at one time thought seriously of locating his proposed college in New York. But he could not get the Walpole ministry to hand over the necessary funds.[3] The time was not ripe.

By the 1740's, however, the northern provinces were full of enthusiasm for the funding of new colleges. This was partly due to the growing stability, posterity, and maturity of the colonies, partly to the impetus given religion by the Great Awakening, partly to the denominational rivalries which resulted from the Awakening. Thus the College of Philadelphia began in 1740 and the College of New Jersey in 1746. In New York the first actual move came in 1746 when college enthusiasts prompted the New York legislature to authorize a lottery, the proceeds to go toward the erection of a college. Evidently "The forwardness and activity of the gentlemen of Philadelphia in founding a college ... provoked the gentlemen of New York to emulation...."[4]

It is interesting to note, as Nicholas Murray Butler observed, that great intellectuals in the colonies took part in this movement to found colleges.[5] Benjamin Franklin was extremely active in the start of the College of Philadelphia, Jonathan Edwards was the third president of the College of New Jersey, and Samuel Johnson became first head of King's.

Johnson's role in the initial efforts to get King's started is difficult to trace, but as early as April 1747, he wrote Cadwallader Colden that he was pleased to learn that New Yorkers were resolved to found a school, and offered to do everything in his power to promote it. Colden, however, seemed more intent upon discussing philosophy.[6] George Berkeley, now Bishop of Cloyne, was more helpful. In August 1749, he responded to one of Johnson's requests for advice on the undertaking. He suggested that no charter or statute for creating a college be requested in England lest the business become troublesome, expensive, and dilatory. He proposed that the college begin with a president and two fellows. The curriculum should center on the Greek and Latin classics, but "the principal care must be good life and morals...." If the requirements for degrees were similar to those of Oxford and Cambridge, the new college would gain credit, and this would pave the way for admitting graduates *ad eundem* to degrees from the English universities. Students might be encouraged with small premiums in books, and a distinctive habit; the college quarters should be plain and cheap, but with a room for each student.[7] That Johnson agreed with much of Berkeley's advice is evident in the sequel.

By 1751 the college lottery had raised £3,443. In November 1751 the legislature created a board of ten trustees to manage this money, and empowered them to lend it out at interest until a site for the school had been selected. Of the ten trustees, seven were *ex officio*;they were three justices of the supreme court of the colony, the mayor of New York, the provincial treasurer, the speaker of the assembly, and the senior member of the governor's council. To these, three were added by name – William and James Livingston, and Benjamin Nicoll, Johnson's step-son. Seven of these were Anglicans, two Dutch Reformed, only one, William Livingston, was a Presbyterian.[8] This was asking for trouble.

Early in January 1752, the trustees offered to receive proposals for a site for the college.[9] We have noted that in 1704 the vestry of Trinity Church were interested in Lewis Morris's idea of a New York college. They were now ready to demonstrate their interest in a practical way. In March the vestry resolved to offer the trustees a part of the land known as the King's Farm. On April 8, the rector, Henry Barclay, met with the trustees to inform them of the action of the vestry. Although Trinity attached no conditions at this time to its offer, it seems to have been understood that the gift, valued at £7,000 New York currency, "would be a Means of obtaining some Priviledges to the Church."[10] On May 14, 1754, the vestry of Trinity took formal, more specific action. They unanimously agreed to give the incipient college a plot, which was fully described. It was to consist of:

> a street of ninety feet from the Broadway to Church Street and from Church Street all the lands between Barclay's Street and Murrays Street to the water side, upon this condition that the President of the said Colledge forever for the time being be a member of and in Communion with the Church of England, and that the Morning and Evening service in said Colledge be the liturgy of the said Church or such a Collection of Prayers out of said Liturgy as shall be agreed upon by the President and Trustees or governors of the said College.[11]

2. Conflict Begins

William Livingston, the lone Presbyterian on the board, and a bitter political enemy of Chief Justice James De Lancey, who supported the Anglican charter proposal, did not at once object to receiving the offer of Trinity Church. But when, in November 1752, it was proposed that the college be established by royal charter, and that Samuel Johnson have a joint appointment of president of the college and assistant minister of Trinity Church, he went into active and vocal opposition. Fearful of royal incorporation, he advocated control of the college by an act of the assembly, which he thought should provide the charter. And combining Presbyterian bias with Englightenment predilections against "universal priestcraft and Bigotry," he insisted that no religion should be taught, but that the students might read what books of divinity they pleased in their chambers. As for religious exercises, they should consist only of reading the Scriptures, and using prayer in which all Protestants might join. Livingston was convinced that if Anglicans controlled the college, they would ruin it or "the Country, and in fifty Years, no Dissenter however deserving, will be able to get into any office."[12]

Although Livingston's motives appear to have been religious and not political, politics, as always, got entoiled in religious arguments. And New York's political factions periodically used religious labels and prejudices to serve their partisan purposes. The Church of England was identified with the royal prerogative, personified by a royal governor. A royal charter for the college represented the governor's encroachment on legislative interests and power. Executive supporters regarded the legislature's activities as usurpatious of gubernatorial rights.

Livingston soon invented an engine of opposition to the Churchmen's proposals. On March 22, 1753, assisted by John Morin Scott and William Smith, Jr., fellow opponents of the De Lancey regime, he started an essay-journal called *The Independent Reflector*. Until November these attacks were continued. Eight essays in all were devoted to the college issue, and several others to related topics, such as prayer, the clergy, and creeds. For Protestant Dissenters, periodically alarmed by proposals to provide Anglican bishops in the colonies, and fearful that an episcopate must inevitably lead to Church establishment and more royalist influence, the college issue carried with it particularly dangerous implications. Adherents of Chief Justice De Lancey, who also held the lieutenant governorship (1753-1755, 1757-1760), supported the Anglican charter proposal, although many of them in the assembly were Dissenters, and as such, sympathized with Livingston's stand in *The Independent Reflector*.

The first of the *Reflector* essays, that of March 22, may stand as a fair sample of the rest. In it the writer not only voiced the suspicion that

Episcopalians sought to use the college as a buttress to their hierarchical system, but also called for a broader, more useful variety of education than one centered in religion and the classics. "The true Use of Education," *The Reflector* insisted, "is to qualify Men for the different Employments of Life...." Freedom of thought and candid inquiry were to be preferred to endless disputation of dogma. A week later the writer argued that a college must admit all varieties of Protestants and prevent any of them from preaching their own doctrines "enforced by the Authority of a Professor's Chair...." In short, if a college were "entirely managed by one Sect," there could be no safeguard against "tincturing the Minds of the Students with the Doctrines and Sentiments of that Sect."[13] And in order for a college to serve public purposes, it was clear to *The Reflector* that it must be dependent upon the representatives of the community – the colonial legislature. If the college was not to be an engine of party – a buttress to the royal executive and his ecclesiastical supporters – it must be chartered by the provincial assembly and not by the Crown acting through its vice-regal agent, the governor.

Successive issues of the paper, especially those of April 12, 19, and 26, elaborated upon these themes, explaining why the alarm raised about the college was justified, and how legislative incorporation would promote more generous donations and benefactions to the school. Appealing to the Dutch Reformed, Presbyterians, Quakers, Huguenots, Moravians, Lutherans, Anabaptists, and even Anglicans, *The Reflector* exhorted them to defeat the scheme by expostulating with their assembly representatives.[14]

But Livingston's approach to the college proposal was not merely a negative one. In the April 19 issue, he offered eleven points to be included in a legislative act to incorporate the college. The governor, the council and the assembly should jointly name the trustees, who were to serve at the pleasure of the appointers. No Protestant should be excluded because of his religious persuasion. The trustees should in turn name the president, who with them would appoint other officers of the college. The president and the trustees should make by-laws, subject to the approval of the legislature. The act of incorporation ought to include as many rules and directions for the college as could be foreseen as necessary.[15]

In regard to freedom of religion Livingston was emphatic. No particular form of religion or religious service should be established in the college, and both faculty and students might attend any Protestant church at their pleasure. The college should have morning and evening prayers, but these were to be non-denominational. There should be no professor of divinity; divinity should not be taught, and no degrees were to be conferred in that field. Teachers and students should have free access to all books in the library, but there must be no public disputations on theological subjects. Finally, the assembly was to maintain a close control of college affairs. Only thus could the college be kept from becoming "A Cage ... of every unclean Bird. – The Nursery of Bigotry and Superstition. – An Engine of Persecution, Slavery and Oppression."[16]

As might well have been expected, this strong language called for appropriate replies. Between April and October 1753, the Anglicans counter-attacked with essays in *The New-York Mercury*, and a short-lived paper called *John Englishman, In Defence of the English Constitution*.[17] The participants on the Anglican side were William Smith, Franklin's coadjutor in the foundation of the College of Philadelphia, the elder Samuel Seabury, James Wetmore of Rye, and Johnson himself. In June 1753, Johnson reported to the Archbishop of Canterbury, "We have several of us been writing in the church's defense against them and endeavoring not without some success to defeat their pernicious scheme."[18] The issue had become quite clearly wider than the relation of the Church to a college in embryo; it was closely related to the whole matter of Anglican advance in the northern colonies, an outreach and influence which were causing great alarm to the Dissenting interest. By the end of 1753 this flurry of paper war had pretty well died out. In November 1753, *The Reflector* came to an end, very likely because James De Lancey, now lieutenant governor, put pressure on James Parker, the printer. Parker depended upon the assembly for its patronage to him as public printer, and he alleged being threatened with a loss of business unless he stopped publishing the offensive paper.[19] In February 1754, Livingston managed to fire one last broadside; the Anglicans did not trouble to reply. Ten months passed without newspaper agitation over the college. The battle seemed to have been won, and Anglicans evidently assumed that De Lancey would provide a college charter on their own terms.

3. Negotiations with Johnson

Meantime, in July 1753 the New York Assembly took further steps to bring the college into reality. An act was passed to continue for nearly four years an excise duty. From this excise the trustees were to be paid £500 a year. The act allowed the trustees to pay the salaries of the "head of the seminary" and any other teachers or officers. As Livingston claimed, the measure virtually placed the college in Anglican hands, because seven of the ten trustees were Churchmen.[20]

Armed with the law, the trustees now began serious negotiations with Samuel Johnson, whom they knew was a well qualified educator. They also dealt with Chauncey Whittlesey of Yale, whom they planned to appoint as tutor. Johnson visited New York some time in the autumn of 1753, and no doubt consulted with the trustees. On November 22, they decided to make him a formal offer of the presidency, with a salary of £250, to begin on May 1, 1754. Recognizing that this stipend was "inadequate to his merit," the trustees relied upon the vestry of Trinity Church to help persuade Johnson to accept. In December some of the trustees who were also vestrymen arranged to name Johnson an assistant minister of Trinity with a salary of £150.[21]

By January 7, 1754, William Livingston had prepared the letter of the trustees to the Rector of Stratford, officially tendering him the post of "chief master or head of our seminary...." They apologized for the stipend, which they felt was inadequate, but appealed to Johnson's generosity and known interest in education. They would make no plan for curriculum until they had the benefit of the advice of both him and Whittlesey. They also sent Johnson a copy of the act of assembly which provided for the financing of the enterprise through the excise tax. Significantly, too, on January 7 *The New-York Gazette* carried an advertisement of a second lottery for founding the college.[22]

Johnson hesitated. On January 17 he answered the letter of the trustees, expressing his appreciation of the honor of being unanimously chosen to head the intended college, and he offered his best wishes for the project. But he feared that his "advanced years, verging apace towards the decline of life," his lack of immunity to smallpox, and his duty to his dear people at Stratford, together with the importance of his virtual leadership of the Church in Connecticut, would not incline him to accept. He asked for time to deliberate and to consider who might succeed him at Stratford. He feared that the stipends from the trustees and from Trinity Church might not be adequate to the cost of living in New York City. As it was questionable whether his agreement with the trustees would hold good, once a legal college corporation was set up by charter, he was "unwilling to part with a certainty for an uncertainty." He therefore declined appointment until the college was duly incorporated.[23]

Johnson's New York friends brought the matter to a head by stating frankly that they felt the prestige of his name was essential to the existence of the college, and that unless he would assume the presidency they would throw up the project. This appeal to Johnson's strong sense of duty had effect. He agreed to go to New York "by the middle of April and make a trial but would not absolutely accept till the Charter should be passed and he should see what sort of college it was to be."[24]

At the end of March, Johnson made his semi-annual report to the secretary of the S. P. G. He announced his intended visit to the trustees, "in order to consider the matter more nearly...." He suggested that John Beach might be his successor in Stratford, but until such a successor could be found, his parish could be served by neighboring clergy and by his son William as lay reader.[25] Apparently, his mind was pretty well made up.

4. Johnson Takes Over

Johnson set out from Stratford on April 15, 1754, determined to make his trial of the as yet unchartered college. Whittlesey had finally declined appointment as tutor; therefore, for the time being Johnson must work single-handed. By May 16 he and the trustees had prepared a draft of a charter, constituting the college, and providing that a building be erected on the land offered by Trinity Church. The trustees also accepted the church's offer of its vestry room as a temporary place for instruction, and agreed that Johnson's salary should begin from the time he left Stratford. Tuition was set at twenty-five shillings per quarter. William Livingston of course raised objections, which he embodied in a twenty-point argument, but to no avail.[26]

Before proceeding further, the trustees sent two of their number to wait on Lieutenant Governor De Lancey. They received his permission to offer a petition for a royal charter. The charter petition proposed that in consideration of the gift of land from Trinity Church, the head of the college should be a member of the Church of England, and that the daily services of the college should be the liturgy of the Church or prayers taken out of the liturgy. There was to be a board of governors to regulate the college and to appoint its officials.[27]

On May 20 the trustees approved the petition. Livingston naturally objected vigorously, again bringing forward his twenty points. Among these the following were perhaps the major ones. The college's use of Anglican liturgy was "a manifest encroachment on the rights and privileges" of the King's dissenting subjects, and especially objectionable because all inhabitants of the province, not merely the Anglican minority, contributed to the support of the college by assembly legislation. Livingston argued that Trinity Church's gift of land had been unconditional; technically this was correct, but Churchmen had acted on an assumption that the college would be suitably linked to the Church as the charter petition now proposed; the trustees, Livingston went on, had no power to accept a condition without consent of the legislature, nor even to fix the location of the school – but only to receive proposals subject to the legislature's decision. Moreover, a Churchman as president would tend "to raise animosities ... by introducing a discrimination of privileges," whereas the trustees' authority did not allow for prescribing any such religious test. Dissenters would likely send their children – and their money – out of the province for their education, rather than enroll them in a Church college. And above all, any charter ought to come from the legislature which had passed the acts for raising funds for a college and naming trustees in the first place.[28]

But Livingston was over-ruled. On May 28, 1754, the trustees formally presented the petition to the lieutenant governor and his council. Again Livingston, with the support of James Alexander and William Smith, Jr., his fellow Presbyterians on the council, opposed the measure, but once more he lost out.[29] It is worthy of note that the two Dutch Reformed trustees did not join him in opposition. In fact, all through this period of contest the Dutch Reformed Church, although the largest in the colony, seems to have raised no objection to the manifest advantage the Anglicans were gaining.

Despite the willingness of Lieutenant Governor De Lancey to grant a college charter, the business was delayed. Johnson summed up the situation as of the end of May in a letter to his son William Samuel:

> All that is wanted of the Assembly is to vest the lottery money in the corporation to be made by the charter, which as there are but two Presbyterians and two or three corrupted Dutchmen and one English, they [the trustees] do not doubt it will pass; but this they say is not at all necessary for my security with regard to the salary which is already vested in the trustees by the Assembly for seven years, and they are ready to give me any security, and the Reflectors none of them object anything to me, only that they would not have it confined forever to the Church that the head must be of that Communion, and the prayers of our Liturgy.[30]

Johnson thought that Trinity Church's gift of £7,000 worth of land on the conditions aforementioned would force the assembly to yield. He was not ready to resign his Stratford rectorate, however, lest untoward developments leave him with neither the college post nor his old parochial cure. Still, Johnson rather expected the college project would succeed; he was reassured that the lieutenant governor treated him so kindly, and was certain "of his interests and approbation." Moreover, he was comforted by being "universally treated with great kindness and respect...." But the move for a royal charter now suffered a delay until autumn. Johnson's son William thought the New York Churchmen were comparable "to the man's fine race horse – he had every good quality only he wanted courage!" But nothing would be "safe till the Assembly have passed the charter."[31]

When William Livingston's protest against the charter was printed for public circulation, Johnson wrote both his sons on June 10, wishing they might find time to write a reply to it. A lawyer's paper deserved a lawyer' s answer.[32] But William Samuel declined to write it.

"You know," he replied, "I am generally averse to disputes of this kind, as tending more to irritate the passions than to convince the understandings of the people." Polemical essays tended to be read only by persons already firmly committed to one side or another of an issue. Moreover, he wisely warned his father that as head of the college, Samuel should do nothing to suggest that he was the head of a party, lest it compromise his position.[33] In the end, when an answer to Livingston's protest was published in December 1754, it was written by Johnson's step-son, Benjamin Nicoll, as "A Brief Vindication of the Proceedings of the Trustees Relating to the College."[34] As a trustee and a lawyer, Nicoll was perhaps the proper person to carry on the fray.

By the time Nicoll issued the "Vindication" the college had received a charter. He deplored those who persisted in "kindling the fire of dissension," and pooh-poohed the alarms raised against a pretended Anglican plot against New Yorkers' liberty and property. Were not the trustees, most of them Anglicans to be sure, honest men? Why else had they been appointed? Were they not interested in the liberty, property and the welfare of their fellow citizens? New York had too long neglected education, yet the trustees, like the assembly, were interested in promoting it. By contrast, the abusive and audacious *Reflector* had raised clamors "against priests and priest-craft," only to "set the different sects of Christians at variance with the Church of England, and to embarrass and obstruct the affairs of the college … that in the interim the favorite College of New Jersey … might take such root, as not easily to be hurt" by anything New York might do to erect a college for itself. After reviewing in detail the history of the college movement from the 1753 excise act (for applying funds to the college) to the issuance of the charter in 1754, Nicoll pointed out that the New York Legislature must have assumed that the Crown would issue the charter and that it was reasonable for the trustees to proceed to ask for it. The lottery acts had, after all, merely provided the funds, and did not even "hint how and in what manner the said college should be founded…." Was it not the Crown's "sole right" by law to create bodies politic? The trustees had "done nothing but what they had a right to do …" – to "begin the education of youth, to pay masters, and conduct and regulate a seminary of learning;" as they had no authority to make rules and orders, they reasonably proceeded to ask for a charter under which such regulations could be made. Next, Nicoll dealt with Livingston's protest by alleging that his "twenty curious and finespun reasons against a charter" were unanswerable because "nobody ever thought they deserved, or required an answer." Livingston had set up a straw man, "a mere chimera ... of his own over-heated brain," which he called "Trinity-Church-College." Anyone could read the charter to see that Trinity Church had no authority in the corporation. (Of course some of its laymen had been trustees and were governors.) And could any reasonable man suppose that the college corporation members had "any design against the liberties and privileges of a province, in which their whole fortunes lie...?" Closing his paper, Nicoll expressed the hope that "every impartial and honest man" would agree to "unite our interest and vigorously oppose those, who under a false pretense of patriotism, are endeavoring to throw all into confusion, in order to answer private purposes and views detrimental and destructive to the public good."[35]

In the meantime Johnson had gone to work making plans for opening school. From the end of May to July 1754 he advertised in *The New York Gazette* that he would examine candidates for entrance each Tuesday and Thursday from 9 to 12 A. M. Actually teaching was to begin on July 1 in the vestry room of Trinity Church's new school house. Admission requirements included the ability "to read well, and write a good legible hand;" knowledge of the "first five rules in arithmetic on as far as division and reduction;" a good knowledge of Latin and Greek grammar with the ability to give a good account of two or three of Tully's orations; the first books of the *Aeneid*, and the first chapters of the Gospel according to St. John in Greek. Johnson carefully endeavored to quiet fears about religion, and in his own moderate style he replied to William Livingston's exaggerated charges against the influence of Churchmen in the college; "there is no intention," Johnson announced, "to impose on the scholars the peculiar tenets of any particular sect of Christians; but to inculcate upon their tender minds, the great principles of Christianity and morality in which true Christians of each denomination are generally agreed." As for morning and evening worship, the collegians would have lessons, prayers, and praises of the liturgy of the Church, as are, for the most part, taken out of the Holy Scriptures," and such as the trustees would agree upon. Everyone would be left to judge particular doctrines for himself. Reminiscent of his recent quarrel with President Clap of Yale was the provision that each student would attend Sunday services of whatever church his parent or guardian selected.[36]

It must be emphasized that in Johnson's day there was a general acceptance of the notion that education must be linked to religion, and more particularly that schools not only ought to teach religion and morality, but also that some form of religious service was a proper part of the college regimen. It was rather unusual for anyone to propose, as Livingston did, that no doctrinal material of a particular body of Christians be taught. Yet even Livingston admitted that there should be general services of worship in which all Protestant Dissenters could participate along with Anglicans. He took a dim view of Johnson's advertisement that "The chief thing that is aimed at in this College is to teach and engage the children to know God in Jesus Christ, and to love and serve Him...."[37] This sounded to him like promoting the interests of the Church of England and its natural ally, the Crown, as against the general voice and interests of the people represented in the colonial assembly.

The final part of Johnson's advertisement for opening the New York school included the profession that the college would not only "instruct and perfect youth" in the traditional, classical disciplines, but would also offer training in more utilitarian subjects such as surveying, navigation, geography, husbandry, commerce and government, and in "the knowledge of all nature in the heavens above us, and in the air, water and earth around us ..., and of everything useful for the comfort, the convenience and elegance of life...." Everything, however, must lead the students "to the knowledge of themselves, and of the God of nature, and their duty to Him, themselves, and one another...." Upon such an ambitious undertaking Johnson prayed God "it may be attended with all the success" the public could wish for; for his part, he pledged to "contribute my endeavors to the utmost of my power...."[38]

5. The College Opens

During the first week of July 1754, Johnson admitted eight pupils to the still unchartered college. The trustees had ordered the academic year to begin on the second Tuesday in May, but they were forced to permit the delay of actual instruction until July 17. "The Matricula or Register of Admissions and Graduations" gives the following list of students at the opening, with typical notations about their subsequent status. They were:

> Samuel Verplanck [B. A. 1758]
>
> Rudolph Ritzema [B. A. 1758]
>
> Phillip Coutland [B. A. 1758]
>
> Robert Bayard – After about two years he went into The Army.
>
> Samuel Provo[o]st [B. A. 1758]
>
> Thomas Marston – After about 2 years he went to merchandize.
>
> Henry Cruger – After about 3 years he went to England.
>
> Joshua Blenmore [Bloomer, B. A. 1758][39]

It is noteworthy that Ritzema was the son of the senior minister of the Dutch Reformed Church. That his father sent him to King's is further evidence of the good relations between Anglicans and Dutch Reformed during this period of religious strife. Provoost became the first bishop of New York and proved himself a Churchman of a far different stripe from Johnson.

Johnson thus began tuition in the vestry room of Trinity Church. The work was interrupted between September 1 and November 10, when he felt compelled to return to Stratford because of the dangerous illness of his eldest son.[40] But the president was indefatigable despite distractions.

Ever since he had been subject to the bare bones offered at the Collegiate School at Saybrook Johnson had been thinking about college curricula. During his brief period as tutor at New Haven he had been a curriculum reformer. Now, having matured his ideas, he was free to put them into practice. Instruction for the first year students evidently followed the lines laid out in the laws and orders of the college adopted in June 1755. These, of course, were Johnson's handiwork, and they were an elaboration of his 1720 views on "The Best

Method" of college studies. Latin and Greek classics, Hebrew for ministerial students, rhetoric, geography, and chronology were first year studies. During the second and third years the subjects were logic, mathematics, mathematical and experimental philosophy, together with agriculture and merchandise, "something of the classics and criticism all the while." Fourth year classes studied metaphysics, logic, moral philosophy, principles of law and government, and history, sacred and profane. One textbook that we know was used in King's College during Johnson's tenure and for a short time thereafter was his own *Elementa Philosophica*, which had been first published by Franklin in 1752 and in a third edition in England by 1754.[41] This was very much a reformed curriculum. The learned languages still held a prominent place, but Johnson had added to them a considerable amount of science, history, and what would be called today vocational courses.

Johnson was troubled of course in opening the first academic year without a firm foundation on which to build his work. The charter having "passed in council" was "preparing for the seals," he wrote Thomas Sherlock, the Bishop of London, on July 6. But the question of the assembly's approval remained unsettled, and the school needed its financial support if it was ever to advance beyond the stage of an embryo. Johnson could only deplore the "most virulent and active faction of Presbyterians and Freethinkers" who busily agitated against the proposed charter. If the Dutch Reformed inhabitants remained "steady in their union" with the Churchmen, he could hope for assembly endorsement of the school. William Livingston, however, was carefully organizing the opposition in preparation for the autumn session of the assembly. By August assemblymen were receiving petitions against granting "any further fund for the college till its constitution and government be settled by an act of legislation." Churchmen were "making interest with the members, to nod over the affair, and leave it to the management of the trustees." To one correspondent Livingston snidely observed that most of Dr. Johnson's students were admitted "though utterly unqualified, in order to make a flourish." Meeting for morning prayers in Trinity Church, they "are like to make as great progress in the liturgy as in the sciences," he sneered. As for Johnson's advertisement promising to "teach the knowledge of all nature in the heavens above us," Livingston scoffed, "Whether he intends to descend as low as he soars on high, and conduct his disciples to the bottom of Tartarus, he doth not inform the public."[42]

By Monday, November 4, 1754, however, Henry Barclay had great news for Johnson, who was still at the bedside of his son in Stratford.

> On Thursday last the charter passed the Governor and Council, and was ordered to be forthwith engrossed. On Friday, the trustees appointed by act of assembly, according to the order of the House, delivered in a report of their proceedings conformable to the act, which report was signed by all but William Livingston, who objected to the report as not being complete, because no notice was taken of the proceedings with regard to the charter, which the Governor and the rest of the gentlemen thought unnecessary. Whereupon Livingston delivered in a separate report in full, containing his famous protest, etc ... We were all afraid that this would have retarded the sealing of the charter, and some well-wishers to the thing would have consented to the retarding of it, had not the Governor appeared resolute and come to town on Saturday and fixed the seal to it; and to do him justice, he has given us a good majority of churchmen, no less than eleven of the vestry [of Trinity Church] being of the number. There are but eight of the Dutch Church, most of them good men and true, and two Dissenters.[43]

The Board of Governors, which would now take the place of the trustees, numbered forty-two. Seventeen of these were *ex officio*; heading the list were the Archbishop of Canterbury and the Earl of Halifax. Included were various provincial officers. But also ex officio were the senior minister of the Dutch Reformed Church, and the Huguenot, Lutheran, and Presbyterian ministers. William Livingston was a member. Although Anglicans were safely in command, every religious group had representation and a chance to speak its mind. This was not true of contemporary Yale.

Although the charter (dated October 31) was duly sealed on November 2, Johnson was horrified when late in the same month the opposition "went so far as to draw up and print a form of Charter and offer it to the Assembly, wherein not even Christianity itself, was to have any preference to any other, or to no religion at all; and no sort of religion was to be taught in the college for fear of prejudice; though the boys were to be encouraged to dispute all points of religion pro and con, etc."[44] This proposal was accompanied by the usual barrage of pamphlets from the Livingstonians, and Churchmen rushed into print with counter-arguments, Johnson maintaining his usual silence. The newspaper war continued well into 1755, and William Samuel suggested that his father consider carefully whether he ought not to "retire from this bustle and racket" and return to Stratford where his parishioners earnestly wished him to continue his ministry.[45] Johnson, however, was determined to stand by the college. In the end the assembly laid by their draught, and no more was heard of it. "However, they stood it out," as Johnson said, "against granting the money...."[46]

One further provision of the charter as issued by the governor and council must be noted. In consideration of the gift of land by Trinity Church for a building, it was provided that the president of the college "for the time being, shall for ever hereafter be a member of ... the Church of England, as by law established...."[47] Johnson was also listed as a governor by reason of his presidential office. So far, Livingston had failed completely in his attack on the college. The charter had been issued, and not by the assembly. The Board of Governors had a secure Anglican majority. Johnson was firmly seated in the president's chair. But Livingston persevered. A frontal attack having failed, he would move against the enemy's flank. The college, if it was to succeed, must have money, and money could only be appropriated by the assembly. The £500 a year from the excise was secure. But with the lottery funds, the case was otherwise. Eventually, in December 1756, the assembly compromised; the quarreling interests then agreed to divide the lottery monies between the college and New York City. The latter used its share to build a jail and a house of detention for infected seamen. William Smith wryly observed that the accommodation consisted of dividing the money "between the two pest houses." Thus "Anglicans secured their charter college but without [further] public support." The opposition "failed to secure their free college but denied the Episcopalians sanction for their own."[48]

By December 1754, Johnson felt sufficiently sure of his position to resign his place in Stratford. On December 3, he wrote the Secretary of the S. P. G. doing so. Lacking a president's house, which he hoped would be provided in 1755, Johnson decided to lodge with his stepson, Benjamin Nicoll, for the winter.[49]

6. The Governors Act

The governors adopted the college's first laws and orders on June 3, 1755, when the second academic year began. The six articles indicate clearly the calibre of Johnson's leadership for they are obviously the product of his mind. The article on admissions specified entrance requirements such as Johnson had advertised in 1754, and every entering student was required to sign a copy of the college rules to signify his acquaintance with them.[50] Article two, "Of Graduation," specified an examination at the end of the fourth year of study, and about six weeks before commencement, which was set as the second Wednesday in May. The degree of Master of Arts might be conferred on the holders of the bachelor's degree who "diligently pursued their studies for three years" after graduating, provided they had been "guilty of no gross immorality...." Only the college governors could waive these terms under extraordinary circumstances, and for each degree granted the recipient must "pay a pistole to the president."[51]

The article on moral behavior stipulated what offenses merited fines, admonition, or the ultimate punishment of expulsion if the offender proved contumacious. There was admonition for drunkenness, fornication, lying, theft, swearing or cursing, frequenting houses of ill fame or keeping company with persons of known scandalous behavior. There were fines for fighting cocks, playing cards, dice, or any unlawful game, fighting, maiming, slandering or grievously abusing any person. Those guilty of dilapidations to the college or injury to anyone's person or property must make good all damages. Related to this article was another concerning "Behavior towards Authority and Superiors." Here, too, were Samuel Johnson's views of order and decency. Students who were disobedient, insulting, disrespectful, or contemptuous in their language might be fined up to five shillings for the first offense, and had to submit to "open admonition and confession...." If they persisted in such behavior, expulsion would follow.

All students must treat the president and all other superiors "as common decency, and good breeding require, such as rising, standing, uncovering the head, preserving a proper distance and using the most respectful language...." Failure to do so would bring punishment at the discretion of the president, the tutors or the governors.[52]

Article six described the "College Exercises and Due Attendance." It included the curriculum as previously outlined, required declamations and dissertations, fines for improper behavior during recitations, attendance at study, prayers and meals. No one was to leave his chambers except for these purposes or except by permission of the president or tutors. The stated vacations were the month after commencement, one week at Michaelmas, a fortnight at Christmas, and Good Friday to Friday in Easter week.[53]

In article three Johnson spelled out the requirements for public worship. Admonitions and ultimately expulsion threatened anyone who did not "behave with the utmost decency at public worship, or in the hall." That meant no "talking, laughing, justling, winding, etc."[54] Here, too, Johnson endeavored to satisfy critics like William Livingston. Although there were morning and evening services, read every day by the president or one of the tutors, they were variations of Morning and Evening Prayer from *The Book of Common Prayer*. Included was "A Prayer Peculiar to the College." Actually it was a series of prayers: one for divine blessing on the students' endeavors, a collect for the day or the season, and any of the occasional prayers (as for the *embertides*), a general intercession for "all sorts and conditions of men" which came from *The Book of Common Prayer*, as did the prayer of St. Chrysostom and "the grace."[55] Johnson's college prayer reflected the peculiarities of his composition, but like most eighteenth century prayers, it was a bit long. Yet so saturated was he with the style of the beloved English liturgy that his product stands up well beside the masterly liturgical craftsmanship of Archbishop Cranmer.

7. The Second Year

The second academic year opened in May 1755 with six more students admitted to the college. Johnson's son William, Master of Arts of Yale College, was appointed as fellow or assistant tutor.[56] As the president proceeded to implement the college regimen he had devised, he was comforted by having settled his wife and family in New York. They had arrived on May 9 after a sea voyage from Connecticut. "The confusion and trouble of packing and moving" were over, and "the prospect relating to the college" was no longer so dark. Indeed the future of the college seemed promising. The Dutch Reformed minister had persuaded several of his laymen of the college's merit, so that Johnson now thought the institution had a majority in the assembly for its support. He was perhaps too sanguine; there were still many difficulties to overcome, the chief being now financial. But a subscription for the school building was being planned, and at least he was head of a college in being.[57]

Chapter XII

Praeses Collegii Regis

1. A New Governor and Patron

The opening of the second year of King's College, in May 1755, found Johnson securely seated in his place as president. He now felt sure enough of his position to move his family to New York. The college organization was complete, with its predominantly Anglican Board of Governors, but its policy was to be comparatively tolerant. The anti-college furor was slowly dying down, though it was not yet at an end. In mid-May, Johnson wrote William Samuel that within a week or ten days past, affairs had "surprisingly taken a very favorable turn." Two of the Board of Governors, Henry Beekman and Philip Verplanck, men whose very names were redolent of the old Dutch stock of the colony, were men of great weight in the assembly, who having "not before appeared very well affected ... seem now very hearty...." The Dutch Reformed minister had persuaded several of his laymen that the college should have their support, "so that we have now a majority in the House...."[1]

Johnson was a little over-enthusiastic. There were still many difficulties to overcome. At the end of October 1755 he wrote the Bishop of London, "Our infant college goes on very heavily – partly by reason of the difficulties of the times, we being here in a state of war [the

Great War for the Empire, 1754-1763], and partly through the violent opposition that continues to be made to it by an importunate clamorous faction." By the narrowest of majorities the assembly had postponed the college governors' petition for the lottery funds; they now had "little hopes of ever obtaining that money [nearly £5,000] and see no other way now" to build the college "but by subscription … which will probably raise 2000 or 2500 pounds and we are about beginning to build;" because this would be insufficient, Johnson asked the help of friends in England and the West Indies.[2]

But there were also happier prospects. In the fall of 1755 James De Lancey, who had served for two years as acting governor of New York, was replaced by the new appointment from England of Sir Charles Hardy. Sir Charles had hardly landed when the persevering William Livingston saw that he was presented with an address attacking the young institution. The result is best told in Johnson's letter of December 12 to William Samuel:

> We seem to have good hopes of a kind friend to the church and college in our new governor. You will see our address and his answer next post. When upon my reading our address to him, he gave his answer into my hand, he told me he understood there was a subscription paper about and he would gladly see it. Yesterday Oliver [De Lancey] and I went to wait on him with it … behold when he came to put to paper it was to our surprise not 2 or 3 but no less than 500 [pounds] that he put down, and today behold the astonishment in all faces, of joy on our side and confusion on the Presbyterians. This gives us to hope that our subscription will now go on vigorously and rise handsomely and even that the assembly may yet before it rises grant us the 5000....[3]

Despite all disappointments, Johnson was the eternal optimist. This last hope, as we have seen, was not to be fulfilled, but at least the college was eventually to get half of the lottery money. Sir Charles continued to be a good friend to the college as long as he was governor. In the preceding May the Board of Governors had determined that the college was now strong enough to proceed with its building program, and set up a subscription list to provide funds for this purpose.

It was to this list that the governor had contributed his five hundred pounds. Encouraged by this, the Board began to buy building materials. Just about the time the new governor arrived, the president's son William left. We have seen him acting as tutor to the college, but he had a strong vocation to the priesthood, and his father was the last man in the world to stand in the way of that. Johnson planned that when William returned in priest's orders, the S. P. G. would appoint him to a Westchester vacancy, close to his father. He was replaced as tutor by Leonard Cutting, a young graduate of Cambridge University, who proved highly acceptable.[4] At first, everything went well with William in England. He was confirmed by the Bishop of Oxford, and ordained deacon a few weeks later in Fulham Palace chapel. On Lady Day, March 25, 1756, he was ordained priest by the Bishop of Carlisle. In May and June he was made Master of Arts by both Oxford and Cambridge Universities. And then, as in the parallel case of Daniel Browne, came tragedy. Smallpox, that bane of Johnson's existence, struck, and on June 20 William died. The grief of the father, with his strong attachment to his sons, may well be imagined. It found expression in his letters to William Samuel.[5] But Johnson was a Christian and a priest, and his firm belief in immortality sustained him in his trial.

2. The Third and Fourth years of the College

The third year of King's College opened brightly in May 1756. The opposition to the institution had died down. Twelve new students were admitted, so that both Johnson and Cutting had their hands full with their teaching responsibility. Having disposed of his house and lot in Stratford, in May Johnson moved his family into a house in Spring Garden, convenient both to the college and to Trinity Church, where he took some services.[6] Meanwhile, construction on the college building had begun.

On the afternoon of August 23, 1756, Governor Hardy laid the cornerstone of the new college building. A procession, which included Lieutenant Governor De Lancey, Johnson, the Board of Governors, Tutor Cutting, and the entire student body, marched to the site "near the river on the northwest side of the city...." After Sir Charles had laid the stone, marked with a Latin inscription, toasts were drunk to the governor, to the prosperity of the college and the advancement of true religion, loyalty and learning under Hardy's administration, and to the King and the success of his arms in the war then raging. Johnson delivered a short congratulatory speech in Latin, and closed with a prayer that the college might be ever enriched by God's blessing, and that it might "increase and flourish and be carried to its entire perfection; and to the glory of His name, to the advancement of His true religion and good literature, and to the greatest advantage of the public weal, to all posterities forevermore." The governors and pupils each laid a piece of the foundation. The affair ended with "a very elegant Dinner, after which all the usual loyal Healths were drunk, and Prosperity to the College; and the whole was conducted with the utmost Decency and Propriety."[7]

But after this climax came anti-climax. All of Johnson's joy with the progress of the college was turned into mourning. On September 12 he received word of William's death in far off England.[8] In November 1756, smallpox broke out in New York. Johnson's panic fear of the dread disease had been strengthened, if possible, by William's death. Furthermore, it had been stipulated in his original agreement to take over the presidency, that if smallpox broke out in the city he was allowed to leave. He now exercised his right, and fled to Westchester with his family. Welcomed by the De Lanceys, he stayed with them over a year.[9]

As there were now about thirty students in the college, spread over three classes, Cutting, thus left deserted, could not manage the situation, especially when the fourth academic year brought eleven more students to the rolls.[10] The Board of Governors therefore employed Daniel Treadwell, a young man recently graduated from Harvard, to whom they gave the resounding title of Professor of Mathematics and Natural Philosophy. He took office on November 1, 1757, teaching the subjects indicated in his title and also Latin and Greek to the freshmen. For this he was paid one hundred pounds a year, provincial currency. The vestry room which had served from the beginning as the schoolroom of the college was now too small for the purpose, and Cutting was obliged to take his classes in his own lodgings.

Johnson was not the man to sit idle in his Westchester refuge. He took one private pupil, for he must teach. He continued his usual avid reading, particularly the Scriptures in the original.[11] But he also found one other great area of usefulness. The parish of St. Peter's, Westchester, was one of the oldest in the colony, and had been a strong parish. But the current incumbent, the Reverend Thomas Standard, was old and ailing. At the end of 1757 Johnson wrote to the secretary of the S. P. G., describing the situation, and what he had done:

> Dr. Standard lives at East Chester, another parish of his where he makes a shift to officiate now and then, but he is so infirm that he scarce ever expects to see this parish again. Wherefore that I might not be useless in this interim I have been officiating for him here, and I hope not without some good effect. Religion was sunk to a very low ebb indeed. There were but one man and four women communicants at the first communion, at the last there were five men and seven women, and the congregation are much increased.[12]

Thus Johnson was able to fill the very vacancy he had designed for his dead son, and shortly after he left, a new priest was sent from England to carry on. In March 1757, he was cheered by the news that William Samuel had a daughter, and he was therefore a grandfather. Though he had hoped for a grandson, the president decided that "In these evil days ... the tender sex are by much the best of the two, be sure they seem so in these parts."[13]

In May 1757 the fourth year of King's College opened, with the president still absent.[14] Eleven more students were enrolled. College finances were looking up. A Mr. Murray had given the remainder of his estate to the college, and Johnson thought this would amount to seven or eight thousand pounds. He also anticipated from the subscription list some £3500 additional. This would pay salaries and go a long way toward the completion of the building.

The lot given by Trinity Church for the college building lay on the west side of Broadway, at Barclay Street, and faced the Hudson River. On this it was proposed to erect a structure in the traditional form of a quadrangle surrounding an area one hundred feet square. On one side were to be a chapel, a hall, and a library. The plan called for a structure 180 feet by 30 and three stories high. Johnson expected that it would be finished in the summer of 1758. The rest would require the assistance of friends in England, but a solicitation was retarded because of what Johnson called the "difficulty of the present times." His references to the Great War for the Empire were generally passing ones, but it is easy to sense the impact it had on the college's affairs.[15]

3. Return to New York

The Johnsons spent the winter of 1757-58 at Westchester. In January 1758, evidently during a visit to New York, Johnson solicited books for the college library from a Reverend Dr. Bristow of London, who (Johnson had heard) was interested in such a donation.[16] Bristow, in fact, gave his library to the S. P. G., suggesting that it might give the books to King's or other such institutions. Years passed before the college received any of the bequest, and evidently not all of it was forthcoming. Yet Johnson was not one to miss a likely opportunity.[17] Meantime, he turned to the new Archbishop of Canterbury, Thomas Secker. It was politic to solicit Secker's patronage not only for the colonial Church but for the infant college.[18] The college governors followed suit in 1758 by petitioning the Bishop of London and the Earl of Halifax. Reporting their progress in pushing the cause of higher education, they suggested the need of "the charitable assistance of our mother country;" the S. P. G. was also asked for help. Of course the Earl was expected to aid them because he was "one of the first members" of the corporation named in the charter, and also because he had "extensive influence in the state," was interested in the colonies, and was deemed a person of "beneficent disposition, and public spirit" – or so the governors imagined and flattered."[19]

In March 1758 Johnson and his family returned to New York. All winter Charity had been ill, and now she grew worse in spite of all the physicians could do. Describing her feverish suffering to William Samuel on May 29, Johnson seemed resigned to her imminent death and Johnson bade his son hurry his arrival "as you may chance to be here before her funeral...." He warned William to beware of contracting small pox in the vicinity of New Rochelle and Kingsbridge, "where you may do well to have some tar to smell to, and tobacco in your mouth … Take care, dear son," he pleaded, "you do not overdo yourself. You are now my all in effect."[20]

Charity died on June 1, and her body was interred in the chancel of Trinity Church. Poor Charity. She and Johnson had been happily married for over thirty-two years. She had brought him a sizable dowry; she had managed his house well; she had found hospitality for students, friends, casual visitors; she had borne him two sons. She had been a good wife, and Johnson was genuinely grieved. But she remains a shadowy figure, always efficient, always in the background.

Charity's death delayed the first commencement of the college, which was held, not in May, but on June 21. Johnson was gratified that "the whole process was attended with much applause and followed with an elegant entertainment." His joys seemed often to be mingled with sorrow.[21] The graduates numbered eight bachelors of arts, and thirteen masters – a strange difference until one recalls that both in England and America at this period the master's degree did not pre-suppose a year of graduate study, but was usually given *honoris causa*. Of the eight bachelors, five – Verplanck, Ritzema, Van Cortlandt, Provoost, and Bloomer – were of the original freshman class; the other three were transfers.

The recipients of the master's degree were the two tutors, Cutting and Treadwell, and seven "ministers and others." Three of these were fellow priests of the Anglican Church, whom Johnson had been instrumental in sending into the ministry – Isaac Browne, Thomas Bradbury Chandler, and Ebenezer Punderson.[22]

"The Order of Holding Commencement" was compiled by Johnson and reported in full in *The New-York Mercury* on June 26. From the vestry room of Trinity Church the academic procession moved to the recently built St. George's Chapel, where the exercises were held. In the procession were:

> The President, with his Honor the Lieutenant Governor, who, by his presence graced the Solemnity, were preceded by the candidates for Bachelor's and Master's Degrees, with their Heads uncovered, and were followed by the Governors of the college, the clergy of all denominations in this

city, and other gentlemen of distinction of this and the neighboring provinces.[23]

After the opening prayers Johnson delivered "a learned and elegant *Oratio Inauguralis*" from the pulpit. Then the students displayed their talents. The bachelors' exercise was begun by Samuel Provoost, later Bishop of New York. It proved so engaging that he won "the admiration and applause of all present." Then the undergraduates disputed a metaphysical thesis, and Philip Van Cortlandt gave a "genteel English oration, on the advantages of a liberal education...." Tutors Treadwell and Cutting disputed a thesis with Timothy Wetmore on the earth's revolution around the sun and the theory of gravity. Then "the President descended from the pulpit, and being seated in a chair, in a solemn manner, conferred the honors of the college" upon the candidates for degrees. Tutor Cutting's concluding valedictory oration, in proper academic Latin was "universally esteemed a masterly preformance." Dr. Johnson made "a solemn pathetic exhortation, to the Bachelors" which left "a lasting impression on the minds of all the pupils." The came the closing prayers, basically taken from *The Book of Common Prayer*. The "procession returned back to the City-Arms, where an elegant entertainment was provided by the governors of the college." The *Mercury* reporter thought the "numerous assembly of people of all orders" was sincerely pleased "to see the exercises performed in a manner which must reflect honor upon the college and incite every friend of his country, to promote so useful, so well regulated an institution."[24] And one can well imagine the pride and joy in Johnson's heart when he saw this conclusion of years of struggle and effort.

In July, Johnson escaped to the country for a time, probably as a relief from his recent bereavement, but also to visit friends and to carry on parochial work in the Westchester parish. From New York he wrote William Samuel that he had returned to the city after "riding every day for ten days in perfect health, and vigor...."[25]

The fifth academic year (1758-59) passed very prosperously and without notable difficulty for the president. Ten new students were enrolled. Cutting was doing well as a tutor. Johnson himself was teaching the New Testament in Greek, logic, metaphysics, and ethics, and Hebrew to those who wanted it. He also read the daily services. And all the while he could watch the steady progress of the college building.[26]

In June 1759, the sixth year of the college opened. Commencement this year, unlike the grandiose affair of the preceding one, was called by Johnson "a small private one," as there were but two candidates for the bachelor's degree. But there were four new students entering. On June 25, shortly after commencement, Johnson suffered another personal loss. His step-daughter Gloriana, who had managed the housekeeping since the death of her mother, died, and Johnson was forced to hire a housekeeper.[27]

Some consolation came to Johnson in the fact that he had been elected a member of the S. P. G. This was more than a gratification. His appointment, he told the Secretary of the Society, would give him "greater weight in endeavoring to be somewhat useful in promoting the pious views of the Society in these parts...." He also re-iterated hopes that an English subscription might be taken for the college, but he doubted its success unless some energetic gentlemen would undertake it – "hardly practicable unless we could send somebody from hence which is also difficult." Perhaps the S. P. G. would help.[28]

The college was proving to be a burden, and early in 1759 Johnson evidently turned his thoughts to preparing the way for a successor. The Archbishop of Canterbury replied to his overtures, saying he hoped that many years would pass "before there be occasion to de-liberate on that head. Pray, will it not be proper," he asked, "that I should send over a proxy, as a governor of the college? And will you permit me to nominate you?" Grateful for Secker' s compli-ment concerning the matter of a successor, he said, "I thank God, I seem to have a very firm health; but my condition here is very precarious, chiefly by reason of the small-pox...." This "especially (together with my advanced years) makes me thoughtful how my college may be provided for." Johnson was glad that the Reverend East Apthorp of Cambridge, Massachusetts was "so near, who I be-lieve would be immediately pitched upon; his youth would be the only Objection."[29]

It was evidently about this time that Johnson draughted a statement to the college governors which he intended should be read "at their next meeting after my decease or dismission." Using a text from He-brews 11:4, "being dead yet speaketh," Johnson asked leave to sug-gest a few things he thought of the utmost importance to the future work of the college. The first point to keep in view, in his opinion, was the need for giving children a truly Christian education, if they were to promote the true happiness of society. Therefore he recom-mended that prayer and scripture lessons be always used. Pupils should constantly attend public worship and read and pray daily. The president should always take the tuition of the youngest class and carry them through the Greek New Testament, "and not only make them understand the words but the things...." They must be-come not only learned men, but good men. He also recommended that they should study moral philosophy so as to "learn the lan-guages and religion and morality at the same time." The study of He-brew should be encouraged so as to foster reading the Old Testament as a proper introduction to the New. And finally, he touched on the issue of his successors: "it is highly fit and necessary that the presi-dent ... should always be ... a serious Christian ... a clergyman, a di-vine as well as a philosopher, and a master of polite learning and eloquence," and preferably a fellow of the University of Oxford or Cambridge. Johnson hoped that the governors would "take in good part what I have here suggested" and that God would prosper the college so that it might make "truly religious and virtuous" people, "flourishing and happy to the end of time, and give us all a happy meeting in a blessed and glorious eternity."[30]

Although Johnson's plans for retirement were perhaps a trifle pre-mature, he became certain that the smallpox again made residing in New York very dangerous. In October 1759, the disease in its most virulent form again broke out. For a time Johnson remained in the city, avoiding exposure by holding classes in his own dwelling.

But eventually the dread malady appeared almost at his door, and he withdrew to a farmhouse in the suburbs. There he remained until it was certain he had not himself contracted smallpox. Then he went to Stratford, and spent the winter with William Samuel, "but with much concern for his College."[31] Naturally, it suffered. Cutting did his best, but Treadwell, who had seemed a very promising teacher, was sickening with consumption, and died in the early spring. The assistant Johnson had hired to take his place turned out to be "but a poor hand of it. So that the college suffered greatly...."[32]

Aside from these circumstances, the college underwent the pains of other difficulties. As Johnson told East Apthorp in December 1759, half of the £3,400 raised by lotteries and the assembly's vote of £500 a year for seven years was lost because of "the quarrel raised by a few virulent Dissenters...." And although another £4,000 had been subscribed, this and other monies would soon be spent on the construction of the building and payment for apparatus. Salaries for the president and the two tutors had to be paid from bequests totalling £9,500, and from the tuition from students, which came to only about if £150 a year. Moreover, the college lacked a library until a bequest of 1,500 volumes expected from an English member of the S. P. G. was actually delivered. The college statutes were in an imperfect state, and the plan of education could not yet be carried out in full. Johnson had to admit students who were "very raw" and poorly trained by the "miserable" grammar schools. Modern educators who find college students ill prepared for advanced studies will observe that little has changed in this respect since the eighteenth century. Like them, Johnson found himself obliged to cover ground that should have been traversed in the lower schools. Unlike some modern educators, Johnson endeavored, while he taught students Latin and Greek, "in these evil times to make them intelligent and serious Christians" too.[33]

4. Life in the New Building

In mid-May 1760 Johnson returned to New York which he found "now so stript that it seemed almost a wilderness to him and never appeared as it had before." In large part his dismay was caused by the death of his step-son, Benjamin Nicoll in April – another "fatal disaster" for the college. Nicoll had ably served on the board of governors as a right hand to Johnson, who described him not only as "one of the chief lawyers," but also "the darling of the city" and "the life and soul of the whole affair" of establishing King's, where "everything depended on his activity and influence...." Nicoll had been an affectionate son, and his loss was "a most fatal shock" to Johnson "to whom he was very dear and very helpful." As always, the president struggled to keep up his spirits, this time "by an indefatigable application to reprieve the damage the College had suffered in his absence."[34]

Not everything about the infant school was gloomy, however. The new college hall was not yet complete, but it was nevertheless ready to accommodate the students. Johnson described it as "a very neat and commodious building 180 feet in length by 30, three stories, in a very delightful situation near Hudson's River opening to the harbor."[35] Here the president now set up housekeeping, a little over forty years after he had first done the same at Yale College.[36] A Mr. Willet was chosen steward to supervise the lodging and feeding of students.[37] The college governors named a committee, Johnson himself, the Reverend Messers. Barclay and Auchmuty of Trinity Church, and John Livingston, to establish the weekly rates for meals and the daily bill of fare. Three meals a day cost eleven shillings per week, payable quarterly. Lower rates were fixed for students who took one or two meals a day. The diet specified the main dishes. Evidently the traditional days of abstinence were not observed, as Friday called for mutton and soup, with fish on Saturday. The students celebrated Sunday with roast beef and pudding, had mutton and roast veal on Monday, and corned beef and mutton chops on Tuesday. Wednesday called for pease porridge and beef steak, Thursday, corned beef and mutton pie. Breakfasts were Spartan; coffee or tea, with bread and butter. So was supper: "bread, butter and cheese, or milk, or the remainder of the dinner."[38]

Johnson held the third King's commencement, the first in the college's new quarters, on June 26, 1760. Six young men were made bachelors of arts. Four of them, Samuel Bayard, Anthony Hoffman, Philip Livingston, and Robert Watts, came from leading families in the colony. In wig and gown, Johnson's large frame must have been impressive as he sat in his president's chair to admit each candidate to his degree. The formula ran, "The President, inclosing both hands of the candidate clasped together in his hands shall say: *Ego ex authoritate hujus Academiae, Regio Diplomate constitute, admitto Te, ad Baccalaureatus in Artibus Gradum.*" Then, delivering to each a little book, a Psalter or Testament, he added a further Latin exhortation.[39] It was almost like an ordination. Johnson further marked the occasion by a "short congratulatory speech in Latin to the Governors on their now first meeting in the College Hall...." As usual, the exercises were followed by a very elegant dinner.[40]

As one year ended another began, and a new class of six boys was admitted. Among them were two of the most outstanding political leaders of the Revolutionary generation – Richard Harrison and John Jay.[41] During the seventh academic year (1760-61) Johnson and Tutor Cutting "were obliged each to do double duty" except for a little help they received from a Mr. Giles, who taught mathematics. The president fully realized that his absences, together with the long illness and death of Treadwell, who had been so promising, had caused the college great damage. Half a dozen students had left. In July 1760, Johnson repeated his earlier request to Archbishop Secker to help provide two more tutors.[42] Short-handed, he managed to struggle through the school year.

Again the smallpox was in town, but Johnson did not run away this time, although the disease was as near as the corner tavern. He had suffered the additional misfortune of breaking his shin in getting out of a carriage. Confined to his quarters from Christmas until well into February 1761, for exercise he ran "frequently up garret, besides walking a great deal the length" of his two rooms. This, with "five recitations (lectures we call them), two of which are equal to two sermons, seem exercise enough to answer the end," he thought. Thus, he managed to keep up his teaching. And as always he read. Smollett he decided he did not quite like: "I fear he has no religion," he told William Samuel.[43] Still unable to recruit any teachers in England, his difficulties he felt were much aggravated by the death of Benjamin Nicoll. Without his step-son "it was no easy matter to prevail upon the Governors to give much attention to the affairs of the College."[44]

In November 1760, Archbishop Secker had responded to Johnson's reports of ecclesiastical and academic affairs by sending his proxy as a governor of the college, and apologizing that he had not found proper persons to assist at King's. One good man was evidently "tinctured with Mr. Hutchinson's notions," and so was unacceptable. Another was ingenious, but had too high an opinion of himself, and lacked dignity, prudence, and temper. Another was too unknown. Still another, Myles Cooper, did not meet the Hebrew requirement and would not likely accept an inferior position. Thus the prelate judged "you had better wait than have a wrong person sent you from hence."[45]

As Secker posted his missive to New York, Johnson was again writing of his pressing need for a tutor to teach mathematics and experimental philosophy, and "a vice-president in due time...." He dutifully submitted prayers for the college for his grace's correction, wondering if he had varied too much in adapting the Prayer Book to local uses. Despite his need for help, Johnson rejoiced: "My college begins to lift up her head and flourish...." Writing also to the secretary of the S. P. G., the president stressed his sorrow at finding "so little hopes of a collection for my college at home," but he had not "expected much unless some gentleman, one or more, either there or sent from hence could be procured to solicit a subscription in person." Nor had he yet been able "to procure a proper gentleman to go from hence...." Without the solicitation, however, the new building had cost so much that it was difficult to provide sufficient salaries. Again, he asked that the Society send the library which had been donated, and for which a room would be ready by the following summer.[46]

By the commencement of June 3, 1761, the building was finished. The year past Johnson viewed as noteworthy only "on account of hard services which made him more and more weary of his station" – and of his situation as a widower.[47] Still, there was cause for rejoicing. Among the recipients of degrees was Agur Treadwell, who had graduated at Yale but now added a King's B. A. to his titles. He would soon go to England for ordination – another in the long list of men shaped for the priesthood in part by Johnson. And Johnson was doubtless gratified that three of King's first graduates were now made masters of arts. So were William Samuel, and three of Johnson's ministerial colleagues, the Reverends Samuel Seabury, Jr., James Scovil, and Samuel Peters.[48]

5. Johnson Remarries

Always a man devoted to his family and concerned for domestic comforts, Johnson found his household affairs "Much upon the decline for want of a careful and disinterested housekeeper."[49] His first attempt at remarriage has not been noted by his previous biographers. Soon after coming to New York, Johnson had made the acquaintance of Mrs. Anne Watts. Not much can be discovered about the lady, except that she was a widow, the mother of the Robert Watts who graduated in 1760, and well connected; the Watts family definitely belonged to the upper crust of the colony. In February 1757, Johnson being then in Westchester, he wrote Mrs. Watts, saying, "I shall never cease to have the deepest sense of gratitude and love for the great and unmerited benevolence with which you have been pleased to distinguish me." In amiable fashion, and in the manner of a pastor and friend, Johnson recounted how he had returned "to the study of the Holy Scriptures ... in the pure and noble original" after "long wandering after the wisdom of this world" and eagerly pursuing "the philosophy so much in vogue...." Here, of course, was no hint of impropriety, for Johnson's wife was very much alive. He suggested that others of leisure should also spend more time "in this noble study [as], me thinks they would soon be convinced that besides necessary business, scarce anything else deserves their notice, if they would come to it as new born babes,etc."[50]

Mrs. Watts replied in August, thanking the doctor because he had "shown me great kindness which I was unworthy of and you will add to your former kindness if you will tell me plainly of my faults and show me where I fail and what it is in me that is an obstacle to the sweet and powerful influences of Grace...."[51] Mrs. Watts was troubled about the state of her soul, and leaned in the direction of Calvinism. She wanted to be sure that she was saved. This Johnson took care to correct.[52]

In the year following Charity's death, in January 1759, Johnson again wrote Mrs. Watts a letter with a purpose. It is so charming in its unconscious humor that we cannot forbear quoting it at some length.

Dearest Madam: –

> I humbly beg you will forgive me the liberty I am now presuming to take, and put the kindest construction you can both on it and the method I venture to take in addressing you with such a view. The thing that I have the assurance to ask and beg of you is no less than this, that you will

think favorably of becoming the endearing and endeared partner and companion of the little remaining part of my life, and I take this method of first making such a proposal because of the great difficulty I should labor under in expressing myself in presence, and because I mortally hate to be talked of in relation to such an affair....

Indeed, Madam, I blush to have it imagined that one of my sacerdotal character and advanced years should think of taking such a step at all, but the necessitous condition I am in, or at least very probably shall be by reason of the infirm and uncertain condition of my dear daughter ... must be my excuse, to say nothing of the little capacity I have for economical affairs; so that in truth if my daughter should fail or be much enfeebled, it looks as if I must otherwise break up house keeping and become a lodger, there being no other person besides you, of whom I have long had the highest esteem, that I can endure the thought of ... I am entirely disinterested, and seek not anything of yours but you....

He added in a postscript, "I will presume to wait on you if you can be at leisure and by yourself in the dusk of the evening of the 25th of this month...."[53] Unfortunately, we do not have the particulars of Mrs. Watts's reply. But it was unfavorable; Johnson's candor and practicality were not perhaps the best approach to marriage.

His next attempt met with success. William Beach, as we have seen, was reputed the richest man in Stratford, and he was a benefactor of the parish. His daughter had married William Samuel. William Beach had now died, leaving a widow, Sarah. To her Johnson's thoughts now turned. On October 27, 1760, he wrote her daughter, Mrs. William Samuel, whom he had apparently already consulted about the matter, remarking, "As to what you say in answer to my former letter: it seems the general opinion of my friends here that I must get somebody and there is it seems a general talk that it is to be Mrs. Beach, though I know not how they came by it...."[54] Evidently there was no difficulty in settling this matter, and on June 18, 1761, Samuel and Sarah were married.

As with Charity Nicoll, Johnson found Sarah "a lady of much worth who had long been a person of excellent economy...." They were married in Stratford, and at the end of a brief holiday, they embarked for New York, where the business of the college once more claimed the president's energies and attention.[55] He enjoyed the company of his granddaughter Charry, whom he and his new wife had brought back from Connecticut, and he wrote the girl's father in October that he "was never happier in life than now...." Charry grew "apace in body and mind," and he thought "after all her childish incogitency she will make a worthy woman." Sarah "without scarce a harsh word has made even Horace a good boy ... so that we have a pleasant quiet family. And what greatly adds to my pleasure," he said, "is that providence has sent us a good teacher of mathematics and experiments from Ireland – bred at Glasgow ... and the scholars are so pleased ... So I hope we are now getting out of the clouds."[56] Thus, new-found domestic comforts were enhanced by academic gains. Later that month Johnson rejoiced that he was again a grandfather and "that our good God, hath at length given us a son that seems likely to stand; but let us rejoice with trembling lest we be yet again disappointed ... I would have the child christened Samuel William, and be usually called Billy, if you think proper ... I give you joy of having seen your 34th year," he wrote William Samuel, "and bless God that I this day begin my 66th."[57] Johnson's successor at Stratford baptized the boy according to his grandfather's wishes.

6. Search for a Successor

All in all the academic year 1761-62 seemed to be a marked improvement over the previous one. In view of the difficulty of procuring a new tutor from England, the college governors eased Johnson's burdens by appointing Robert Harpur, trained at Glasgow, as professor of mathematics and natural philosophy.[58] Johnson was anxious that the college start a good grammar school, so that entering students might be better qualified for college work, but this did not come to pass until the president retired.

Johnson spent his eighth year at King's dealing largely with two major problems. One was the choice of a successor. The other was raising funds; here Johnson had to prod the governors into action.

Such an enterprise was bound to be competitive, for all of the colonial colleges were vying for English aid. In February 1762 Provost William Smith of the College of Philadelphia set out for England to solicit gifts for his college. Whereupon Dr. James Jay, brother of John Jay, a New York physician trained in Edinburgh, designing a voyage to England, offered to collect for King's. Johnson quickly seized the opportunity, and by the end of April he persuaded the governors to arm Jay with addresses to the King, the archbishops, the two universities, and the S. P. G.[59] Archbishop Secker, always zealous for the welfare of the colonial Church, saw that competition between two fund-raising projects would be harmful, so he managed to unite the two American colleges in a common solicitation, with the agreement that the funds thus gathered would be divided equally. In August 1762, King George granted a patent, naming trustees to receive and disburse the monies, which were to be collected for a year beginning at Michaelmas.[60]

When Johnson heard of the order for the English collection, he shared the "glorious news" with his son. Although he hoped that £10,000 might be raised for each college, the results were less sizable. After expenses were paid, King's received about £5,000. This, with Mr. Murray's legacy, which netted about £8,000, and other scattering donations, provided enough money to insure the payment of salaries.[61]

While the major business of finance thus proceeded apace, President Johnson and Tutors Cutting and Harpur carried on with the work of tuition. Six new students had been admitted in 1761, bringing the student body to a total of about a score.[62] In April 1762, the college building was fully completed. It was designed to be the first side of a quadrangle, but lack of funds prevented any further construction during Johnson's tenure as president.[63]

On June 19, 1762, Johnson presided at his fifth commencement. It was to be his last. Still fearful of the smallpox, he insisted on being taken to the chapel in a closed carriage. Included in the ranks of the nine bachelors of arts were two men who had formerly been students at Yale – evidence of Johnson's power of attraction. Once again Johnson conferred master's degrees on two fellow Anglican clerics – Bela Hubbard and Samuel Andrews. This brought the total number of Anglican priests thus honored during Johnson's presidency to eight.[64]

The president delivered an exhortation to the graduates which turned out to be a valedictory. It was a typical Johnson statement of the purposes of a college education. "Upon the whole, be persuaded to think," he exhorted, "as in a just estimate, the truth is, that the characters of a true gentleman and a true Christian are entirely coincident, and can never be separated ... Fear God, and keep his commandments, for this is the whole – the whole duty, and the whole happiness of man."[65] Learning was valuable, not for its own sake, but because true learning was rooted in religion, and religion had to be demonstrated in conduct. Here Puritan and Anglican were in complete agreement.

As early as 1759, Johnson began to think seriously about retirement. This involved the choice of a fit successor, as Johnson was determined to leave the college in good hands. His first choice was the Reverend East Apthorp, a distinguished layman of Boston who had been ordained to the Anglican ministry. On December 1, 1759, Johnson wrote Apthorp, giving him a complete description of the college, its finances, and its curriculum. But the S. P. G. determined that Apthorp should be first minister of the new church it was setting up in Cambridge. And after an exchange of correspondence during the winter of 1759-60, Apthorp decided that it was "very doubtful whether the honor and advantage" of the college presidency "should at any time induce me to desert it."[66] Johnson then turned to his correspondent Archbishop Secker for help, feeling that a graduate of Oxford or Cambridge would give the college needed prestige.[67] Secker replied on November 4, 1760, mentioning a number of possibilities. Among them was Myles Cooper, whom the archbishop described as follows:

> One Mr. Cooper, a Fellow also of Queens' College, [Oxford], hath been recommended to me as a grave and good man, and very well affected to the government; well qualified for the inferior tutor's place, but not inclined to accept it; not unskilled in Hebrew, and willing to take the vice-president's office; but not of an age for Priest's Orders till next February. I am afraid, though I have not seen

him, that he should appear too young; but have given no decisive answer.[68]

After considerable correspondence, Johnson and the Board of Governors accepted the Archbishop's suggestion.[69] In the fall of 1762, Cooper, now twenty-five and in priest's orders, landed in New York. On November 15, he met the board, was elected a Fellow and Professor of Moral Philosophy. It was specified that he was to assist Johnson in the government of the college, and it was clearly understood that he was to succeed to the presidency.[70] One of Johnson's notable characteristics was his ability to attract younger men, and attach them to his personality and his ideals. Cooper immediately fell under the spell, and became a firm disciple of the older man. And despite his misgivings about Cooper's youth, Johnson discovered him to be a "worthy and well accomplished young gentleman...." Cooper "was with him as a son with a father, and his conduct was very amiable...."[71]

By this time, Johnson had definitely turned his thought to retirement, encouraged to do so it seems by difficulties with the college governors concerning their failure to provide a good grammar school to prepare students for entry to King's. But this was not the only cause. Johnson increasingly felt that the burden of work was too great for his age. Another extended smallpox epidemic had also hindered the duty he owed to Trinity Church. Cooper could now easily assume the presidency, and Johnson was convinced that he was well qualified for it. Thus, in November he warned the governors to prepare for his resignation as soon as he could conveniently arrange it.[72]

It is also evident that at this time there was some friction between Johnson and the board. His salary had proved inadequate to his expenses. New York was more expensive than Stratford to live in, and the war, like all wars, had forced up the cost of living. In January 1763, Johnson prepared a statement of his case with the governors, which he intrusted to friends like Daniel Horsmanden to be read to the entire board if "it were found absolutely necessary." In it he summed up all his difficulties – money, smallpox, tutors, the grammar school. Moreover he was also disturbed when "He was not indeed very politely treated at the meeting" of the governors, some of whom had "since unkindly talked of dismissing him without any consideration ...." This they might do had he misbehaved, but Johnson insisted that "this cannot with the least truth be pretended (the worst that can be said being he has perhaps a little too much tenderness and lenity in discipline)...." Convinced that he had "faithfully and laboriously borne the burden and heat of the day" and was "now declining and that it was not owing to any real fault of his that the college has prospered no better," he asked "whether it can consist with equity and gratitude and the honor of this corporation that he should retire without some valuable consideration?"[73]

In November 1762,when William Samuel had heard of his father's difficulties, he promptly wrote to Daniel Horsmanden, one of the college governors: "Poor old Gent. How hard it is after a life spent in the service of mankind that his well meant and real services should be contemned." In strongly intimating that the governors owed his father some recompense, William Samuel stopped short of demanding a pension; but he did ask that the governors "not put any open contempt or affront upon him (this certainly his services have not merited)." His father's name would "be eternally remembered as a shocking instance of the baseness, ingratitude and barbarity of the Governors ... who when they were in necessity drew him from a certain subsistence for life which they induced him to relinquish for their sakes ... to found a college for the benefit of their posterity, and the moment they could do without him dismissed him to starve the remainder of his days or be supported by his friends." The loyal son thanked Horsmanden for "the kind intimation" of the president's troubles, and promised to advise his father "not to wait for a dismission but to resign and as soon as he can conveniently to retire from among so perfidious a set of people. Indeed were it not so late in the fall," he wrote, "I should advise him to come off immediately, but it will perhaps be necessary [for him] to tarry there till spring."[74]

By early January 1763, Johnson's future was not yet clearly settled. There was a possibility that he might remain as president another year. He was cheered that many New York gentlemen, the college governors and the vestry of Trinity Church had paid him a New Year's day call, "seemingly very affectionately," and he thought he might stay another year if they wished it.[75] Then something occurred which brought about an immediate decision.

At the end of January, Sarah Johnson fell ill. What was first thought to be a cold proved to be the dreaded smallpox. Johnson anticipated the worst. "I hope for a comfortable issue," he wrote on February 3. "If otherwise let us calmly say God's will be done!" At first Johnson left his wife to the nurses and took refuge in Myles Cooper's room, but Cooper and others suggested that he go to the country. He evidently needed little urging. On February 3 he "took leave of his dear College and retired three miles off" to John Watts's country seat, Rose Hill.[76] There he anxiously waited with slender hopes that Mrs. Johnson would recover. He wrote to William Samuel that she lacked "sufficient strength of nature, though she has the best of means and nurses. She has been an unspeakable comfort to me, and the loss of her would be unsupportable ... without the divine aid; but this, which God be thanked, I have so much experienced, I hope will not now desert me."[77] On February 9 she died, "comfortably resigned and without delirium...." She was buried, like her predecessor, in the chancel of Trinity Church. Johnson was not present at the funeral.[78] Death had taken a heavy toll of his family since his coming to New York – his wives, Charity and Sarah, his son William, his stepchildren, Gloriana and Benjamin Nicoll. His faith remained unshaken, but he was tired.

Johnson remained at Mr. Watts's about twenty days, receiving the visits of many friends when "at length a favorable time for sleighing offered ... he wrote a decent compliment with his resignation to the Governors and committed the care of his affairs to Mr. Cooper and his friend Mr. [Nicholas W.] Stuyvesant," a tutor. He would not return to the city, but he hired a driver with a sleigh to take him back to Stratford.[79] No doubt he followed the Boston Post Road, which ran from Manhattan through southwest Connecticut and beyond, passing through towns in which much of his earlier missionary work had contributed so much to the growth of the Episcopal Church – Stamford, Norwalk, and Fairfield. Beyond, lay other towns which now had Episcopal churches – New Haven, Branford, Guilford, and New London. On February 25, 1763 Johnson, now in his sixty-seventh year, was back home in Stratford.

Samuel Johnson had "made King's College possible."[80] Although it was not his greatest accomplishment, he has been perhaps most readily and easily identifiable – almost ironically so – as the first president of the school. That he should have been asked to lend his prestige to the founding of the new institution was a fitting climax to his practical services to education. It is difficult to measure such intangibles as prestige, but there is no doubt that Johnson's fame as an educator was well deserved and that New Yorkers benefitted when they pressed him to serve as president of a college even before it was certain of an existence. All his life he had taught – children, young men, ministerial candidates. Franklin and others recognized his wisdom and abilities and valued his advice on educational matters. And what was feebly started in the way of Johnson's curricular changes at King's "was made into an effective progress: at the College of Philadelphia" where William Smith directed affairs.[81]

King's College suffered from Johnson's several absences when he fled New York to escape the smallpox. It also suffered from its very birth pangs and precarious infancy, and for these hardships Johnson is not particularly culpable. Although his accomplishments were far from spectacular, they are not to be under rated, much less despised. True, there were difficulties with the Board of Governors who balked at adding more faculty and at the proposal to institute a school to prepare students for entry to the college. But Johnson was a good layer of foundations. He promulgated the first college statutes, and the second set of rules issued after his departure in 1763 was clearly an elaboration of his own. Johnson's imprint was not only left upon these, but also upon Myles Cooper, his successor. For Cooper the old president felt the affection as for a son; Cooper went to Stratford in the summer of 1763, and "seldom passed a vacation without making him a visit" for some years thereafter. By this means, and his correspondence, Johnson advised him of everything he "could think of what might be of use...." And Cooper valued the old man's views. Archbishop Secker told Johnson how he had appreciated his successor's numerous civilities and kindnesses even before the young man had replaced the elder.[83]

Johnson worked to provide the first college hall, and he taught the first students of King's. He labored to collect a library, and he modified the curriculum, as he had done decades earlier at Yale – not only in terms of particular courses of instruction, but with a spirit liberal even for his age. "King' s College marked the new tendency, which included a comprehensive program of surveying, navigation, geography, history, husbandry and modern languages, although it was incompletely carried out by Dr. Johnson."[84]

In Samuel Johnson's judgment the prosperity of King's College after 1762 "was the same as when he presided there," and that seems as reasonable an assessment for the period before the Revolutionary War as was his autobiographical profession that "his leaving the College did not at all abate his affection to it or concern for its prosperity," despite the cloud of disgruntlement under which he made his departure.[85] The redoubtable priest was not wont to glorify himself or to gloss over his failings. By May 1766 when Johnson visited "his beloved College and friends at New York," he was gratified by an affectionate and respectful reception. He attended the commencement on May 20 with "the unspeakable satisfaction," as his autobiography asserts, that King's was in "a good flourishing way," the students performing "their exercises exceeding well, and the music (it being in Trinity Church) was exquisitely fine."[86] Had he lived to see the disruption caused by the War of Independence, he would have mourned. But as his device for the seal of the college indicated, he was ever the optimist, chastened by reasonableness; he had shared in a worthy enterprise, expressed by its motto: "*In Lumine Tuo videbimus Lumen*. In Thy light shall we see light."

Chapter XIII

Indian Summer

1. The Return to Stratford

By the end of 1762, the affairs of King's College were in good order. Myles Cooper quickly proved an able assistant, and between him and Johnson there had grown up a feeling of real intimacy and affection. As of January 1763, Johnson's future was not yet clearly settled. Despite his consideration of returning to Stratford in the spring, he thought "perhaps the Governors and doubtless Mr. Cooper will choose that I stay another year round." And he was inclined to stay. Nonetheless, he asked his son to hire a house at Stratford by spring; it was good insurance against uncertainty, and Mrs. Johnson was "utterly averse to giving" William Samuel and her daughter "the trouble of us, and especially the trouble and charge of building another room" for them. William Samuel told his father that he and his wife were sorry that Johnson "or Mrs. should think anything we could do for you should be called a trouble," but he promised to do his father's bidding.[1] Yet other events interfered.

Early in February 1763, there came catastrophe. Once again smallpox, the bane of Johnson's life, was raging in New York. At the end of January Mrs. Johnson fell sick; she had the dread disease. On the 9th of February she was dead. On the 11th Samuel wrote to William

Samuel, announcing the sad event. This precipitated a decision Johnson had been mulling over for some little time. They had "reckoned … within three or four months of retiring together and spending the remainder of our day among our children and theirs with much tranquility."[2] He at once offered his resignation to the governors of the college. When the sleighing became good, his books and valuables were quickly loaded, and on February 25 he arrived in Stratford.

Johnson was now in his sixty-seventh year. He thought of himself as an old man, and pictured his life as one of quiet retirement in the midst of his beloved family. In fact, except for his perennial trouble with the leg which had been broken years before and badly set, he was in excellent health as usual. And the boundless energy which had characterized him throughout his life showed little signs of abatement. His retirement was to be an exceedingly active one.

William Samuel was still living in the house his father had bought about the time of his first marriage. It was large enough so that a sort of separate apartment could be set up within it, giving the father a bedroom and a study, where he could indulge his passion for books. He needed this bit of a retreat, because the house must have been bursting at the seams with family and servants.

On August 10, 1763, Johnson wrote Archbishop Secker, whom he had never met, but with whom he had begun a long and intimate correspondence, describing his situation at Stratford:

> As to myself, I am very happy here as I am, only as I have never for almost 50 years been without some public charge or other, it seems somewhat strange now to be without one. However I hope I may live here to some good purpose, by directing candidates [for holy orders] and others to their studies, and preaching frequently for Mr. Winslow, and so enable him often to preach at destitute places. I hope also, though at this distance to be of some use to the college.[3]

Despite Johnson's general contentment, there was one piece of unfinished business with King's College that rather annoyed him. When the board of governors accepted his resignation on March 2, 1763, they hurried to offer him "grateful sentiments" for his services, and their condolences for the death of his wife. But as for a pension, the board only promised to consider it later.[4] Johnson was obliged to wait until May 1764 for their decision to grant him the annuity.

The £50 a year that the governors finally voted, Johnson surmised was an indication of ill-will; thanking John Watts for his part in providing it, he observed that the amount specified (in New York currency instead of sterling) "seems hardly expressive ... of generosity or a sense of honor and gratitude but rather of a narrow and contracted spirit, and indeed had any good will been meant, I apprehend it would not have been improper to have been expressed as a testimony of it, and it seems to me very hard that it had not at least been ordered to commence from my last payment a year ago." Although Johnson grumbled that he "must live at least ten years to be made as good as I should have been had I never been" president, we must not think that he was himself ungenerous or grasping. Samuel Auchmuty had informed him of the governors' behavior: "some of them bit their lips and swelled" at the very suggestion of making some provision for the retired president, "yet no one said a word" until Judge Daniel Horsmanden asked them what they thought of Auchmuty's motion for a gratuity. Auchmuty also thought the judge's proposal for £50 a year was little enough; and so he told Johnson "I have obtained you something not near enough, but considering their grumbling dispositions more than I expected."[5]

2. Family Circle

To a man with Johnson's strong family feeling, it was a joy to be back in Stratford. First, there was William Samuel. We have seen how close the bond was between father and son. And Samuel now had reason to be proud of his offspring, for William Samuel had made a place for himself in Connecticut. He was one of the best known lawyers in the colony, and like lawyers in that and every succeeding age, he had made a good start in politics. In 1760 he had been elected a selectman of Stratford; in the following year Stratford sent him to the general assembly. In 1765, he was a delegate to the Stamp. Act Congress. And in 1766 he received the crowning honor of being elected to the governor's council, that small and exceedingly select body which really ruled the colony. He was the first Episcopalian to sit in that body.[6] He thus played a considerable part in breaking the taboo against Anglicans in public office in the Puritan colony.

Financially, the family was in easy circumstances. Both of Samuel's marriages had brought him money, which he generously divided with William Samuel. It is estimated that by 1763 the son had an estate of eight thousand pounds, well invested. The father must have had an equal amount.[7] For colonial Connecticut, this was wealth. In addition, there was the pension of fifty pounds per annum which the governors of King's College had awarded Samuel in 1764.[8]

Samuel's relations with his daughter-in-law were excellent. Ann was, it will be remembered, the daughter of Johnson's second wife. But his particular delight was in his grandchildren; there were plenty of them. First came Charity, aged thirteen in 1763. Then there were Sarah, nine, Gloriana Ann, six, Mary, four, and Elizabeth, born the December after Johnson's return to Stratford. But while girls were all well enough in their way, grandfather's favorites were Robert Charles and especially Samuel William, born October 23, 1761.[9] We shall hear more of their dealings later in the chapter. When Johnson made his will on January 1, 1767, his grandfatherly instincts were abundantly evident. The testament was conditional upon William Samuel's predeceasing his father. In that event, grandson Samuel William was to receive a tract of land, but both grandsons were to share the rest of their grandfather's real estate and books. Their mother was to use the remainder of Johnson's "goods and chattles and what money" he had "at interest, towards the better enabling her to give the best education that may be to all my dear Grandchildren, both sons and daughters...."[10]

There were still others in the crowded Johnson household. There were the slaves. One does not ordinarily think of slavery with colonial Connecticut, but Negro house servants were common. During his previous term of office as rector of Stratford, Johnson had baptized many of them. Indeed, except for an occasional Quaker, there seems to have been in this pre-Revolutionary day no particular sentiment against slavery; Johnson took it for granted. But one of his letters to William Samuel, written in 1767, gives us a brief glimpse of the nature of this household slavery:

I told you in my last that we had sold Jenny (at which I believe you are glad) and had Lintot's wench on trial but we did not like her; upon which my daughter (I believe) wisely got Robin, who has been a 12night on trial, and we may have him for 60 pounds, I hope 55. Nothing can be happier than he is, and if he continues to do as well as he has done, nobody needs wish to be happier in a servant than we shall be, and I believe he is in earnest resolved to do his best ....[11]

There was a break in this idyllic family picture in 1766. The colony was deeply involved in the "Mohegan case" – a matter of tangled land titles which involved thousands of acres in eastern Connecticut. To settle it for once for all the government of the colony determined that a special agent must be sent to England. The honor went to William Samuel, who therefore set sail on Christmas Day 1766, only a few days after the birth of Elizabeth.[12] He expected to be gone a year; it was almost five years before he returned. The parting was a great blow to both father and son, but it is a blessing to the historian. The letters Samuel wrote to William Samuel during this period – and he wrote frequently and at length – give us a priceless insight into the home at Stratford.

3. The Inveterate Pedagogue

The departure of William Samuel left his father as acting head of the family. Ann must be comforted; she found the separation from her husband very trying. Above all there were the children. The girls could well be left to their mother's care, but there was little Samuel William, commonly known as Billy. He was Johnson, a boy, and intelligent. He must be educated. And so we have a sort of repetition of the events of 1700. Just as his grandfather had begun the long process of educating Samuel, so must Samuel do the same for his grandchild. In a letter to William Samuel on March 12, 1767, Samuel described the operation:

Billy, who is a lovely child, and if he lives, I think will make just such a man as we would wish. Since you left us, he has taken very much to me, and seems to have as much pleasure with me at least, as with his mates in the street, and is very apt to learn. He has perfectly learned both his Greek and Hebrew letters. I wrote out the Lord's Prayer for him in Greek and he reads it, and has got it by heart, and says it prettily, and spells and reads all the names of the Books in the Hebrew Bible, and as soon as he had got the Lord's Prayer by heart in Greek, of his own accord he was impatient till I wrote it out for him in Hebrew, and is now engaged in learning that by heart ... I believe you will think he deserves you should send him some pretty thing or other....[13]

When the ex-president of a college can thus capture the attention of a five year old, and can thoroughly enjoy doing it, he is a real teacher. The modern progressive educator would doubtless be appalled at this mixture of ancient languages and divinity as the foundation for a curriculum; at least Johnson was aware of the fact that if a language is to be learned, the grade school is the place to start the process. But it might also be remembered that Johnson was an unusual educator even for his own time; "the difference between the old and the new [attitudes toward children] is exemplified by the writings of the Puritan Jonathan Edwards and the Anglican Samuel Johnson, both of Connecticut. Whereas the former collected and published a selection of the most infamous passages from the Old Testament to show God's wrath against infants, the latter insisted upon the intellectual light to be found in children and asserted that we owed them the utmost reverence – *pueris maxima reverentia debetur.*"[14]

Another quotation from a Johnson letter to William Samuel indicates that the grandfather knew when to be indulgent: "My dear Billy abides by me yet ... only now the weather is fine he can't avoid playing more in the streets ... I am going to teach him my English Grammar."[15] This comment, with its mention of "my English Grammar" shows how one thing leads to another. Johnson, in the process of teaching Billy, had found no satisfactory grammar of either English or Hebrew. Very well, he would make such essential tools. He set to work, and the two grammars were published as a single volume in London in the following year.

The teaching of Billy by no means exhausted Johnson's interest in education. His relationship to Myles Cooper, his successor as president of King's College, had become almost a father and son affair. Cooper was a young man for the position, and understandably he depended considerably on the wisdom of the older man. At every vacation he was to be found at Stratford, receiving advice. On May 20, 1766, Johnson was present at the commencement in New York "on which occasion he had the unspeakable satisfaction to find the College in a good flourishing way, and the young gentlemen to perform their exercises exceeding well ...." The commencement was held in Trinity Church, and Johnson commented on the music as being "exquisitely fine."[16] He had developed a great liking for music, and he had few opportunities of hearing it. No doubt he was also gratified that one of his fellow clergymen, Richard Clark, who had graduated during Johnson's presidency in 1762, was now made Master of Arts.[17]

On the following day there was a meeting of fourteen clergy, from New York, New Jersey, and Connecticut, at which it was insisted that Johnson should preside. He had already become a sort of patriarch of the Church of England in the northern colonies, and whenever he was present at a clergy gathering, he was expected either to preside or to preach. The clericus took up the business of a need for bishops, and they petitioned the S. P. G. for support in establishing an American episcopate. Only recently two candidates for holy orders had been lost at sea, thus bringing the number to "ten out of fifty-one (near one in five) who had lost their precious lives in going hence for Holy Orders...."[18] The Church still suffered for want of bishops and would continue to do so, no matter how many men Johnson and others might prepare for the priesthood.

Finally Johnson persisted in operating his one-man seminary. Yale was still producing graduates with a desire for the Anglican ministry, and some were also coming to Stratford from King's College. It was during this Indian summer period that he projected the full-fledged seminary, which we have mentioned in a former chapter.

4. Back in Harness

When Johnson moved to New York, he had been succeeded as rector of Stratford by the Reverend Edward Winslow. Although Christ Church, Stratford, was the mother church of Connecticut Anglicanism, the congregation had always been poor, and had been able to raise little to supplement the fifty pounds allotted by the S. P. G. for the support of the missionary. This had mattered little when Johnson was the rector, for he had money of his own. But Winslow had a large family, and had trouble making ends meet. Therefore he was, as early as 1762, looking about for another place. And as a result, even before he left King's College, Johnson was recommending to the S. P. G. that Winslow be moved to Hartford. Johnson could then resume occupancy of the parish at Stratford, and if the Society would continue the stipend, he offered to use that as a means of paying an assistant.[19] In the end, Winslow moved, but the S. P. G. offered him the mission at Braintree, Massachusetts. And as Archbishop Secker indicated to Johnson in September 1763, the change was made "in order to make room for you at Stratford" because the Society was "very desirous of restoring you to your old station; and if this proposal doth not succeed, they will be glad to have any other method pointed out to them."[20] No other method was required, for Winslow went to Braintree, and Johnson was again rector of Stratford.

And once again, under Johnson's vigorous leadership, Stratford became, but in a modest way, a missionary center. Across the mouth of the Housatonic was the hamlet of Milford; the two places were connected by a ferry. In 1764 a mission was started there, and services were held in the townhouse by Mr. Richard Clark. Mr. St. George Talbot, a wealthy layman of New York City, gave it some financial help, and a church building was projected, but had not been built. In 1766 Johnson took over the mission, which he held until 1771. In June 1770, the church was finally built. This was Johnson's last missionary effort.[21]

In December 1767 Johnson took action to secure an assistant. His age had begun to tell on his activities "as his legs grew troublesome...." He first tried out John Tyler, but he was not very well liked by some of the people. He was therefore dismissed, and replaced by the Reverend Ebenezer Kneeland, Yale class of 1761, who after his ordination had served briefly as chaplain in the British army. Kneeland proved acceptable, and he was permanently engaged, with the understanding that he was to succeed the rector.[22] To one member of the congregation he proved exceedingly acceptable. In May 25, 1769, Johnson wrote to William Samuel:

> I have told you once and again how happy both I and all
> my people are in Mr. Kneeland, and the more I am ac-
> quainted with him the more I am delighted in him. He is
> truly amiable. But (what may perhaps surprise you) he has
> of late desired and, with our approbation, conversed with
> our dear Charry, and a very tender regard to each other ap-
> pears to obtain between them; insomuch that he has ex-
> pressed a great desire to marry her, and desires me to send
> you the enclosed letter to ask your favor and approbation.
> I will only say further that it seems very probable that a
> greater happiness than riches can afford may arise from
> admitting of such a union.[23]

Obviously the consent of the father was received, and in October of the same year Johnson had the gratification of presiding at the marriage.[24]

During his last years Johnson's service to the Church of England in the colonies was not confined to his work at Stratford. We have noted his activity at clergy conferences, where he was invariably asked to preside or to preach. And he continued to be what he had been for many years, an invaluable link between the Church in England and the Church in the colonies, writing assiduously both to the English bishops and archbishops, and to the secretaries of the S. P. G., giving them his mature advice in strategy and placement. The story of his role in the struggle to obtain an American episcopate has also been noted. Curiously enough, this campaign reached its climax during Johnson's retirement at Stratford, and then, like him, declined as the momentum of the American Revolution seemed to gather more force.

5. Intellectual Life

The "impatient curiosity to know" which had been evident in the child of five was still active in the man of sixty-odd. Unlike many men of his age, Johnson could still be learning some new thing. He deliberately set out a plan of re-educating himself. Much of his time in "this sweet retirement was employed in reviewing all his former studies in almost all parts of learning."

> He especially re-examined with particular care the several conclusions he had gone into in all the former stages of his life and read over again with much pleasure most of the best books he had formerly read, twenty, thirty or forty, and even fifty years before, and especially several of the best tracts of some of the ancient fathers and philosophers and some of the best moderns who had endeavored to make the study of nature subservient to religion....

> But what he chiefly labored and delighted in this happy interim of health and leisure, was the study of the Holy Scriptures, in their sacred originals, and especially the Hebrew language in which the holy oracles were from the beginning delivered. This was always his delight and therefore now his chief business....[25]

Johnson's English correspondence during these golden years bears eloquent testimony to his still active intellectual interests. He wrote about the study of Hebrew to that great Hebraic scholar, Bishop Lowth, and referred a manuscript of a Hebrew grammar to a correspondent in England for publication. He discussed the study of ancient languages, about which he was much concerned at this time, with the Reverend John Parkhurst, Surrey parson and scholar. With other correspondents he examined the Hutchesonian philosophy which was momentarily current in scholarly circles. He begged William Samuel to send him new books. He was not letting his mind go to seed.

During the period between 1765 and 1770 Johnson wrote two pieces which were never published during his lifetime. One was an autobiography, which Thomas Bradbury Chandler used some years later as the basis for the first published life of Johnson. Indeed, Chandler's book is to a large extent but an extension of the autobiography. Our concern here is with the second of these works. It was entitled *Raphael*, or the *Genius of the English America*. We have already looked into this in our survey of Johnson's ideas on education. Cast in the traditional form of a philosophic dialogue, between the author and Raphael, the guardian angel of New England, it is a queer melange of ideas on such diverse topics as the moral government of the universe, the proper rearing of children and their religious training, public affairs, college education, and the relation of church and state. But it is of the greatest interest to the student of Johnson for the light it throws on Johnson's personality during his later life. In it one finds set forth Johnson's characteristic trust in sheer human reason as a specific for the ills of the world. (Johnson had never read anyone like Freud, nor worked in a slum parish.) In it one finds the writer's delight in physical nature; his confidence that the happiness of man was God's purpose in creation; his emphasis on man's free will; even his conviction that the English Constitution was the perfect form of government. With something like prophetic insight, here Johnson anticipated the nineteenth century Tractarians in holding that the Church was something more than the religious aspect of the state, and should be free from state control. And he talked like a man of the twentieth century when he stated roundly that the whole human race is one community, rising above that extreme localism which so often characterized the American colonist. The whole essay, for all its defects, is shot through with the serene spirit of the kindly old man. It is the work of one who, in spite of the weight of advancing years, in spite of the frustrations of politics and the abortive struggle for an American episcopate, was at peace with the universe.

6. The Elder Statesman

The sort of ripe wisdom that Johnson had come to possess was too valuable to the Church to be lost in the retirement of a country parish, and was still actively aware of a world outside the confines of Stratford, and still actively engaged in its affairs. As the leading strategist of Anglicanism in the northern colonies, he continued to carry on a steady correspondence with the English hierarchy and with the officials of the S. P. G. He was still sending his divinity students abroad, and advising about their placement when they returned in holy orders. He was deep in plans with Sir William Johnson for an Indian school, and for a bishop to be located in Albany. He urged Chandler to carry on his active propaganda for an American episcopate, and at one point made the daring suggestion that the English bishops disregard their Erastian masters, and consecrate bishops for America of their own accord.

We have already mentioned the clergy meeting of May 1766, following the commencement of King's College. On the surface, this meeting accomplished nothing of importance. The one thing that appears to have emerged from it was the usual abortive petition to the English bishops to do something about supplying bishops for the colonies. But in the long perspective of history, this meeting is highly significant. One thing the colonies had to learn at this time, and it proved a hard lesson, was the vital importance of inter-colonial action. Only the year before this meeting, the Stamp Act Congress had met, the precursor of more important congresses to come. The same lesson had to be learned by colonial Anglicanism. Now Samuel Johnson was of all colonial priests the most notable for his intercolonial connections and intercolonial vision. He was the undoubted patriarch of the Church of England in Connecticut – perhaps even of the entire range of the seaboard colonies. Through Cutler and Caner he had close relations with the Church in Massachusetts. He had turned down the rectorship of Trinity parish, Newport. He had lived for eight years in New York City. The most influential priest in New Jersey, Chandler, was his pupil and intimate. He had corresponded with churchmen in Maryland and Virginia. We must look at this clergy meeting of 1766 as a sort of foreshadowing of General Conventions of the Episcopal Church to come – and Johnson presided and gave it direction.

7. Feast Day: the End

Johnson missed his son William Samuel and thought it hard to be deprived of his company at the very time when the old man could have most enjoyed it. Of course it was gratifying that the province of Connecticut had honored William Samuel by its agency to London, but the aging parson seldom wrote a letter in which he did not express hope that his son would soon return. In November 1769, for example, he urged him to finish the business and hurry home.[26] And so anxious was he to see him back at Stratford that in December Johnson wrote Governor Jonathan Trumbull to expostulate with him on the subject:

> I am told the lower house voted to direct him to come home in the spring at all events, but that the upper house

had, by I know not what expressions in his own letters, prevailed on the Assembly to conclude to instruct him by all means to continue longer, leaving however a discretionary power with your Honor to direct otherwise ... Now Sir, I would humbly suggest that this seems to me a very hard case indeed after he has already spent three years from his family in the government service. The truth is that his family and affairs are in a very suffering condition for want of him ... I do earnestly beg of your Honor, to advise with your Council and consider whether it be not expedient and indeed very necessary as soon as may be to instruct my son to return, at least by the beginning of April.[27]

During 1770-1771 Johnson pined even more for the return of William Samuel. Indeed, as one year succeeded another the old man feared that he might never see his beloved son again. But he never lost the faculty for serenity or for contentment with his son's preferment. In one of his many letters he expressed pleasure that William Samuel had met his namesake, the English lexicographer; "it must have been an agreeable curiosity," he wrote in February 1770. "Pray return my compliments to him."[28]

When, on October 1, 1771, William Samuel reached Stratford from his long sojourn in England, the family circle was once again complete. His father felt "great and unspeakable comfort and satisfaction" that he had returned in safety; "great was the divine goodness in the preservation both of him and his family in this long absence and administered matter of inexpressible joy and thankfulness both to him and them."[29] But William Samuel found his father an old man. Samuel's mind was still clear and active, but the vigorous body which had sustained that mind through so many busy years was at last wearing out. The disorder of his legs, which had troubled him for years, grew worse, and his hand shook so that he could barely write the letters he had delighted in composing. Significantly, with William Samuel's reappearance, Johnson concluded his autobiography.[30] And yet he spoke of himself as "the happiest man on earth."[31]

Although Johnson's philosophic and theological bent may have prompted him to write "Reflections on Old Age and Death" earlier in his life, perhaps he penned them in the months of contentment just prior to his death. In any event they are a fitting commentary on the quality of both his life and death:

> … it is only this decaying body that can fade and die: my soul which only is myself shall continue to live, to think and act, and flourish in immortal youth. It shall, if qualified, forever dwell in unfading bliss, with the universal Father of spirits….

> … O Thou Almighty Being, the Great Genius of the World, by whom all things exist … It is on the free exertion of Thy omniscient will and power that all things depend; and Thou art the great source of all being, perfection and happiness!

> Thou, like the sun to this world of bodies, art the glorious sun of the world of spirits; the light and life of every created intelligence; … the life that can never die!

> Thee will I ever devoutly acknowledge, love, revere and adore: – To Thee will I cheerfully resign….

> Let my whole soul be entirely devoted to Thee, and freely conformed to Thy purity, rectitude, truth and goodness; that I may never cease to be happy, both in Thee, my God, and in myself and others, rejoicing together with them in the everflowing streams of Thy inexhaustible benevolence!

The notes of happiness, faith, strength, of purposeful life and service are unmistakable, and also in the closing lines: "*Quod faxit DEUS, Pater O. M. mediante Jesu Christo et renovante Spiritu Sancto; cui JEHOVAE aeterno, Uno, Trino, omnii tribuatur, laus, Honor et Gloria, in secula seculorum. Amen.*"[32]

Johnson had expressed the wish that he might die, like his old friend, Bishop Berkeley, in the full possession of his faculties. His wish was granted. On the morning of January 6, 1772, the Feast of the Epiphany, he again stated this desire. And as he sat in his chair, talking with his family, he died, without the least struggle or groan. On January 9, he was buried in the chancel of Christ Church, Stratford. All the clergy of the neighboring towns attended. John Beach was to have preached the funeral sermon, but he fell ill, and his composition was later printed. Instead, another of Johnson's pupils, the Reverend Jeremiah Leaming preached on a topic of which Johnson's life had been a constant testimony: "The True Christian's Support under Affliction."[33] It, too, was published in 1772.

Myles Cooper, Johnson's successor at King's College and his friend, composed an inscription for the great Churchman's monument. It is an exceedingly apt commentary on the Connecticut parson – a summary of Johnson's exemplary life and work:

> If decent dignity, and modest mien,
> The cheerful heart, and countenance serene;
> If pure religion, and unsullied truth,
> His age's solace, and his search in youth;
> If piety, in all the paths he trod,
> Still rising vig'rous to his Lord and God;
> If charity, through all the race he ran,
> Still wishing well, and doing good to man;
> If learning, free from pedantry and pride, –
> If faith and virtue, walking side by side;
> If well to mark his being's aim and end, –
> To shine, through life, a husband, father, friend:
> If these ambition in thy soul can raise,
> Excite thy reverence, or demand thy praise;
> Reader – ere yet thou quit this earthy scene,
> Revere his name, and be what he has been. [34]

Epilogue

In some respects Samuel Johnson was both a representative of his age and a man who was ahead of his times; in others, he was out of step with them. "Advanced" in terms of his educational views, steadfastly Catholic in his fundamental theology, he was, in the context of the religious furor of the Great Awakening and the political turmoil known as the American Revolution, a man who listened to a different drummer – different at least from most other American colonists. His life is of course a commentary on the temper of his era. His death in 1772 was perhaps fortunate. "It was well that he went, for he could not have prevented the calamities of the war, and they would have rent his heart asunder." Johnson perceived the dangers of the Revolutionary upheaval, and like so many other men of conservative bent, he was almost constitutionally unable to stem the tide or to swim with it. Yet he saw "with clear vision the needs of the church, and labored assiduously to supply them. Happily he was spared the hour of her disaster; but his influence wrought mightily in her reconstruction when once the time of her deliverance came."[1]

Two of Johnson's contemporaries, James Duane of New York and Ezra Stiles of Connecticut, offered perceptive commentaries on Samuel Johnson's character and achievement. Duane, like Johnson an Anglican and a conservative, wrote William Samuel on February 18, 1772:

> Your father, whose every word and action was benevolence itself, during his residence here, acquired, nay commanded, the love and esteem of all who had the honor of his acquaintance. The severity of letters, or of age, was no bar to an intimacy with a soul which embraced in fond affection the whole human race. Good humor, affability and condescension, cheerfulness, and an uncommon liberality of sentiment, sweetened every conversation, rendered instruction pleasing, and attracted the love and confidence of the most unthinking.[2]

Ezra Stile's assessment of Johnson, longer and less flattering, is nonetheless trenchant. Stiles graduated from Yale in 1746 when the influence of Johnson among the Yale students was at its height. After graduation, he made a considerable study of the varieties of Christianity in the colonies, and at one time Johnson had hopes of adding him to his list of converts. Indeed, Stiles was approached by Anglicans who wished him to join them and accept the Stratford parish when Johnson became president of King's College.[3] But this "gentle Puritan" preserved his allegiance to the Standing Order, and became mildly anti-Anglican. He was ordained to the Congregational ministry, and settled at Newport, Rhode Island. After the War of Independence he became president of Yale. He was one of the most intelligent of the New England clergy, and his *Literary Diary* is justly famous. In it, he was in the habit of writing obituaries; the longest of these is that of Samuel Johnson. Beginning with a resume of the main points of Johnson's career, Stiles offered a personal estimate as follows:

> He was an excellent classical Scholar, even a good Critic in Latin, Greek, and Hebrew. In 1729 to 1732, he was occasionally acquainted with *Dean Berkeley* then living on Rhode Island; He persuaded the Dean to believe, that *Yale College* would soon become Episcopal, and that they had received his *immaterial philosophy*. This or some other Motive influenced the Dean to make a Donation of his Rhode

Island Farm 96 Acres, with a Library of about a Thousand Volumes to Yale College in 1733....

Dr. Johnson was a Man of general, but not of profound and solid or deep Erudition. Rev. Mr. Ruggles of Guilford used to say of him, "Dr. Johnson was always of the Opinion of the last Book he read." He printed several Things – controversial on prelacy and Liturgy 1736 – an Introduction to Study of the Sciences 1744 – several Sermons – but his *Noetica* or Principles of human Knowledge an 8vo Volume was his most considerable Work. He was a very indifferent Writer, especially of Sermons. But a very considerable Reader all his Days. He was pleased with *polite Writings*, had some Taste for *History* particularly of the Classics, and for the periodical Productions of the day as they came forth. He loved to see what was going forward in the learned World but was not himself very learned. Some Geniuses, with half the Observation and Reading of Dr. Johnson, would make ten times greater Men. His theological Acquirements were ordinary and so were his performances. In Conversation very social, instructive, agreeable – much of the Gentleman.[4]

Stiles not only was erroneous in several of his facts, but also saw Johnson through the spectacles of a partisan Dissenter. Yet he and Duane reached similar conclusions about Johnson; both agreed that he had in some degree made a mark on his times, and both judged him an attractive personality. But something more than this is needed in summarizing Johnson's accomplishment.

When he made his fateful decision, on the Dark Day at Yale, there was in Connecticut but one Anglican parish – the embryonic church at Stratford, with no building, and frequently no priest. When he died, there were in that little colony forty-three Anglican parishes or missions with forty buildings erected, and staffed by sixteen priests. Throughout the eighteenth century, the Church of England was growing in all the northern colonies, but nowhere was that growth as rapid and extensive as in Connecticut. Of course this was not all the work of Samuel Johnson. Many other forces had entered in. But in outline, his specific contributions had been sizable, indeed greater than perhaps any other single person's.

Johnson had first of all made Stratford a missionary center, visiting personally the nearby communities, with the result that churches were formed in Fairfield, Newtown, and all over Fairfield County.

He had steadily kept in mind, as fields for Anglican missionary work, not only the rest of Connecticut, but Long Island, Rhode Island, western Massachusetts, eastern New York and the Mohawk Valley. Repeatedly forwarding petitions from interested groups of lay people, he prodded the S. P. G. and missionaries into action.

He had fought the fight against unjust church taxation, and helped secure for Anglicanism at least a limited toleration in a hostile colony.

He had, by the operation of his one-man seminary, produced enough clergy to keep all the new missions he had recommended in some sort of operation. And he had attracted, or in some measure influenced, some forty men to the Anglican ministry.

He had, by means of numerous clergy conventions, taught the clergy of Connecticut – and of other colonies – to work together, to be conscious of their corporate existence. What he had accomplished during his lifetime is doubtless easier to determine than what his influence wrought in his successors. But that the present Diocese of Connecticut finally reached 137,000 baptized members, that one person in twenty in Connecticut is a member of the Episcopal Church – a figure far beyond the national average – is in some degree due to the fact that Samuel Johnson once lived and worked there.

Johnson's influence, then, did not end when his body was laid to rest in Christ Church, Stratford. We have already mentioned the fact that after the War of Independence, the Connecticut clergy were the first to meet and act as a body. They were the first in the American states to elect a bishop – and that a man whom Johnson had sent to England with a recommendation for ordination. Connecticut, then, was the first of the new American dioceses to emerge from the catastrophe of the war with a complete diocesan organization.

After diocesan organization came national organization. The story of the successive conventions from 1785 to 1789 has been well told, in great detail, by Clara Loveland.[5] They were, as she makes clear, stormy conventions that nearly ended in a schism instead of unity. Interestingly, she never states, though the implication is there in her details, that this was a churchmanship fight, a battle over the basic constitution and theology of the new organization. That the American Church emerged with a separate house of bishops, with complete power to initiate and to block legislation in the general convention, was due to the persistent action of Samuel Seabury, Jr., and the Connecticut Church, backed by the rest of New England, and New Jersey under the leadership of Thomas B. Chandler. That the Church was kept committed to the Catholicity of the historic creeds and the doctrine and discipline set forth in the *Book of Common Prayer* was also in large measure due to the steadfast loyalty of Johnsonian Churchmen.

Johnson, it will be especially remembered by every thoughtful reader of this volume, was a High Churchman – the first of American High Churchmen. True, he never sported a biretta nor wore Eucharistic vestments, he never swung a thurible and he never recited the rosary. But then, none of these are of the essence of High Churchmanship. Johnson was a High Churchman of the old school, who had learned from his reading of the Fathers and the Caroline divines to regard the Church of England as a basically Catholic body, and the apostolic succession of bishops as essential to a true church. He came to love the *Book of Common Prayer* as the best expression of corporate worship, and to set a high value on the grace conveyed by the sacraments. He was, if not the first American priest to grasp these things clearly, the first to propagate them effectively. He perpetuated and enriched a noble tradition.

We have no indisputable documentation to prove his transmission of these things to Bishop Seabury. But Seabury was a student at Yale when Johnson's influence there was at its peak; he went to England for ordination with Johnson's recommendation. As bishop, he advocated the doctrines Johnson had labored to spread.

Of the effect of Johnson on a still more important High Churchman than Seabury we have clear evidence. The first biography of Johnson was written by his favorite pupil, Thomas Bradbury Chandler. Chandler died before the book was published, and it was edited and seen through the press in 1805 by his son-in-law.[6] That son-in-law was John Henry Hobart. Hobart added to the book a long appendix, in which he stated, with characteristic Hobartian flair, the leading features of Johnson's theological emphasis. As Bishop of New York from 1811 to 1830, Hobart was the strongest leader the High Church party ever had in this country. Like Johnson, he trained pupils, and through his pupils the tradition passed on, through Bishops William Whittingham, Jackson Kemper, Benjamin and Henry Onderdonk, George Washington Doane, to such later men as Frederic D. Huntington, Francis Hall, James DeKoven, and William T. Manning.[7] Whether one accepts the tradition or not, it became one of the major features of the life and thought of the American Episcopal Church.

One last result of Johnson's work remains to be noted. The rapid expansion of the Episcopal Church in up-state New York after the War of Independence is one of the most dramatic events in American church history. The settlers who flowed into this region came largely from Connecticut, and many were Episcopalians. In community after community, from Schenectady west to Buffalo, we find the same thing happening. A group of Connecticut settlers gather into a frontier hamlet. They have brought with them in their scanty baggage copies of the *Book of Common Prayer*. And so they form themselves into a congregation, appoint one of their number lay reader, and Sunday after Sunday meet together for prayer book worship until a priest finally arrives and they become an incorporated parish. Four strong dioceses of the Episcopal Church – Albany, Central New York, Rochester, and Western New York – came into being largely because Connecticut Churchmen, trained into the tradition established by Samuel Johnson and his pupils, resolved to take their beloved Church with them into what was then the frontier. In view of his rather more limited accomplishments at King's College or as educator, philosopher, author and champion of an episcopate, these are perhaps among the most enduring monuments of Samuel Johnson. When it appeared that Episcopalians were repudiating Catholic Faith and Order in 1976 in ways that doubtless would have shocked Johnson and Seabury that heritage was defended by those who organized the Anglican Catholic Church which remained loyal to the exemplary work of the American Dr. Johnson.

Appendix A

A table showing the growth of the Anglican Church in Connecticut before 1772.[1] The list includes parishes and mission stations established during the period 1707-1772, with the date of their commencement, and whether each had a building and a resident priest, in 1772.

Date	Location	Building	Resident Priest
1707	Stratford	yes	yes
1723	West Haven	yes	yes
1724	Fairfield	yes	yes
1725	New London	yes	yes
1732	Newtown	yes	yes
1732	Redding	yes	
1734	Hebron	yes	yes
1737	Poquetanuch	yes	
1737	Waterbury	yes	yes
1737	Derby	yes	yes
1737	Norwalk	yes	
1739	Ridgefield	yes	
1739	Plymouth	yes	
1740	North Bloomfield	yes	yes
1740	Roxbury	yes	
1740	Woodbury	yes	yes
1740	Wallingford	yes	yes

Date	Location	Building	Resident Priest
1742	Stamford	yes	yes
1742	New Milford	yes	yes
1744	Guilford	yes	
1745	Litchfield	yes	
1747	Norwich	yes	yes
1747	Bristol		
1747	North Guilford	yes	
1748	Bridgeport	yes	
1749	Greenwich	yes	
1749	Huntington	yes	yes
1750	Middletown	yes	yes
1752	New Haven	yes	yes
1752	Branford		
1754	Sharon		
1759	North Haven	yes	
1760	Cheshire	yes	
1760	Tashua	yes	
1762	Hartford	yes	
1762	Easton	yes	
1764	Danbury	yes	
1764	Milford	yes	
1764	Oxford	yes	
1764	New Preston	yes	
1764	Watertown	yes	
1765	Northford	yes	
1771	Brooklyn	yes	

Appendix B

The following is a list of Yale students who entered the ministry of the Church of England between 1722 and 1772. The year of their graduation or departure from Yale follows each name; at least two, Punderson and Clarke, were educated at Yale but did not receive their degrees there. Where these men are treated in the body of this book, only their names have been given below. Otherwise, we include some biographical data. The information comes largely from Dexter, Yale Graduates.

Samuel Johnson, 1714.

Daniel Browne, 1714.

James Wetmore, 1714. Ordained to the Congregational ministry, 1718. Ordained priest in England, 1724. Assistant at Trinity Church, New York, 1724-1726. Rector at Rye, New York, 1726 until his death in 1761. Wrote controversial pamphlets in the press war between Anglicans and Dissenters.

John Beach, 1721.

Daniel Dwight, 1721. Congregational chaplain at Fort Dummer. Ordained in England, 1729, and worked in South Carolina.

Jonathan Arnold, 1723. Succeeded Johnson as Congregational minister at West Haven. Received first communion from Johnson at Easter 1734. Ordained in England in 1736, worked in Connecticut and on Staten Island.

Henry Caner, 1724.

Ebenezer Punderson, 1726. Ordained to the Congregational ministry, 1729. Converted by the Reverend James McSparren in 1734. Ordained in the Church of England the same year, and held parishes at New Haven and Rye. "The Church in America has had few missionaries to match this now almost forgotten circuit-rider, who was never quite at ease out of the saddle."[1]

Isaac Browne, 1729. Brother of Johnson's friend Daniel. Ordained in 1733, he held the parish in Newark, New Jersey until the Revolutionary War, when he went to Canada.

Solomon Palmer, 1729. Congregational minister, ordained in 1735. In 1754 ordained priest of the Church of England and worked mainly in Litchfield, Connecticut.

John Pierson, 1729. Received first communion from Johnson in 1732. Ordained in 1733, and ministered thereafter at Salem, New Jersey.

Ebenezer Thompson, 1731. Admitted to communion by Johnson in 1734. Worked as lay reader at Simsbury. Ordained in 1743, and settled at Scituate, Massachusetts, where he remained until his death in 1775.

Henry Barclay, 1734.

Ebenezer Dibble, 1734. Licentiate in the Congregational Church. Ordained in England in 1748, he was rector at Stamford and Greenwich for fifty years.

Richard Caner, 1736. Brother of Henry Caner. Ordained in 1741, he served at Norwalk and on Staten Island.

Barzillai Dean, 1737. Converted while in college, admitted to communion in Stratford. Ordained in 1745, he was lost at Sea on the way back.

Hezekiah Watkins, 1737. Congregational licentiate. Admitted to communion by Johnson, ordained in England in 1743, and served at New Windsor and Newburgh, New York.

Christopher Newton, 1740. Licensed in Congregational Church. Ordained priest in the Church of England in 1755. He was missionary at Ripton until his death in 1787.

Joseph Lamson, 1741. Admitted to communion by Johnson in 1743. Ordained in 1745; followed Henry Caner as rector at Fairfield.

Richard Mansfield, 1741. Converted in 1744, ordained 1748. Rector of Derby, Connecticut until 1820. Yale gave him a D.D. in 1792 – the first Anglican priest to be so honored by Yale.

Ichabod Camp, 1743. Licensed in the Congregational Church, ordained priest in England in 1752, missionary at Middletown, Connecticut.

Jonathan Copp, 1744. Convert in 1747, ordained in 1750, missionary in the southern colonies.

Thomas Bradbury Chandler, 1745.

Jonathan Colton, 1745. Ordained in England in 1752, died of smallpox on the way back.

Jeremiah Leaming, 1745.

William Sturgeon, 1745. Son of a Congregational minister, converted about the time he graduated. Ordained in 1747, then became assistant at Christ Church, Philadelphia.

William Johnson, 1748.

John Ogilvie, 1748. Lay reader at Norwalk in 1749. Ordained possibly in Scotland. Army chaplain at Albany and missionary to the Mohawks. Chaplain again during the Great War for the Empire (1754-1763), later assistant at Trinity Church, New York.

Samuel Seabury, 1748.

James Greaton, 1754. Ordained in 1760, later succeeded Timothy Cutler at Christ Church, Boston.

Luke Babcock, 1755. Ordained in 1769, missionary at Yonkers, New York. Imprisoned as a Tory, and died of the effects in 1777.

Abraham Beach, 1757. Converted about 1764, he studied under his uncle John Beach and Johnson, and was ordained in 1768. He served at Perth Amboy and New Brunswick, New Jersey. He lived until 1828. (Johnson's connection with the Beach family is further illustrated by the fact that he married Sarah Beach, the widow of Abraham's uncle William.)[2]

Samuel Peters, 1757. Ordained in 1759, he was missionary at Hebron until the Revolution. He hoped to be made bishop. In 1781 he published a history of Connecticut, notorious for its anti-Puritan bias and inaccuracy.

James Scovil, 1757. His father was a convert. In 1758 the Episcopalians of Waterbury raised money to send him to England for ordination. After ordination in 1759 he became rector of Waterbury, where he remained until 1785.

Thomas Davies, 1758. Ordained in 1761, he was missionary at New Milford and parts adjacent until his death from tuberculosis in 1766.

Bela Hubbard, 1758. He studied under Johnson at King's College. Ordained in 1764, he was missionary at Guilford, then rector of a church in New Haven. He became one of the leading priests of the Diocese of Connecticut, and was given a D.D. by Yale in 1804.

Roger Viets, 1758.

Samuel Andrews, 1759. Ordained in 1761, he was missionary at Wallingford. He was fined and confined to his house during the Revolution.

Agur Treadwell, 1760. Ordained in 1762, he was missionary at Trenton, New Jersey until his death in 1765.[3]

Ephraim Avery, 1761. His father was a Congregational minister. He was ordained in 1765, and served at Rye, New York.

Abraham Jarvis, 1761.

Ebenezer Kneeland, 1761. Ordained in 1766. Served first as chaplain in the British army, then as assistant to Johnson at Stratford. He succeeded as rector of Stratford.

John Lyon, 1761. Ordained in 1764, he served as missionary in Massachusetts and Delaware.

Gideon Bostwick, 1762.

Richard Clarke, 1762. He was baptized by Johnson, received his B.A. and M.A. from King's College.[4] Ordained in 1767, he was missionary at New Milford.

John Tyler, 1765. Became an Anglican in his boyhood. He studied under Johnson and functioned as lay reader in Guilford. Ordained in 1768, he served at Norwich until his death in 1823.

James Nichols, 1771. He was one of the last to go to England for ordination. A Loyalist during the Revolution, he later was rector at Arlington, Vermont. He was suspended from the ministry in 1819.

Footnotes

The essential list of sources for the Bibliography is indicated by the footnotes.

Footnotes for Preface

1. E. Edwards Beardsley, *Life and Correspondence of Samuel Johnson*, D. D. (New York, 1874).

2. Herbert and Carol Schneider (eds.), *Samuel Johnson, President of King's College: His Career and Writings* (4 vols.; New York, 1929). Hereafter cited as Schneider, *Johnson Writings*.

3. Larry Lee Bothell, Princeton University doctoral dissertation (1967), "Cloak and Gown: A Study of Religion and Learning in the Early Career of Samuel William Johnson of Connecticut;" Joseph Ellis, Yale University doctoral dissertation on Johnson as the Puritan mind in transition and his "The Puritan Mind in Transition: The Philosophy of Samuel Johnson," *William and Mary Quarterly*, 3d. Ser., XXVIII (1971); Norman S. Fiering, "President Samuel Johnson and the Circle of Knowledge," *ibid.*, XXVIII (1971); Donald F. Gerardi, Columbia University doctoral dissertation on the American Dr. Johnson: the Eighteenth Century Clergyman as Intellectual and Educator; also, Peter Carroll of the University of Minnesota projects "A Study of Samuel Johnson as a case study of the provincial mind... ." *The Connecticut History Newsletter,* VI (1970), 6. See also Theodore Hornberger, "Samuel Johnson of Yale and King's College: A Note on the Relation of Science and Religion in Provincial America," *The New England Quarterly*, VIII (1935); Vincent Buranelli, "Colonial Philosophy;' *William and Mary Quarterly*, 3d Ser., XVI (1959), 359. Johnson's central role in eighteenth-century Anglicanism is examined in Gerald Joseph

Goodwin, University of Wisconsin doctoral dissertation (1965), "The Anglican Middle Way in Early Eighteenth-Century America: Anglican Religious Thought in the American Colonies, 1702-1750." Joseph Ellis's *The New England Mind in Transition: Samuel Johnson of Connecticut, 1696-1722* (Yale University Press, 1973) is the most recent work approaching a biography of Johnson, but is devoted mostly to intellectual history, and leaves out or barely sketches many points of Johnson's life. Its value is the assessment of Johnson's intellectual activities, but Ellis does not appreciate the character of Johnson's conversion to Anglicanism, and is more impressed by the similarities between Johnson's Puritanism and Anglicanism than by the differences. Peter N. Carroll's *The Other Samuel Johnson: A Psychohistory of Early New England* (Associated University Presses, Inc., 1978) yielded some highly questionable results and reflects the persistence of old views, the secularism of our age, and a preference for Freudian psychology and for treating religion merely as a social phenomenon.

4. Isaac Woodbridge Riley, *American Philosophy: The Early Schools* (New York, 1907).

5. Schneider, *Johnson Writings*, II, 21.

6. Claude M. Newlin, *Philosophy and Religion in Colonial America* (New York, 1962).

7. Carl Bridenbaugh, *Mitre and Sceptre: Transatlantic Faiths, Ideas, Personalities, and Politics, 1689-1775* (New York, 1962). Bridenbaugh cites Johnson's "Sound judgment, moderation in speech and action ... skill in tactics and grand strategy," but emphasizes how he "harped" on the subject of episcopacy and how his "religious partisanship blinded him to many of the verities of American life." (pp. 74-75.) But Bridenbaugh's work is a queer combination of excellent research with a perverse thesis about "Anglican aggression." He himself overlooks some of the verities of American colonial life – such as the Anglican struggle for toleration in Connecticut and the rest of New England. He fails to appreciate that it was a revolt of the religiously underprivileged who struggled as much for a parity with Protestant Dissenters as for any kind of dominant position. And he prefers to overlook the Dissenters' aggression and their failure to understand that Anglicans could have legitimately claimed what Protestants had achieved in the colonies – toleration and a full ecclesiastical organization. Although Bridenbaugh tells admirably the story of the Dissenters' transatlantic operations, he has adopted their prejudices and, like them, refuses to believe the Anglicans' professions that they had no designs against the religious liberty of others.

Footnotes for Chapter I

1. George L. Walker, *Thomas Hooker* (New York, 1891), 34ff.

2. Charles M. Andrews, *The Colonial Period of American History* (4 vols.; New Haven, 1934-1938), II, 105.

3. Edwin Oviatt, *The Beginnings of Yale, 1701-1726* (New Haven, 1916), 48, 49.

4. Edward E. Atwater, *History of the Colony of New Haven to its Absorption into Connecticut* (New Haven, 1881), 185.

5. Edward R. Lamberts, *History of the Colony of New Haven Before and After the Union with Connecticut* (New Haven, 1838), 31-34.

6. Andrews, *The Colonial Period*, II, 192-193.

7. "The Charter of Connecticut, 1662," *Tercentenary Commission of the State of Connecticut Committee of Historical Publications. No. 3* (Nos. 1-60; New Haven, 1933-1936), 17; Andrews, *The Colonial Period*, II, 137-139.

8. Williston Walker (ed.), *The Creeds and Platforms of Congregationalism* (Boston, 1960), 11-19, 29-40, 134-135, 139, 143-148, 171-200, 203-237, 245-266, 465-508.

9. Herbert W. Schneider, *The Puritan Mind* (Ann Arbor, Mich., 1958), 23-24.

10. Edmund S. Morgan, *Visible Saints. The History of a Puritan Idea* (New York, 1963), 113.

11. Cotton Mather, *Magnalia Christi Americana. or, the Ecclesiastical History of New England* (2 vols.; Harvard: Silas Andrus, 1820), II, 184.

12. Williston Walker, *The History of the Congregational Churches in the United States* (New York, 1894), 45.

13. The first step toward religious liberty in Connecticut seems to have been taken in 1669. After the Hartford church split over acceptance of the Halfway Covenant, those who wanted it asked the General Court to permit a division of the church and to exempt those withdrawing from the old church from paying the local taxes levied for its support. The Court allowed pious and peaceable dissenters from the Covenant a practice of their beliefs so long as they were orthodox and sound in other matters. But of course this was not toleration for non-Puritan Christians. Paul Wakeman Coons, "The Achievement of Religious Liberty in Connecticut," *Tercentenary Commission of the State of Connecticut Committee of Historical Publications, No. 60* (Nos. 1-60; New Haven, 19331936), 10-11.

14. J. H. Trumbull and C. J. Hoadley (eds.), *The Public Records of the Colony of Connecticut* (15 vols.; Hartford, 1850-1890), I, 111-112, 311-312; V, 50-51.

15. Mather, *Magnalia*, II, 239-258; Schneider, *Puritan Mind*, 86-91; Walker (ed.), *Creeds and Platforms*, 245-266. For more detailed discussion of the origins and workings of the half-way covenant see Robert G. Pope, *The Half-Way Covenant: Church Membership in Puritan New England* (Princeton, N.J., 1969) and Ross W. Beales, Jr., "The Half-Way Covenant and Religious Scrupulosity: The First Church of Dorchester, Massachusetts, as a Test Case," *William and Mary Quarterly*, 3d. Ser., XXXI (1974), 465-480. Further disarray and change in New England is discussed in James W. Jones, *The Shattered Synthesis: New England Puritanism before the Great Awakening* (New Haven, Conn., 1973).

16. Richard L. Bushman, *From Puritan to Yankee* (Cambridge, Mass., 1967), 148.

17. Oviatt, *Beginnings of Yale*, 116.

18. Bushman, *Puritan to Yankee*, 151. The act providing for the Saybrook Platform is in *Public Records of Connecticut*, V, 51-52.

19. *Public Records of Connecticut*, IV, 216. A convenient summary of how and why the ordination of ministers by laymen came to be replaced by ordinations by ministers is given by J. William T. Youngs, Jr., "Congregational Clericalism: New England Ordinations before the Great Awakening," *William and Mary Quarterly*, 3d. Ser., XXXI (1974), 481-490. Because of various social turmoil the ministers tended to become more and more presbyterian and sacerdotal, thus emphasizing "their distinct professional standing."

20. Evarts B. Greene and Virginia D. Harrington, *American Population Before the Federal Census of 1790* (New York, 1932), 47-48. The 30,000 souls included about 150 Anglicans.

21. Oviatt, *Beginnings of Yale*, 260-262.

22. Edmund S. Morgan, *The Puritan Family* (New York, 1966), 89.

23. *Public Records of Connecticut*, IV, 363-365.

24. Our discussion of the Stratford Anglicans is based largely on Kenneth W. Cameron's annals and collection of documents, *The Genesis of Christ Church, Stratford, Connecticut* (Stratford, 1957), 3, 50-52.

25. *Ibid.*, 5-6, 57-58; *Public Records of Connecticut*, I, 437-438.

26. Cameron, *Genesis of Christ Church*, 10-11.

27. The rumor about Reed is only hearsay, but it seems to be borne out by letters of Colonel Caleb Heathcote to the Secretary of the S. P. G. in 1707, *Ibid.*, 12, 20-21,23-24.

28. *Ibid.*, 18-19,21-23.

29. *Ibid.*, 18-19, 25. The activities of Heathcote and Muirson are discussed in greater detail in Samuel M. Garrett, "George Muirson And The Mission Into Connecticut," *Historical Magazine of the Protestant Episcopal Church*, XLIII (1974),125-168, which includes one of Muirson's letters to John Chamberlayn, Jan. 9, 1707/8, describing the situation in Connecticut.

30. *Public Records of Connecticut*, V, 50-51.

31. Cameron, *Genesis of Christ Church*. 27-28.

32. *Ibid.*, 28.

33. *Ibid.*, 33.

34. Herbert and Carol Schneider (eds.), *Samuel Johnson, President of King's College: His Career and Writings* (4 vols.; New York, 1929), I, 11. The quotations are Johnson's. Hereafter cited as Schneider, *Johnson Writings*.

35. Bray also organized a Society for the Promotion of Christian Knowledge (S. P. C. K.) to provide libraries for colonial Anglicans. And one of the byproducts of Bray's associates was the foundation of the colony of Georgia in 1733 -- another example of the far-flung reaches of Anglican humanitarianism and English empire-building in the eighteenth century.

Footnotes for Chapter II

1. Old Style. All dates are left as they appear in the sources cited.

2. Schneider, *Johnson Writings*, I, 3.

3. *Ibid.*, I, 3-4.

4. *Ibid.*, I, 4.

5. Franklin B. Dexter (ed.), *Biographical Sketches of the Graduates of Yale College* (6 vols.; New York and New Haven, 1885-1912), I, 52-56.

6. Schneider, *Johnson Writings*, I, 5.

7. Louis Leonard Tucker, *Puritan Protagonist: President Thomas Clap of Yale College* (Chapel Hill, N.C., 1962), 8-10.

8. Oviatt, *Beginnings of Yale*, 256, offers a map of Saybrook.

9. *Ibid.*, 239.

10. Dexter, *Yale Graduates*, I, 115.

11. Schneider, *Johnson Writings*, II, 51.

12. *Ibid.*, II, 57.

13. *Ibid.*, I, 7.

14. Oviatt, *Beginnings of Yale*, 257.

15. *Ibid.*, 290.

16. *Public Records of Connecticut*, V, 353, 355-356, 360; Sheldon S. Cohen, "The Diary of Jeremiah Dummer," *William and Mary Quarterly*, 3d Ser., XXIV (1967),419-420.

17. Oviatt, *Beginnings of Yale*, 298ff. *Papers in Honor of Andrew Keogh, Library of Yale University* (New Haven, 1938), 7-44 gives the list of books that Dummer collected. Cotton Mather's library of between 3,000 and 4,000 titles accumulated by 1728, and William Byrd II's of about 3,600 in 1744 were among the few, if not the only, collections larger than Yale's. Louis B. Wright, *The Cultural Life of the American Colonies*, 1607-1763 (New York, 1957), 145.

18. Franklin B. Dexter (ed.), *Documentary History of Yale University* (New Haven, 1916), 63; *Public Records of Connecticut*, V, 528-529.

19. Dexter, *Documentary History of Yale*, 64; Schneider, *Johnson Writings*, I, 7-8; *Public Records of Connecticut*, VI, 30. Curiously enough, before the college was settled at New Haven, the representatives had voted to locate it at Middletown. And in May 1717 they voted for "some place at or near the Connecticut River." In May 1718 the house responded to a general tide of dissatisfaction by a decision for a Connecticut River location; until the matter was resolved, it was decided that public funds be divided among tutors at Wethersfield, Saybrook and New Haven and that commencements should be held alternately at Wethersfield and New Haven. *Ibid.*, VI, 30n.

20. Strangely enough, Dexter does not mention the revolt either in *Yale Graduates* or the *Documentary History of Yale*. The story is as Oviatt, *Beginnings of Yale* tells it. But that Oviatt was not romancing is proven by the mention of the affair in Johnson's autobiography, Schneider, *Johnson Writings*, I, 7-8.

21. Schneider, *Johnson Writings*, I, 6.

22. *Ibid.*, I, 10-11.

23. *Ibid.*, I, 11.

24. *Ibid.*, III, 297.

Footnotes for Chapter III

1. Dexter, *Documentary History of Yale*, 73-74.

2. *Ibid.*, 76; Schneider, *Johnson Writings*, I, 8.

3. Dexter, *Documentary History of Yale*, 92. The trustees reaffirmed their action of October 1716 on April 5, 1717, and again appealed to the General Assembly in regard to the location of the school. *Ibid.*, 89. *Public Records of Connecticut*, VI, 30n refers to the issue causing "much feeling" in several sessions of the assembly.

4. This description is based on Thomas Bradbury Chandler, *The Life of Samuel Johnson, D. D.* (New York, 1805).

5. Tucker, *Puritan Protagonist,* 82.

6. Dexter, *Yale Graduates*, I, 163.

7. William Stevens Perry, *The History of the American Episcopal Church, 1587-1883* (2 vols.; Boston, 1885), I, 214.

8. *Public Records of Connecticut*, V, 37-39.

9. Dexter, *Documentary History of Yale*, 146.

10. Dexter, *Yale Graduates*, I, 200.

11. Dexter, *Documentary History of Yale*, 28, 179-180, 184-186. Cf, *Public Records of Connecticut*, VI, 83-84.

12. Henry B. Parkes, Jonathan Edwards: The Fiery Puritan (New York, 1930), 44-45.

13. Dexter, *Documentary History of Yale*, 187-191. *Cf. Public Records of Connecticut*, VI, 101.

14. Parkes, *Jonathan Edwards*, 60.

15. Dexter, *Documentary History of Yale*, 189. *Cf. Public Records of Connecticut*, VI, 100.

16. Dexter, *Documentary History of Yale*, 198.

17. Schneider, *Johnson Writings*, I, 497-526.

18. *Ibid.*, III, 3-8.

19. *Ibid.*, III, 3-5. In a day when so much church controversy dealt with trivialities like the wearing of a surplice or the sign of the cross in baptism, it is interesting that Johnson got down to fundamentals.

20. *Ibid.*, III, 5-6.

21. *Ibid.*, III, 7.

22. *Ibid.*, III, 8.

23. Dexter, *Yale Graduates*, I, 124.

24. Schneider, *Johnson Writings*, II, 8.

25. *Ibid.*, I, 500.

26. Whittlesey's son eventually became a tutor at Yale, where he was reputed to be tainted with the Arminian "heresy."

27. Perry Miller, *Errand into the Wilderness* (Cambridge, Mass., 1956), 112.

Footnotes for Chapter IV

1. Schneider, *Johnson Writings*, I, 13.

2. Raymond W. Albright, *A History of the Protestant Episcopal Church* (New York, 1964), 63.

3. E. Edwards Beardsley, *Life and Correspondence of Samuel Johnson, D. D.* (2d. Ed.; New York, 1874), 15.

4. Schneider, *Johnson Writings*, I, 14; s. D. McConnell, *History of the American Episcopal Church From the Planting of the Colonies to the End of the Civil War* (New York, 1890), 127ff.

5. Perry, *History of the American Episcopal Church,* I, 247-248. Perry adds that "at the same time two more, and these pastors of great note, gave their assent, of whom the one, Mr. Buckely, of Colchester, declared Episcopacy to be *jure divino*, and the other, Mr. Whiting, of some remote town, also gave in his opinion for moderate Episcopacy." There is some evidence that John Buckley, Harvard 1699, had Episcopal leanings. Whiting cannot be identified.

6. Schneider, *Johnson Writings*, I, 14.

7. *Ibid.*, I, 62. Note how the very language of The Book of Common Prayer had crept into Johnson's thought and writing. The end of this passage comes directly from the Litany.

8. *Ibid.*

9. Francis L. Hawks and William Stevens Perry (eds.), *Documentary History of the Protestant Episcopal Church in the United States of America, Containing Numerous Hitherto Unpublished Documents Concerning the Church in Connecticut* (2 vols.; New York, 1863-1864), I, 63.

10. *Ibid.*, I, 67-71.

11. *Ibid.*, I, 75-78.

12. Schneider, *Johnson Writings*, I, 14.

13. In a letter to the Bishop of London in 1727, Johnson said: "Absolute lay ordination is the avowed principle of some of the chief of their ministers, and has been frequently practiced in the country, and even in this town, though now, of late, their ministers generally ordain." Here Johnson probably overstated his case. Hawks and Perry, *Documentary History*, I, 108.

14. Oviatt, *Beginnings of Yale*, 407.

15. Schneider, *Johnson Writings*, I, 6f.

16. Perry, *History of the American Episcopal Church*, I, 250-251.

17. Schneider, *Johnson Writings*, I, 15-16.

18. E. Edwards Beardsley, *The History of the Episcopal Church in Connecticut* (2 vols.; New York, 1866-1868), I, 42-43. Arminius is the Latinized form of the name of Jakob Hermanns (1560-1609) who was a Dutch theologian, a professor at the University of Leyden. In reaction against the Calvinist doctrine of predestination he arrived at the contrary doctrine that "the providence of God, while sovereign, is exercised in harmony with the nature of the creatures governed, *i.e.,* the sovereignty of God is so exercised as to be compatible with the freedom of man." Thus, anyone who challenged predestination was labeled "Arminian," even though, like Johnson, he had never read a line of Arminius, and had arrived at the doctrine of man's free will by the study of Catholic theologians.

19. Beardsley, *Life of Johnson,* 23. A comparison of Johnson's journal (microfilm copy in the New York State Library) with Beardsley's transcription shows that Beardsley included everything of importance in the journal and that the transcription in his *Life of Johnson* is faithful to the original. The reader may be consistently referred to Beardsley.

20. *Ibid.*

21. *Ibid,* 25.

22. Schneider, *Johnson Writings*, I, 16-17.

23. Beardsley, *Life of Johnson*, 28. Checkley was already known to Cutler, and it has been stated that he was influential in swinging Cutler to Anglicanism.

24. Perry, *History of the American Episcopal Church*, I, 264. Perry's allegation that Checkley was on the same ship that took Cutler and his friends to England is contradicted by Johnson's travel journal as quoted above.

25. Schneider, *Johnson Writings*, I, 18.

26. *Ibid.*, II, 8.

27. Beardsley, *Life of Johnson*, 31.

28. *Ibid.*, 29.

29. *Ibid.*, 30.

30. *Ibid.*, 34.

31. *Ibid.*, 35. The Articles were of course the Thirty-Nine Articles of Religion.

32. *Ibid.*, 36.

33. *Ibid.*, 41.

34. Beardsley, *History of the Episcopal Church in Connecticut*, I, 51; Schneider, *Johnson Writings*, I, 19.

Footnotes for Chapter V

1. Hawks and Perry, *Documentary History*, I, 61.

2. Beardsley, *History of the Episcopal Church in Connecticut*, I, 51-52.

3. Samuel Orcutt, *History of the Old Town of Stratford* (2 vols.; New Haven, 1886), I, 292, 295.

4. *Ibid.*, I, 297.

5. *Ibid.*, I, 318-319.

6. According to Orcutt, it was designed by Thomas Salmon, vestryman and schoolmaster, who had some English training as an architect, and who was eventually to design the far different second church.

7. Manuscript Parish Records, Christ Church, Stratford, Connecticut, indirectly indicate the practice of monthly celebrations of the Holy Communion by reference to communion alms collections on those days. Hereafter cited as MS Church Records (Stratford).

8. MS Church Records (Stratford), I, 40.

9. *Ibid*., I, 45; II, 36, 39. The Puritans were apt to allege that men joined the Anglican church to avoid paying local church rates to the Congregational establishment. The above evidence shows the falsity of this charge.

10. Schneider, *Johnson Writings*, III, 224-225.

11. Hawks and Perry, *Documentary History*, II, 55.

12. Schneider, *Johnson Writings*, III, 227, 229, 239, 243-244, 255. These are quotations from the semi-annual reports required by the S. P. G. The 1754 report notes that Johnson's predecessor had baptized 60, which brings the total to 1,021, and had admitted 74 communicants, which brings the total to 517.

13. Hawks and Perry, *Documentary History*, I, 131

14. For Johnson's reports see Schneider, *Johnson Writings*, III, 224, 233, 239, 243, 247. For evidence "that New England Anglicanism in its area of greatest numerical strength – the farm community and the rural village – was in good part a lower class movement," see Bruce E. Steiner, "New England Anglicanism: A Genteel Faith?," *William and Mary Quarterly*, 3d. Ser., XXVII (1970), 122-135.

15. Nelson Rollin Burr, *The Story of the Diocese of Connecticut* (Hartford, 1962), 66-67; MS Church Records (Stratford), II, 81, undated entry probably from 1763: "Voted that ten shillings of the money collected at the communion be paid monthly to Thomas Stratton, who undertakes for the same to lead upon the organ."

16. Schneider, *Johnson Writings*, I, 133.

17. William H. Wilcoxson, *History of Stratford, Connecticut* (Stratford, 1939), 210.

18. Schneider, *Johnson Writings*, I, 20.

19. *Ibid*., I, 20, 203.

20. *Ibid*., I, 68.

21. *Ibid*., I, 56, 69-70.

22. Chandler, *Life of Samuel Johnson*, 133.

23. Hawks and Perry, *Documentary History*, I, 94; cf. Schneider, *Johnson Writings*, III, 218, 223.

24. *Ibid*., I, 58, 145-11,6.

25. In his journal Johnson made this entry on the birth of William: "O my God I give this child as well as the other to Thee! Bless them both. Let them live to do a great deal of good in the world and (if it may be thy will) let me live to see them

well educated and engaged in thy service! Give them sound and healthy constitutions, capacious understandings, teachable and obedient tempers and above all sanctified hearts and virtuous lives, that no iniquity may have dominion over them!" *Ibid.*, I, 70.

26. George C. Groce, Jr., *William Samuel Johnson: A Maker of the Constitution* (New York, 1937).

27. Schneider, *Johnson Writings*, I, 126-127.

28. *Ibid.*, I, 184-185.

29. Hawks and Perry, *Documentary History*, I, 89.

30. *Ibid.*, I, 81, 140.

31. Schneider, *Johnson Writings*, III, 217.

32. MS Church Records (Stratford), I, 42-43.

33. Hawks and Perry, *Documentary History*, I, 101.

34. *Ibid.*, I, 127.

35. Schneider, *Johnson Writings*, I, 89-92.

36. Beardsley, *History of the Episcopal Church in Connecticut*, I, 56.

37. Burr, *Diocese of Connecticut*, 30-31; see also Joseph J. Ellis, III, "Anglicans in Connecticut,1725-1750: The Conversion of the Missionaries," *New England Quarterly*, XLIV (1971),66-81. However, Ellis's conclusion that Johnson had to behave like a Puritan and "formulate pragmatic policies that closely resembled the policies of the New England churches" (p. 81) is over-simplified and his estimate too categorical that "Anglicans in Connecticut failed."

38. *Public Records of Connecticut*, VII, 106-107. The law provided that all residents of a Congregational parish must pay the religious tax levy, but that taxes paid by Anglicans would be delivered "unto the minister of the church of England living near unto such persons;" and Anglicans were excused from paying levies for building Congregational meeting houses.

39. Hawks and Perry, *Documentary History*, I, 199-200.

40. William Howland Kenney III, "George Whitefield, Dissenter Priest of the Great Awakening, 1739-1741," *William and Mary Quarterly*, 3d. Ser., XXVI (1969),75-93.

41. Schneider, *Johnson Writings*, III, 228.

42. Hawks and Perry, *Documentary History*, 1,180-181.

43. See for example Edwin S. Gaustad, *The Great Awakening in New England* (New York, 1957); C. C. Goen, *Revivalism and Separatism in New England, 1740-1800: Strict Congregationalists and Separate Baptists in the Great Awakening* (New Haven, 1962); William W. Sweet, *Religion in Colonial America* (New York, 1942); Glenn Weaver, "Anglican-Congregationalist Tensions in Pre-Revolutionary Connecticut,' *Historical Magazine of the Protestant Episcopal Church*, XXVI (1957), 269-285.

44. Schneider, *Johnson Writings*, I, 157.

45. Bruce E. Steiner, "Samuel Seabury and the Forging of the High Church Tradition: A Study in the Evolution of New England Churchmanship, 1722-1796" (unpublished Ph.D. dissertation: University of Virginia, 1962), 82-83.

46. Schneider, *Johnson Writings* I, 105-107.

47. See Appendix A.

48. Steiner, "Samuel Seabury and the Forging of the High Church Tradition," 19-23, 53-59, 64-65, 73-74.

Footnotes for Chapter VI

1. Schneider, *Johnson Writings*, I, 502-506.

2. *Ibid.*, II, 263-270.

3. *Ibid.*, II, 309-320.

4. *Ibid.*, I, 29.

5. *Ibid.*, III, 19.

6. *Ibid.*

7. *Ibid.*, III, 37-38.

8. *Ibid.*, III, 118.

9. *Ibid.*, II, v, 357-518.

10. *Ibid.*, I, 29-30, 117; III, 161*ff.*

11. *Ibid.*, I, 20-23, 76-79.

12. *Ibid.*, II, 305.

13. *Ibid.*, II, 327. Writing to Bishop Berkeley in 1752, Johnson described Franklin as "one Mr. Franklin, an ingenious public-spirited gentleman of Philadelphia, a zealous promoter, and one of the founders of their college...." *Ibid.*, II, 329.

14. *Ibid.*, I, 140-142, 154.

15. *Ibid.*, I, 155.

Footnotes for Chapter VII

1. Hawks and Perry, *Documentary History*, I, 105.

2. *Ibid.*, I, 113.

3. *Ibid.*, I, 128.

4. *Ibid.*, I, 145.

5. Groce, *William Samuel Johnson*, 5-6.

6. Hawks and Perry, *Documentary History*, I, 213-214.

7. Tucker, *Puritan Protagonist*, 169.

8. Hawks and Perry, *Documentary History*, I, 152.

9. Burr, *Diocese of Connecticut*, 30.

10. Emest, Hawkins, *Historical Notices of the Missions of the Church of England in the North American Colonies* (London, 1845), 214-215.

11. Hawks and Perry, *Documentary History*, I, 140.

12. *Ibid.*, I, 245.

13. *Ibid.*, I, 223.

14. See Appendix B.

15. Burr, *Diocese of Connecticut,* 56.

16. George E. De Mille, *A History of the Diocese of Albany* (Philadelphia, 1946), 5.

17. Schneider, *Johnson Writings*, I, 155.

18. *Ibid.*, III, 274.

19. *Ibid.*, I, 439.

20. Hawks and Perry, *Documentary History*, fI, 136.

21. John Langden Sibley, *Sibley's Harvard Graduates, 1642-1689* (vols. 1-3; Boston, 1873-1885) and Clifford K. Shipton (ed.), *Sibley's Harvard Graduates, 1690-1763* (vols. 4-15; Boston, 1933--).

Footnotes for Chapter VIII

1. Schneider, *Johnson Writings*, I, 149.

2. *Ibid.*, I, 150.

3. *Ibid.*, I, 295.

4. *Ibid.*, I, 420.

5. *Ibid.*, I, 295.

6. *Ibid.*, I, 392.

7. *Ibid.*, I, 88.

8. *Ibid.*

9. *Ibid.*, I, 297-301.

10. *Ibid.*, I, 361.

11. *Ibid.*, I, 452-453.

12. *Ibid.*, II, 359-441.

13. *Ibid.*, I, 183.

14. Adam Leroy Jones, *Early American Philosophers* (New York, 1898: reissued 1958),42. Jones notes how Johnson recognized "an important pedagogical principle which is valid today."

15. Schneider, *Johnson Writings*, II, 360-361. See also Graham P. Conroy, "Berkeley and Education in America," *Journal of the History of Ideas*, XXI (1960), 211-221.

16. Schneider, *Johnson Writings*, II, 422-424.

17. Jones, *Early American Philosophers*, 43.

18. Schneider, *Johnson Writings*, II, 424.

19. *Ibid.*, II, 224.

20. *Ibid.*, II, 428.

21. Jones, *Early American Philosophers*, 44.

22. Schneider, *Johnson Writings*, II, 428-435.

23. *Ibid.*, II, 521-600.

24. *Ibid.*, II, 555.

25. *Ibid.*, II, 556.

26. *Ibid.*, II, 561.

27. *Ibid.*, II, 562-563.

28. *Ibid.*, II, 565.

29. *Ibid.*, II, 566.

30. *Ibid.*, II, 568.

31. Jones, *Early American Philosophers, 22, 45.* See also Lawrence A. Cremin, *American Education: The Colonial Experience, 1607-1783* (New York, 1970), 461-462 *et passim.*

32. Vincent Buranelli, "Colonial Philosophy," *William and Mary Quarterly*, 3d. Ser., XVI (1959), 353, 358-359, 362.

33. W. T. Jones, *A History of Western Philosophy* (New York, 1952), 761.

34. *Ibid.*, 762; Jones, *Early American Philosophers*, 27-29.

35. *Ibid.*, 24.

36. Schneider, *Johnson Writings*, II, 309-312.

37. *Ibid.*, II, 313-320.

38. Jones, *Early American Philosophers* offers an excellent, brief review of Johnson's development of Berkeley's idealism. Buranelli, "Colonial Philosophy" discusses the need for studies of colonial philosophy and for a detailed examination of Johnson's system. Joseph J. Ellis III has responded to Buranelli's call with "The Puritan Mind in Transition: The Philosophy of Samuel Johnson," *William and Mary Quarterly*, 3d. Ser., XXVIII (1971),26-45. It is a fine essay which explains in greater detail how Johnson combined Berkeley's system with his Yale training and Platonism. See also Norman S. Fiering, "President Samuel Johnson and the Circle of Knowledge," *Ibid.*, XXVIII (1971), 199-236.

39. Robert A. Whittemore, *Makers of the American Mind* (New York, 1964), 56; Jones, *Early American Philosophers*, 30-31.

40. *Ibid.*, 31.

41. Schneider, *Johnson Writings*, III, 400.

42. *Ibid.*, III, 161-183. It was followed in 1746 by a letter to Jonathan Dickinson after the latter attacked the argument. *Ibid.*, III, 184-205.

43. *Ibid.*, III, 167-168.

44. *Ibid.*, III, 176-177.

45. *Ibid.*, III, 412.

46. *Ibid.*, III, 563.

47. *Ibid.*, III, 592.

48. *Ibid.*, III, 549.

49. E. Clowes Chorley, *Men and Movements in the American Episcopal Church* (New York, 1946), 176.

50. Schneider, *Johnson Writings*, I, 270-271.

51. *Ibid.*, I, 268.

Footnotes for Chapter IX

1. William Wilson Manross, *History of the American Episcopal Church* (New York, 1935), 45. See also L. L. Brown, "Henry Compton, 1632-1713, Bishop of London, 1675-1713," Historical Magazine of the Protestant Episcopal Church, XXV (1956), 9-71; John Clement (comp.), "Clergymen Licensed Overseas by the Bishops of London, 1696-1710, 1715-1716," *Ibid.*, XVI (1947), 318-349.

2. Hawks and Perry, *Documentary History*, I, 97.

3. *Ibid.*, 1, 106.

4. *Ibid.*, I, 117-120.

5. *Ibid.*, I, 119.

6. See for example the petitions from laity of Reading and Newtown (1732), Stamford and Litchfield (1747). *Ibid.*, I, 149-151, 233-236.

7. *Ibid.*, I, 128.

8. *Ibid.*, I, 146.

9. *Ibid.*, I, 173-174, 187, 192, 197, 216.

10. Possibly the transcript is erroneous here. The sentence makes no sense if "Mr. Dean" refers to Barzillai Dean, who was lost at sea.

11. *Ibid.*, I, 222-223.

12. *Ibid.*, II, 37.

13. *Ibid.*, II, 73-74.

14. *Ibid.*, I, 110.

15. *Ibid.*, I, 198.

16. *Ibid.*, I, 207, 217, 221, 226; in October 1746, Johnson suggested two possible candidates for the New London church, 223.

17. *Ibid.*, I, 237.

18. Schneider, *Johnson Writings*, I, 145, 151, 158-159, 161, 163; III, 238, 243, 246; cf. William Wilson Manross (comp.), *The Fulham Papers in the Lambeth Palace Library* (Oxford, 1965), XXI, 32-41. Although this reference is a catalogue, the microfilm of the manuscript papers will hereafter be cited as Manross, *Fulham Papers* with the appropriate manuscript volume and folio numbers, as above. In many instances Schneider, *Johnson Writings* and Hawks and Perry, *Documentary History* contain the same sources; because they are more conveniently accessible and as reliable for coverage as the microfilm of the manuscripts, the authors have preferred to cite them instead of Manross.

19. Hawks and Perry, *Documentary History*, I, 311.

20. *Ibid.*, I, 310-314.

21. *Ibid.*, I, 51. See also Schneider, *Johnson Writings*, I, 290, 307, 351-352 and Nelson R. Burr, *The Anglican Church in New Jersey* (Philadelphia, 1954), 579-581.

22. Hawks and Perry, *Documentary History*, I, 148.

23. *Ibid.*, I, 259-260.

24. *Ibid.*, I, 95.

25. *Ibid.*, I, 106.

26. *Ibid.*, I, 124-125.

27. *Ibid.*, I, 277-286. See also Maud O'Neil, "A Struggle for Religious Liberty: An Analysis of the Work of the S. P. G. in Connecticut," *Historical Magazine of the Protestant Episcopal Church,* XX (1951), 173-189, and Ellis, "Anglicans in Connecticut, 1725-1750 ...," 66-81.

28. Henry Wilder Foote, *Annals of King's Chapel* (2 vols.; Boston, 1882), I, 338.

29. Manross, *Fulham Papers*, IV, 182-184.

30. Steiner, "Samuel Seabury and the Forging of the High Church Tradition," 169-

171, 343. See also Hawks and Perry, *Documentary History*, I, 170-171; Schneider, *Johnson Writings*, III, 233.

31. Hawks and Perry, *Documentary History*, I, 157-158. Cf. Steiner, "Samuel Seabury and the Forging of the High Church Tradition," 340-341.

32. Hawks and Perry, *Documentary History*, I, 167.

33. *Ibid.*, I, 168.

34. *Ibid.*, I, 170-171.

35. *Ibid.*, I, 270.

36. *Ibid.*, I, 317.

37. Morgan Dix (ed.), *A History of the Parish of Trinity Church in the City of New York* (4 vols.; New York, 1898-1906), I, 314. See also Steiner, "Samuel Seabury and the Forging of the High Church Tradition," 341-344, 350-354.

38. Dix, *History of the Parish of Trinity Church,* I, 314-315. Walter Herbert Stowe (ed.), "The Seabury Minutes of the New York Clergy Conventions of 1766 and 1767," *Historical Magazine of the Protestant Episcopal Church*, X (1941), 124-162. For reference to a clergy meeting at Stratford in October 1766 see the Connecticut Clergy's petition to the Bishop of London, Oct. 8, 1766 in Manross, *Fulham Papers*, I, 308-309.

39. Steiner, "Samuel Seabury and the Forging of the High Church Tradition," 350-364. See also Clara Loveland, *The Critical Years: The Reconstruction of the Anglican Church in the United States of America, 1780-1789* (Greenwich, Conn.; 1956).

40. Tucker, *Puritan Protagonist*, 150.

41. *Ibid.*, 171-172.

42. *Ibid.*, 173.

43. *Ibid.*, 176.

44. Schneider, *Johnson Writings*, I, 174-175.

45. Tucker, *Puritan Protagonist*, 167n, 178.

46. Schneider, *Johnson Writings*, I, 176-180.

47. *Ibid.*, I, 178.

48. *Ibid.*, I, 180-182.

49. Tucker, *Puritan Protagonist*, 180.

50. Schneider, *Johnson Writings*, I, 190.

51. *Ibid.*, I, 191.

52. Hawks and Perry, *Documentary History*, I, 181.

53. *Ibid.*, I, 181-182.

54. *Ibid.*, I, 183; Schneider, *Johnson Writings*, I, 109; cf. Manross, *Fulham Papers*, I, 282-285.

55. Schneider, *Johnson Writings*, I, 130.

56. Manross, *Fulham Papers*, I, 289-290. Manross's catalogue (p. 15) says the letter "Acknowledges what appears to be appointment as Commissary, though language is vague." Indeed, the text of the letter does not appear to support the notion of Johnson's commissioning at all.

57. Hawks and Perry, *Documentary History*, I, 265-266.

58. Schneider, *Johnson Writings*, III, 237. When Johnson answered the letter, he asked Sherlock to excuse him for his inability to comply with this particular request. Manross, *Fulham Papers,* I, 291-293. But he never hesitated to offer advice or information, whether requested or not, whenever he considered himself qualified to speak.

59. Steiner, "Samuel Seabury and the Forging of the High Church Tradition," 66.

Footnotes for Chapter X

1. Schneider, *Johnson Writings*, III, 255. A general discussion of the problem is provided by Mary Kent Davey Babcock, "Difficulties and Dangers of Pre-Revolutionary Ordinations," *Historical Magazine of the Protestant Episcopal Church*, XII (1943), 225-241; See also George Woodward Lamb (comp.), "Clergymen Licensed to the American Colonies by the Bishops of London: 1745-1781," *Ibid.*, XIII (1944), 128-143, and John Clement (comp.), "Anglican Clergymen Licensed to the American Colonies, 17101744," *Ibid.*, XVII (1948), 207-250.

2. The standard works on the issue are Arthur Lyon Cross, *The Anglican Episcopate and the American Colonies* (Cambridge, Mass., 1924) and Carl Bridenbaugh, *Mitre and Sceptre: Transatlantic Faiths, Ideas, Personalities, and Politics, 1689-1775* (New York, 1962). Bridenbaugh assumes that the episcopal issue was one of religious and civil tyranny. An apologist for the Dissenters, he disregards English and colonial spokesmen who denied any intent of arming American bishops with civil and ecclesiastical power over non-Anglicans, accuses the Churchmen of crassly playing for power and place, and uses language that is gratuitous, immoderate, and distorts the truth. Note for example his references to the "drive for ecclesiastical power,"

(as if the matter was as simple as all that) to "nine Episcopal clergymen [who] ostentatiously appeared at the Yale Commencement," and "Lust for Dominion...." (pp. 76, 85, 116.) For an antidote to Bridenbaugh's excessive partisanship, see Jack M. Sosin, "The Proposal in the Pre-Revolutionary Decade for Establishing Anglican Bishops in the Colonies," *The Journal of Ecclesiastical History,* XIII (1962), 76-84. Also typical of historians' unflattering and inaccurate interpretation of Anglican activity is Charles H. Maxson, *The Great Awakening in the Middle Colonies* (Chicago, 1920; Peter Smith reprint, 1958). Asserting the democratic character of the Awakening and the Church of England's appeal to "a small aristocratic body, centering in an official class," Maxson insists that "The clergy therefore sought the advancement of their interests by intrigue with the authorities in England. They were suspected by the people of being the emissaries of a foreign government." (p. 149.) In fact, the Church did not become "more and more a small aristocratic body," and in Connecticut and New England the exact reverse was true, as is shown by Bruce E. Steiner, "New England Anglicanism: A Genteel Faith?," *William and Mary Quarterly*, 3d. Ser., XXVII (1970), 122-135.

3. Schneider, *Johnson Writings*, III, 3-8.

4. *Ibid.*, I, 64.

5. *Ibid.*, III, 9-16.

6. *Ibid.*, III, 217-218.

7. *Ibid.*, III, 218. See also Ruth M. Winton, "Governor Francis Nicholson's Relations with the Society for the Propagation of the Gospel in Foreign Parts, 1701-1727," *Historical Magazine of the Protestant Episcopal Church,* XVII (1948), 274-286.

8. Schneider, *Johnson Writings*, III, 219-221.

9. *Ibid.*, III, 219.

10. Steiner, "Samuel Seabury and the Forging of the High Church Tradition," 343; Schneider, *Johnson Writings*, III, 221-222.

11. Hawks and Perry, *Documentary History*, I, 102.

12. Schneider, *Johnson Writings*, I, 86.

13. *Ibid.*, I, 87-88.

14. *Ibid.*, I, 93.

15. *Ibid.*, I, 94-99.

16. E. Edwards Beardsley, *The History of the Episcopal Church in Connecticut* (New York, 1865), 107-110.

17. Cross, *Anglican Episcopate*, 109-110.

18. Schneider, *Johnson Writings*, III, 228-229. See also Steiner, "New England Anglicanism: A Genteel Faith?," 122-135. For a general resumé of the Church's growth see Frederick V. Mills, "Anglican Expansion in Colonial America, 1761-1775," *Historical Magazine of the Protestant Episcopal Church*, XXXIX (1970), 315-324.

19. Schneider, *Johnson Writings*, I, 103, 109, 112.

20, Cross, Anglican Episcopate, 122-123.

21. Schneider, *Johnson Writings*, III, 240.

22. *Ibid.*, I, 144-145,

23. *Ibid.*, III, 237.

24. *Ibid.*, III, 240-243.

25. Cross, Anglican Episcopate, 113-122, 246, 254-256.

26. Schneider, *Johnson Writings*, I, 151, 158-165; III, 244-246.

27. *Ibid.*, II, 332-335, 345-351; III, 248-253.

28. *Ibid.*, III, 248-253.

29. *Ibid.*, II, 332- 335.

30. *Ibid.*, I, 195-196.

31. *Ibid.*, I, 231-241.

32. *Ibid.*, I, 243-244.

33. Steiner, "Samuel Seabury and the Forging of the High Church Tradition," 239.

34. Schneider, *Johnson Writings*, I, 243-244.

35. *Ibid.*, I, 255-256.

36. *Ibid.*, II, 336- 339.

37. *Ibid.*, IV, 42-45.

38. *Ibid.*, III, 256-260.

39. *Ibid.*, I, 282-287.

40. Sosin, "The Proposal … for Establishing Anglican Bishops in the Colonies," 80.

41. Schneider, *Johnson Writings*, IV, 69-70.

42. *Ibid.*, I, 293-300; IV, 70-73.

43. *Ibid.*, I, 297-300.

44. Sosin, "The Proposal ... for Establishing Anglican Bishops in the Colonies," 76-77.

45. Schneider, *Johnson Writings*, III, 260-263.

46. *Ibid.*, I, 316-322.

47. *Ibid.*, I, 322-323.

48. *Ibid.*, IV, 83-85.

49. Bridenbaugh, *Mitre and Sceptre*, 221; Schneider, *Johnson Writings*, I, 43-44. For detailed discussions of the various campaigns of pamphlet warfare see Bridenbaugh, *Mitre and Sceptre,* 207-313 and Cross, *Anglican Episcopate*, 139-214.

50. Bridenbaugh, *Mitre and Sceptre*, 224-225.

51. Cross, *Anglican Episcopate*, 150-151.

52. Schneider, *Johnson Writings*, I, 44, 337; III, 279.

53. *Ibid.*, I, 44.

54. *Ibid.*, III, 269~271.

55. *Ibid.*, III, 272-275.

56. *Ibid.*, III, 277-278.

57. Beardsley, *History of the Episcopal Church in Connecticut* (1865), 232-233; Bridenbaugh, *Mitre and Sceptre*, 224-229, 240.

58. Schneider, *Johnson Writings*, III, 284-285.

59. Cross, *Anglican Episcopate*, 153-159.

60. Schneider, *Johnson Writings*, I, 352-354.

61. *Ibid.*, I, 354-355.

62. Steiner, "Samuel Seabury and the Forging of the High Church Tradition," 350-351; Schneider, *Johnson Writings*, I, 355-357.

63. Sosin, "The Proposal ... for Establishing Anglican bishops in the Colonies," 81-82.

64. Steiner, "Samuel Seabury and the Forging of the High Church Tradition," 352-354; Walter Herbert Stowe (ed.), "The Seabury Minutes of the New York Clergy Conventions of 1766 and 1767," *Historical Magazine of the Protestant Episcopal Church*, X (1941), 124-162; Schneider, *Johnson Writings*, I, 360-361.

65. *Ibid.*, I, 361.

66. *Ibid.*, I, 362-364.

67. *Ibid.*, I, 366-369, 384-391, 415-417, 432-434, 436-438, 442-448.

68. *Ibid.*, I, 403.

69. *Ibid.*, 366-369; Hawks and Perry, *Documentary History*, II, 101.

70. Schneider, *Johnson Writings*, I, 47, 369-371, 376-377. See also K. Clowes Chorley, "Minutes of the Conventions of the Clergy of Connecticut for the Years 1766, 1784 and 1785," *Historical Magazine of the Protestant Episcopal Church*, III (1934), 56*ff*.

71. Schneider, *Johnson Writings*, I, 372-373; the copy of this letter, dated November 1, is in James Sullivan, Alexander C. Fliek, Milton W. Hamilton (eds,), *The Papers of Sir William Johnson* (13 vols.; Albany and New York, 1921-1962), V, 406-408.

72. *Ibid.*, V, 432-434, 460-462, 471-472, 586-587, 733-734, 840-841; VI, 164-165; Schneider, *Johnson Writings*, I, 373-375, 411-412; Frank J. Klingberg, "Sir William Johnson and the Society for the Propagagation of the Gospel (1749-1774)," *Historical Magazine of the Protestant Episcopal Church*, VIII (1939), 4-37.

73. Schneider, *Johnson Writings*, I, 378-381.

74. *Ibid.*, I, 384-387.

75. *Ibid.*, I, 395-397.

76. *Ibid.*, I, 398-399.

77. *Ibid.*, I, 401-403; Cross, *Anglican Episcopate*, 253.

78. Schneider, *Johnson Writings*, I, 403-406.

79. Steiner, "Samuel Seabury and the Forging of the High Church Tradition," 356-358; Cross, *Anglican Episcopate*, 161-164, seems to suggest that Chandler's Appeal was an answer to Charles Chauncey's open letter (of Dec. 1767) against the Bishop of Llandaff's sermon, but in any event Chandler began work on the Appeal before Chauncey published his letter, See also *Papers of Sir William Johnson*, V, 835-843; VI, 11-13, 77-79; Schneider, *Johnson Writings*, I, 432-434.

80. Cross, *Anglican Episcopate*, 161-212 and Bridenbaugh, *Mitre and Sceptre*, 289-313 offer full discussions of the polemics.

81. Charles C. Tiffany, *A History of the Protestant Episcopal Church in the United States of America* (New York, 1895), 153; see also Bridenbaugh, *Mitre and Sceptre*, 294-296.

82. Schneider, *Johnson Writings*, I, 438-439; *Papers of Sir William Johnson*, VI, 164-165.

83. Schneider, *Johnson Writings*, I, 436-441.

84. *Papers of Sir William Johnson*, VI, 291-294, 414-416.

85. Schneider, *Johnson Writings*, I, 448-449.

86, *Ibid*., I, 449-450.

87. Steiner, "Samuel Seabury and the Forging of the High Church Tradition," 508.

88, *Ibid*., 335-336.

89. Schneider, *Johnson Writings*, I, 475-478.

90. Beardsley, *History of the Episcopal Church in Connecticut* (1865), 282-283.

91. Cross, *Anglican Episcopate*, 231-238; Schneider, *Johnson Writings*, I, 482-484. Frank Dean Gifford, "The Influence of the Clergy on American Politics from 1763-to 1776," *Historical Magazine of the Protestant Episcopal Church*, X (1941), 104-123; Ray Hiner, Jr., "Samuel Henley and Thomas Gwaitkin: Partners in Protest," *Ibid*., XXXVII (1968), 39-50; George William Pilcher, "The Pamphlet War on the Proposed Virginia Anglican Episcopate, 1767-1775," *Ibid*., XXX (1961), 266-279; George William Pilcher, "Virginia Newspapers and the Dispute over the Proposed Colonial Episcopate, 1771-1772," *The Historian,* XXIII (1960). See also Frederick V. Mills, "Anglican Resistance to an American Episcopate, 1761-1789" (unpublished Ph. D. dissertation: University of Pennsylvania, 1967).

92. Sosin, "The Proposal … for Establishing Anglican Bishops in the Colonies," 82-83. English Dissenters, cooperating with their American counterparts through correspondence and leaders like colonial agent Jasper Mauduit, lobbied against all plans for an episcopate – plans which in fact the government did not intend to act upon. The Earl of Hillsborough thus informed Thomas Lucas, chairman of a London committee of Dissenters in 1772, that both prelates and politicians "from political principles could not adopt such a Measure," although they believed Anglicans had "an undoubted Right" to bishops. In short, those principles were that an episcopate was too dangerous, too antagonistic an issue to pursue, for they

had nothing to gain and everything to lose by doing so. In typically Whig libertarian fashion they showed no desire to disturb long established religious practices! *Ibid.*, 83-84.

93. Schneider, *Johnson Writings*, I, 482-484; IV, 284, 354.

94. *Ibid.*, I, 480.

Footnotes for Chapter XI

1, Tucker, *Puritan Protagonist*, 264 (quoting Yale President Charles Seymour).

2. Don R. Gerlach, *Philip Schuyler and the American Revolution in New York, 1733-1777* (Lincoln, Nebr.; 1964), 100-110 *et passim*.

3. Horace Coon, Columbia: *Colossus on the Hudson* (New York, 1947), 36-38.

4. Schneider, *Johnson Writings*, I, 32.

5. *Ibid.*, I, v, vi.

6. *Ibid.*, I, 32; II, 296-305.

7. *Ibid.*, I, 134-135.

8. Milton M. Klein (ed.), *The Independent Reflector or Weekly Essays on Sundry Important Subjects More particularly adapted to the Province of New York By William Livingston and Others* (Cambridge, Mass.; 1963), 34; Schneider, *Johnson Writings*, IV, 163, 177.

9. Schneider, *Johnson Writings*, IV, 180.

10. Klein, *Independent Reflector*, 35; Schneider, *Johnson Writings*, IV, 180, 184.

11. Dix, *History of the Parish of Trinity Church*, I, 271.

12. Klein, *Independent Reflector*, 36-37.

13. *Ibid.*, 172, 180-181.

14. *Ibid.*, 189, 191-214.

15. *Ibid.*, 199-205.

16. *Ibid.*, 204.

17. *Ibid.*, 38-44.

18. Schneider, *Johnson Writings*, IV, 4.

19. Klein, *Independent Reflector,*, 40-41.

20. Schneider, *Johnson Writings*, IV, 164, 195-196.

21, *Ibid.*, I, 172-173; III, 253; IV, 5-7, 180-181, 196.

22. *Ibid.*, IV, 7-8, 181, 217-218.

23. *Ibid.*, IV, 8-9, 94.

24. *Ibid.*, I, 33. See also I, 180; IV, 181-182.

25. *Ibid.*, III, 253-255.

26. *Ibid.*, I, 33; IV, 182-183.

27. *Ibid.*, IV, 184.

28. *Ibid.*, IV, 183-189.

29. *Ibid.*, IV, 208-211.

30. *Ibid.*, IV, 11.

31. *Ibid.*, IV, 11-13.

32. *Ibid.*, IV, 15-16.

33. *Ibid.*, IV, 17, 18.

34. *Ibid.*, IV, 33, 191-207.

35. *Ibid.*, IV, 191-207.

36. *Ibid.*, IV, 222-224.

37. *Ibid.*, IV, 223.

38. *Ibid.*, lV, 223-224.

39. *Ibid.*, IV, 243-244. Other parts of the Matricula carry amusing and revealing comments on those students who did not complete their degrees: "Abraham De, Peyster -- After 3 years went to nothing"; "James Harris -- After about 2 years he went to Privateering." Others left to study law or to enroll in other colleges; some departed "after having behaved very indifferently" or because they were "very unmanageable." Schneider, *Johnson Writings*, IV, 244-254.

40. *Ibid.*, I, 34.

41. *Ibid.*, II, 250; IV, 228. Johnson's book was the first philosophy textbook printed in America. Berkeleyan in substance, it seems not to have been much circulated or widely accepted, partly because Anglican clerics were neither able to use it nor much interested in it. Scientists and natural philosophers like Franklin and Cad-

wallader Colden thought it ingenious but fantastic. Theologians were preoccupied with works such as Jonathan Edwards 's. *Ibid.*, III, v, 21, 345, 359.

42. *Ibid.*, IV, 20.

43. *Ibid.*, IV, 24-25.

44. *Ibid.*, I, 33-34; IV, 26.

45. *Ibid.*, IV, 31-32. See also IV, 213-214 and Steiner, "Samuel Seabury and the Forging of the high Church Tradition," 316-320.

46. Schneider, *Johnson Writings*, I, 34.

47. *Ibid.*, IV, 219, 221-222. John Howard Van Amringe *et al.*, *A History of Columbia University*, 1754-1904 (New York, 1904), 13 says the provision respecting the president being an Anglican was eliminated after the American Revolution.

48. Klein, *Independent Reflector,* 44-45.

49. Schneider, *Johnson Writings*, IV, 26.

50. *Ibid.*, IV, 222 cf. 225.

51. *Ibid.*, IV, 225-226.

52. *Ibid.*, IV, 226-227.

53. *Ibid.*, IV, 228-229.

54. *Ibid.*, IV, 226.

55. *Ibid.*, IV, 270-271.

56. *Ibid.*, IV, 244.

57. *Ibid.*, IV, 34-36.

Footnotes for Chapter XII

l. Schneider, *Johnson Writings*, IV, 34-36.

2. *Ibid.*, IV, 36-37.

3. *Ibid.*, IV, 37-38.

4. *Ibid.*, I, 36, 228.

5. *Ibid.*, I, 35, 56, 238-240, 245, 248, 255, 257.

6. *Ibid.*, I, 241, 254-255; IV, 244-245.

7. *Ibid.*, IV, 229-230, 271.

8. *Ibid.*, I, 36.

9. *Ibid.*, I, 37 ; IV, 245.

10. *Ibid.*, IV, 245.

11. *Ibid.*, I, 272-273.

12. *Ibid.*, IV, 43.

11. *Ibid.*, I, 271.

14. *Ibid.*, I, 37.

15. *Ibid.*, IV, 42-45.

16. *Ibid.*, IV, 45.

17. The corporation records suggest that the first payment for library books was not authorized until January 1762, and the first reference to a librarian in the records was dated March 1763. The governors allowed a £10 annual salary to Robert Harpur, the mathematics teacher, for serving that function (in addition to his teaching salary), and he was then ordered to catalogue the books. Van Amringe *et al., History of Columbia*, 428-429.

18. Schneider, *Johnson Writings*, I, 276-277.

19. *Ibid.*, IV, 46-48.

20. *Ibid.*, I, 277.

2L *Ibid.*, I, 37, 56.

22. *Ibid.*, IV, 246; cf. I, 37 and Appendix B, Chapter VII *supra*.

23. Schneider, *Johnson Writings*, IV, 280.

24. *Ibid.*, IV, 280-281; cf, 273-277,

25. *Ibid.*, I, 278.

26. *Ibid.*, I, 38.

27. *Ibid.*; see also IV, 247.

28. *Ibid.*, IV, 48.

29. *Ibid.*, IV, 49-52.

30. *Ibid.*, IV, 115-116.

31. *Ibid.*, I, 38.

32. *Ibid*, See also IV, 51-58, 63-70.

33. *Ibid.*, IV, 54-57.

34. *Ibid.*, I, 38-39, 296.

35. *Ibid.*, I, 296.

36, *Ibid.*, I, 39.

37. *Ibid.*, IV, 247.

38. *Ibid.*, IV, 231.

39. *Ibid.*, IV, 275, 277.

40. *Ibid.*, I, 39.

41. *Ibid.*, IV, 247.

42. *Ibid.*, I, 296.

43. *Ibid.*, I , 304-306.

44. *Ibid.*, I, 39.

45. *Ibid.*, IV, 70-73.

46. *Ibid.*, IV, 74-75.

47. *Ibid.*, I, 39; cf. IV, 248.

48. *Ibid.*, I, 39; IV, 248. Cf. Appendix B of Chapter VII *supra*.

49. Schneider, *Johnson Writings*, I, 301.

50. *Ibid.*, I, 272-273.

51. *Ibid.*, I, 273.

52. *Ibid.*, I, 274-276, 279.

53. *Ibid.*, I, 280-281.

54. *Ibid.*, I, 301.

55. *Ibid.*, I, 40, 51.

56. *Ibid.*, I, 314.

57. *Ibid.*, I, 315.

58. *Ibid.*, I, 40; IV, 248.

59. *Ibid.*, I, 40; IV, 81-82.

60. *Ibid.*, I, 40, 321; IV, 82-84, 231-236.

61. *Ibid.*, I, 40-41, 324; IV, 44, 55, 262.

62. *Ibid.*, IV, 248-249; cf. for 1758-1760 in IV, 245-247.

63. *Ibid.*, IV, 81-82.

64. *Ibid.*, I, 41; IV, 249. Cf. Appendix B of Chapter VII *supra*.

65. Schneider, *Johnson Writings*, IV, 278-280.

66. *Ibid.*, IV, 52-58; see also 49-52.

67. *Ibid.*, I, 296; IV, 75-76.

68. *Ibid.*, IV, 71.

69. *Ibid.*, I, 318; III, 262; IV, 76-77.

70. *Ibid.*, IV, 78-82, 85, 249.

71. *Ibid.*, I, 41.

72. *Ibid.*, IV, 85 cf. 97-98.

73. *Ibid.*, IV, 93-97 .

74. *Ibid.*, IV, 86-88.

75. *Ibid.*, IV, 90-91.

76. *Ibid.*, I, 41 cf. 333- 334.

77. *Ibid.*, I, 334.

78. *Ibid.*, I, 335- 336.

79. *Ibid.*, I, 42.

80. Jones, *Early American Philosophers*, 42.

81. Michael Kraus, *Intercolonial Aspects of American Culture* (New York, 1928), 119.

82. Schneider, *Johnson Writings*, IV, 225-229 cf. 237-243.

83. *Ibid.*, I, 43; III, 270-271, 274; IV, 111-114.

84. Kraus, *Intercolonial Aspects of American Culture*, 119.

85. Schneider, *Johnson Writings*, I, 43.

86. *Ibid.*, I, 47.

Footnotes for Chapter XlII

1. Schneider, *Johnson Writings*, IV, 90-92.

2. *Ibid.*, I, 335.

3. *Ibid.*, III, 274.

4. *Ibid.*, IV, 96-97, 249.

5. *Ibid.*, IV, 107, 109.

6. Groce, *William Samuel Johnson*, 52, 66.

7. *Ibid.*, 41.

8. Schneider, *Johnson Writings*, IV, 98.

9. Orcutt, *History of the Old Town of Stratford*, II, 1226.

10. Schneider, *Johnson Writings*, I, 57.

11. *Ibid.*, I, 403.

12. Groce, William Samuel Johnson, 69.

13. Schneider, *Johnson Writings*, I, 394.

14. James Truslow Adams, *Provincial Society* (New York, 1927), 311. See also Chapter VIII *supra*.

15. Schneider, *Johnson Writings*, 1, 401.

16. *Ibid.*, I, 47; IV, 252. The quotation is from Johnson's autobiography.

17. *Ibid.*, IV, 249, 252.

18. *Ibid.*, I, 47.

19. *Ibid.*, I, 325-328.

20. *Ibid.*, III, 277-278, 281, 283. Cf. I, 338, 341.

21. Arthur Lowndes (ed.), *Archives of the General Convention* [of the Protestant Episcopal Church in the United States of America] (6 vols.; New York, 1912), IV, 301.

22. Schneider, *Johnson Writings*, I, 47-48.

23. *Ibid.*, I, 455.

24. *Ibid.*, I, 49.

25. *Ibid.*, I, 45-46.

26. *Ibid.*, I, 462-463.

27. *Ibid.*, I, 464.

28. *Ibid.*, I, 466.

29. *Ibid.*, I , 49.

30. *Ibid.*, Chandler, *Life of Samuel Johnson*, 115.

31. *Ibid.*, 123.

32. Schneider, *Johnson Writings*, II, 603.

33. Steiner, "Samuel Seabury and the Forging of the High Church Tradition," 534.

34. Schneider, *Johnson Writings*, I, 53-55 and Chandler, *Life of Samuel Johnson*, 124-126.

Footnotes for Epilogue

1. Charles C. Tiffany, *A History of the Protestant Episcopal Church in United States of America* (New York, 1895), 156-157.

2. E. Edwards Beardsley, *Life and Times of William Samuel Johnson* (2d ed.; Boston, 1886),203.

3. Edmund S. Morgan, *The Gentle Puritan: A Life of Ezra Stiles, 1725-1795* (New Haven and London, 1962), 109-111.

4. Franklin B. Dexter (ed.), *The Literary Diary of Ezra Stiles* (3 vols.; New York, 1901), I, 205.

5. Clara O. Loveland, *The Critical Years: The Reconstruction of the Anglican Church in the United States of America, 1780-1789* (Greenwich, Conn.; 1956).

6. Thomas Bradbury Chandler, *The Life of Samuel Johnson, D. D.* (New York, 1805).

7. George E. De Mille, *The Catholic Movement in the American Episcopal Church* (2d. ed.; Philadelphia, 1950), 15-27 et passim.

Footnotes for Appendix A

1. Based on the map in Burr, *Diocese of Connecticut*. Cf. Weaver, "Anglican Congregationalist Tensions in Pre-Revolutionary Connecticut," 278, citing Lucy Cushing Jarvis (ed.), *Sketches of Church Life in Colonial Connecticut* ... (New Haven, 1902), 183-184. Weaver includes churches located at Southfield (1725), Simsbury

(1740), and Weston (1744). See also *Historical Resources of the Episcopal Diocese of Connecticut* (Hartford, 1966),269. Note the particular increase of churches during the decade (1740-1750) when the Great Awakening had its most direct impact. Bruce E. Steiner, "Anglican Officeholding in Pre-Revolutionary Connecticut: The Parameters of New England Community;" *William and Mary Quarterly*, 3d. Ser., XXXI (1974), 369-406 suggests that by 1774 there were about 17,200 Anglicans in Connecticut, comprising 9% of the colony's white population. He counts 46 Anglican congregations which erected churches by 1774; of these 25 were organized in 1724-1748 and 20 in 1748-1771; the other one, Stratford, was organized in 1707. Nelson R. Burr, comp., *Inventory of the Church Archives of Connecticut*, Protestant Episcopal (New Haven, Conn., 1940), 65-118, 125-126, 132, 138,237-238.

Footnotes for Appendix B

1. Burr, *Diocese of Connecticut*, 31. The register of King's College graduates indicates that Punderson was "educated but not graduated at Yale College" and that he was made Master of Arts at King's in 1758. Schneider, *Johnson Writings*, IV, 246.

2. Steiner, "Samuel Seabury and the Forging of the High Church Tradition," 621.

3. Treadwell also received a King's College B. A. in 1761. Schneider, *Johnson Writings*, IV, 248.

4. The King's College register indicates that Clarke was educated at Yale but received the King's College degrees in 1762 and 1766. Schneider, *Johnson Writings*, IV, 249, 252.

Index